Southeast Asia and the Enemy Beyond

Institute of Southeast Asian Studies

The Institute of Southeast Asian Studies was established as an autonomous organization in May 1968. It is a regional research center for scholars and other specialists concerned with modern Southeast Asia, particularly the multi-faceted problems of stability and security, economic development, and political and social change.

The Institute is governed by a twenty-two-member Board of Trustees comprising nominees from the Singapore Government, the National University of Singapore, the various chambers of commerce, and professional and civic organizations. A ten-member executive committee oversees day-to-day operations; it is chaired by the director, the Institute's chief academic and administrative officer.

About the Book and Author

This book explores elite perceptions of the external threats facing the members of the Association of Southeast Asian Nations (ASEAN), drawing on Dr. Tilman's interviews with senior political, military, and intellectual leaders in Indonesia, Malaysia, the Philippines, Singapore, and Thailand. He supplements his interviews with an examination of their writings, speeches, and other public statements, which he examines in the context of the history, geography, culture, and governmental structures of each country. He addresses the fundamental questions of the extent to which these perceptions differ and why. His focus throughout is on subjective reality--the world as it is perceived by the leadership of the ASEAN nations.

Robert O. Tilman is professor of political science at North Carolina State University and has published widely on Southeast Asia.

Published under the auspices of the
Institute of Southeast Asian Studies, Singapore

Southeast Asia and the Enemy Beyond

ASEAN Perceptions of External Threats

Robert O. Tilman

Westview Press / Boulder and London

Westview Special Studies on South and Southeast Asia

Published in 1987 in the United States of America by Westview Press, Inc.;
Frederick A. Praeger, Publisher; 5500 Central Avenue, Boulder, Colorado
80301

Library of Congress Cataloging-in-Publication Data
Tilman, Robert O.
    Southeast Asia and the enemy beyond.
    (Westview special studies on South and Southeast
Asia)
    Includes index.
    Bibliography: p.
    1. Asia, Southeastern--Foreign relations. 2. ASEAN.
I. Title. II. Series.
DS526.7.T56 1987   327.59   86-1720
ISBN 0-8133-7130-9

Composition for this book was provided by the author.

Printed and bound in the United States of America

The paper used in this publication meets the requirements
of the American National Standard for Permanence of Paper
for Printed Library Materials Z39.48-1984.

6   5   4   3   2   1

Contents

viii

TABLES

Preface

I have long been fascinated by the distinction between "reality" and "perception," but it was only during a whirlwind lecture tour of Southeast Asia in 1980 that I came to realize the extent to which perceptions may vary from one nation to another, and, within a single country, from one group to another. I returned to my university determined to pursue this question further. Because of my administrative responsibilities at that time I did not progress as rapidly as I would have liked. However, the delay proved to be a useful gestation period for my thoughts and a good excuse for several subsequent trips to the field. Indeed, as the project matured over a five-year period I came to appreciate the underlying similarities of perceptions as much as the differences, and this theme will surface frequently throughout the study.

Although I have been supported by numerous foundations during my more than a quarter-century of research in Southeast Asia, this book is the result of the support of five institutions and programs that have provided the funds to maintain me in Southeast Asia on four occasions since 1980. The lecture tour in 1980 that gave birth to this study was supported by the United States Information Agency (USIA, but at that time the United States International Communications Agency), and, despite a gruelling schedule of forty presentations in ten cities in five weeks, it was a rewarding and instructive experience. The lecture tour was followed by a Fulbright research award to the Institute of Southeast Asian Studies (ISEAS) in Singapore in 1983, fellowships from the Social Science Research Council and the Earhart Foundation for a four-month visit to ISEAS and the region in 1985, and an award from my university to permit me to return to Manila following the People Power Revolution in February 1986. With the exception of the last trip, each visit included a complete tour of ASEAN (except Brunei, which only joined the Association in 1984).

As I have noted elsewhere in this study, the cooperation I have received from the leadership of the ASEAN states goes well beyond what might be reasonably expected from busy leaders. In fact, they gave unsparingly of their valuable time--rarely on just one occasion and frequently many times. Very few of the top leaders proved not to be available at all, and in several cases in which they were not available they put documents and assistants at my disposal that proved to be of great value. If I left the region uninformed or misinformed it is my fault and not theirs.

The reader should be forewarned that I have great respect for most of the leaders with whom this study is concerned and great admiration for their accomplishments. Some are personal friends and will remain personal friends in or out of office. Thus, although I have tried to pursue this study with scholarly objectivity, and I hope I have succeeded, I did not approach it with hostility or even indifference. I was once introduced to a seminar in Bangkok as "an honorary Southeast Asian," and I regard this as one of the highest compliments I have been paid in any introduction. This comment is probably sufficient to give the reader a sense of my own perspectives.

During many visits to the region, ISEAS in Singapore has provided me with comfortable facilities, valuable research materials, a helpful staff, and stimulating colleagues. I owe a great debt to the Institute and its Director. The assistance and hospitality of the Institute of Security and International Studies in Bangkok and the Centre for Strategic and International Studies in Jakarta have also been valuable and appreciated on many occasions.

Finally, my wife has served as a research assistant (unpaid, of course) on most of our travels, and much of the material copied, clipped, or noted was provided by her. She has my gratitude for her scholarly contributions, but, probably more important, for the mobility and flexibility she has had to demonstrate during the past twenty-five years.

Despite my many debts to institutions and individuals, they cannot be blamed for errors of omission or commission. These are mine alone.

Robert O. Tilman

1

The Tiger at the Door:
Threats and Threat Perceptions

*O, wad some pow'r the giftie gie us
To see oursels as ithers see us!*
Robert Burns

Vietnam is . . . a tiger squatting on our doorstep.
Thanat Khoman
Deputy Prime Minister of Thailand
Honolulu, February 1982

*Some countries said that Vietnam is a danger to
Southeast Asia, but the Indonesian Army and people
do not believe it.*
General Benny Murdani
Indonesian Armed Forces Chief of Staff
Hanoi, February 1984

*With respect to policy-making . . . what matters
is how the policy-maker imagines the milieu to be,
not how it actually is.*
Harold and Margaret Sprout, 1957

By common convention a particular animal is
called a tiger, and most of us will recognize a tiger
whether we have ever seen one or not. In most circumstances uncaged tigers should be respected, feared,
and avoided. Our cognitive experiences have taught us
about tigers--albeit thankfully secondhand in most
cases--and when we see a tiger we perceive a threat to
our physical well-being. Dealing with the animal
called a tiger is simple because most who know the
tiger agree that it constitutes a threat. Very few
perceive it otherwise.

When we deal with figurative rather than literal
tigers there is much greater latitude for disagreement. When the former deputy prime minister of
Thailand said that he saw Vietnam as a tiger squatting
on Thailand's doorstep, he meant that Thailand was
facing an external threat from its new next-door

neighbor, Vietnam.[1] Many Indonesian leaders, however, would not agree that Vietnam is a tiger. For many Indonesian leaders there are many tigers in the world, but Vietnam is not one.[2] The Thai leader's identification of a figurative tiger differed from the perceptions of his Indonesian colleagues.

This is a study of figurative tigers as they are perceived by the leaders of the Association of Southeast Asian Nations (ASEAN).[3] The different perceptions held by leaders in each of the ASEAN states are examined,[4] and attempts are made to shed light on the origins of these differences. This is not a subject that lends itself easily to objective inquiry and systematic analysis, but it is important and relatively unstudied.

An author's temptation in an opening chapter is to construct a new "theoretical framework." The landscape is littered with such models of decision making and foreign-policy formulation, most of which were touted as having broad applicability, but in reality end up as theoretical skeletons without empirical flesh or as one-event case studies that prove to be of questionable applicability to other settings.[5] This study breaks no new theoretical ground and claims to "explain" no foreign policies other than those of the five ASEAN states with which this research was concerned.

Like all authors, I have approached my tasks here with certain intellectual and philosophical orientations, of which the reader should be made aware. First, my work is influenced by the "givens" of my own mind-set, or what I have called my "perspectives." Second, I have used a consistent framework to formulate questions and analyze collected material. Although the organization of this book does not follow this framework, as an earlier working paper did,[6] the influence of the framework is clear in each of the subsequent chapters.[7]

PERSPECTIVES

Individuals Matter

Foreign-policy elites operate under various constraints, some of which can be very severe. The international system itself often sets the agenda, defines the options, imposes constraints on the freedom of national policy makers, and forces them to choose options with which they might not feel entirely comfortable. In most states the bureaucracy that undergirds the work of the policy makers is also a constraining influence. Bureaucracies and bureaucrats also set agendas, identify options, and selectively filter or emphasize the information that flows into the hands of the decision makers. Furthermore, both the decision makers and the bureaucrats are products of the society in which they live; in many ways foreign policy is but an external manifestation of the domestic social and political system.[8] Finally, when an individual finds himself in the role of the policy maker, his perception of the role he has assumed may serve to impose constraints on his policy choices.[9]

Although structural and cultural constraints on the latitude of policy makers are real and must be taken into account, individuals are also important, and are often a key factor in the policy-making process.[10] Holsti has suggested seven situations in which the use of the cognitive approach to decision making can be significant, and these are applicable to my argument that individuals matter. In brief, Holsti's situations involve circumstances that require more than the application of standard operating procedures and established decision-making rules; top leaders who define their leadership roles broadly; long-range planning; conditions of great ambiguity with little "reliable" information; information overload requiring discretionary filtering; unanticipated events; and leaders under unusual stress.[11]

To Holsti's catalogue may be added some further circumstances of a more specific nature applicable to the ASEAN countries. Most foreign policy issues are simply not important to most Southeast Asians. For most citizens, foreign policy is precisely what the term conveys--it is foreign. As previous Thai governments have found, they are likely to be more vulnerable to the prices of kerosene or charcoal than to rapprochement with the People's Republic of China. Only when foreign policy touches a domestic nerve, as is the case with the bases issue in the Philippines, is foreign policy likely to get on the agenda of most citizens. Even in the Philippine case a Jeepney drivers' strike in Manila over the high cost of gasoline can cripple the city and put far more pressure on the government than an anti-bases demonstration on Roxas Boulevard.

When foreign policy is largely foreign, individual policy makers are freed from many of the domestic political constraints imposed on First World policy makers. In addition, most Third World policy makers, including those in the ASEAN region, do not have their policies scrutinized daily by a highly competitive, inquisitive, or crusading media. The press tends to be "disciplined," and foreign affairs is not an important topic to much of the public anyway. Finally, the typical foreign affairs bureaucracy is relatively small, and the personal imprint of the top policy maker is frequently apparent.[12] Taken together, at least in the ASEAN countries, individuals matter in the formulation of foreign policy, probably more than they do in First World countries.

Facts Are Ambiguous

In the early days of black-and-white television Sergeant Joe Friday of "Dragnet" would implore his witnesses to give him "the facts, ma'm, just the facts," but at about the same time a distinguished scholar of international relations was telling us that "for any individual . . . or organization, there are no such things as 'facts.' There are only messages filtered through a changeable value system."[13] In spite of his best efforts, Joe Friday frequently discovered that facts are ambiguous.

Are all "facts" relative? Of course not, but only because of commonly accepted conventions that they are facts. Universally, two plus two is accepted as four, twenty divided by ten is two. Beyond these easy examples, however, lie many facts that are subject to widely varying interpretations, just as two witnesses to a murder may have given Sergeant Friday two different set of "facts." Sergeant Friday's task was to discover "reality," but it was of course his reality, which some of the witnesses may never have been able to reconcile with their own realities.[14] The problem of dealing with reality leads to the third perspective from which this study has been approached.

Perception Is Reality

Concern for "what seems to be" in contrast to "what is" is not new. In the "Allegory of the Cave" Plato has his subjects watch shadows cast on the wall of the cave by actual figures they never see. For his subjects, the shadows become reality because for them the figures never existed. But for Plato the subjects are misinformed, and therefore capable of being mislead, because they are ignorant of the true nature of the shadows. Today many of us tend to be less certain of the true nature of phenomena, and more inclined to accept that one man's shadows may be as reliable as another's.

Much attention in recent years has been devoted to investigations of the origins, meanings, and interpretations of these shadows. In the cognitive process information is processed through a set of existing beliefs and from this emerges one's perceptions of the phenomena observed. Cognitive theory concerns itself "with the structure of beliefs. . . and with the manner in which information is processed in reference to existing beliefs."[15] To understand the landscape of beliefs through which information is processed, some scholars, principally from the discipline of psychology, have turned to "mapping."

Psychological, cognitive, social, and cultural mapping is not new; indeed, although it was not called by this term the cognitive map was one of Plato's concerns in the cave. An ambitious project launched by the United Nations not long after its creation sought to map national groups throughout the world on the assumption that wars might be avoided if nations realized that they were following different and sometimes contradictory psychological maps.[16] Recently, cognitive mapping has taken on some very specific connotations, and the process of drawing, interpreting, and utilizing such maps has become much more rigorous and conceptually sophisticated.[17]

Although there is vast disagreement on the makeup, structure, and application of such maps--which is really a more basic disagreement on beliefs and how they affect perceptions and actions--few scholars disagree on the practical significance of the end result. The early observations of Harold and Margaret Sprout, quoted at the beginning of this chapter, have lost none of their validity. To this the Sprouts add: "[There is a] simple and familiar principle that a person reacts to his milieu as he apperceives it--that is, he perceives and interprets it in the light of past experience."[18]

Cognitive theorists generally agree that information filtered through an individual's belief system (cognitive map, psychological environment, or other such terms) produces perceptions, and that individuals are guided by subjective perceptions and not by objective reality, whatever it may be. They also agree that belief systems are constructed on past experiences. However, what constitutes significant past experiences, precisely how these influence perceptions, and how blatant conflicts between facts and beliefs are reconciled are matters of dispute.

Past experiences may serve to create an individual's belief system, but the range of past experiences can cover an almost limitless span of phenomena. Every individual is a member of countless social and cultural networks: most are family members; most were born into or converted to a particular religion; and most grew up speaking a single language and were thus limited in their access to information to those sharing this language. The catalogue can be continued almost indefinitely.

In addition to past experiences that link individuals to groups there are more specific individual experiences that must be taken into account in mapping the cognitive process. A high official in one of the ministries of foreign affairs recounted to me on several occasions how he as a boy witnessed the death of his father, a medical assistant, who was machine-gunned outside a hospital tent by a Japanese soldier for no apparent reason. The attention he gave to the details of the murder made it apparent that it remained a vivid and significant memory. More than forty years later in his position in the ministry he dealt almost daily with matters of state involving Japan. One is left to speculate about how this very personal experience had influenced his cognitive map, altered his perceptions of the motives and behavior of all Japanese, and eventually affected the course of relations between the two countries.

Not all messages that we receive are consistent with our belief system; some are so strange and unexpected that there is no pigeonhole in which they may be filed. We can infer from previous experiences and interpret the unexpected accordingly, or we may suffer selective blindness in what we see and fail to see, accepting information that fits and rejecting information that does not. The mind has an immense capacity to produce consistency between perceptions and beliefs even when the information received may seem highly inconsistent.[19]

Thus, whatever the complexities of the cognitive processes, reality is often relative. Although perceptions alone do not structure policy, they influence policy choices, and this is the subject of this study.

From the Perspective of the Grass

According to a well-known proverb in South and Southeast Asia, "when elephants fight it is the grass that suffers." A modern-day skeptic might amend this to "whether elephants fight or make love, it is still the grass that suffers."

As far as the ASEAN states are concerned, my sympathies lean toward the grass, and I write from this perspective. Elephants are highly visible, frequently examined, and can usually take care of themselves. The grass, which is far more vulnerable, is also much more interesting as a subject for research.

THE FRAMEWORK OF INQUIRY AND ANALYSIS

While the subject of perceptions has been treated extensively in recent years, the literature on threat perceptions is not voluminous. Numerous studies deal with threat realities, and writings on perceived nuclear threats are common. However, studies of reality often substitute the subjective perceptions of the author for those of the actor, and there is little concern about nuclear warfare in the states of ASEAN.[20]

Another genre of threat-perception literature deals with empirically describable perceptions and misperceptions in foreign policy making and international relations.[21] Such studies depend on the historical record and refer to manifest threats and the perceptions and misperceptions of them ("misperceptions" because historically documented outcomes can be cited to disprove the accuracy of the perceptions).

My concern in this study is with something much more ambiguous--ASEAN leaders' perceptions of future developments that will threaten their countries if they occur and the perceived probabilities that these events will take place.[22] The factors affecting perceptions may be considered to fall into several "dimensions," a term employed here to describe a cluster of related influences. In crude terms the following figure illustrates this concept.

PROJECTION -----> TRANSFORMATION -----> PERCEPTION

Dimensions:

1. Structural
2. Geopolitical
3. Historical
4. Sociocultural
5. Economic

The Structural Dimension

Here we are concerned with the political and bureaucratic machinery through which foreign policy is formulated and executed. Central to this is the question "who makes policy?" but there are other considerations. Bureaucracies are rarely neutral because bureaucrats, and through them the bureaucracies they serve, develop vested interests that seem to be conducive to sustaining or nurturing both the bureaucrats and their bureaucracies. Thus, with intent, but more likely as a conditioned reflex, the foreign-affairs bureaucracy may selectively gather, filter, or subtly alter the messages it transmits to the policy makers at the top. In addition, individuals inside or outside the government influence policy makers in interpreting the messages that have been forwarded to them through normal bureaucratic channels, the media, or word of mouth. All of these together constitute the structural dimension, a subject that receives greater attention in chapter 3.

The Geopolitical Dimension

This is probably the most readily apparent cluster of influences. An enemy that is far away, all other things being equal, certainly seems much less threatening than one that shares a common land border. If the USSR occupied the territory that constitutes Canada it is doubtful that the "cold war" would have been limited to verbal exchanges and long-range threats; or perhaps there might have been no cold war at all. Cuba, small and relatively powerless, was perceived as a great threat because of its proximity to the United States. The threat of Russian offensive missiles in Cuba would probably have been of short-term concern to President Kennedy and his advisors if Cuba had been located at the tip of Africa rather than ninety miles off the coast of Florida. On the other hand, under such a circumstance there would have been little strategic need for the introduction of offensive missiles. The Chinese perceive the Russians as a threat, and vice versa, in part because they share a long and poorly demarcated land border. For centuries Europe has been a cauldron of latent and manifest hostility because many nations and claimants to nationhood are packed into a limited geographic area. Throughout history geography has helped to shape the perceptions of the world's policy makers. These influences will be considered frequently in the chapters that follow.

The Historical Dimension

The historical dimension presents numerous complexities, for the influence of history must be considered on at least two levels: personal and collective. First, each policy maker has had unique personal experiences that affect his perceptions. Second, "friend" and "enemy" are defined in textbooks, in popular wisdom, in literature, and in coffeehouse and barroom gossip. In addition, countries sometimes attempt to write or rewrite their national histories to alter or reinforce their own historical memories.

The story recounted earlier of the foreign ministry official who witnessed the murder of his father at the hands of a Japanese soldier is an example of a very personal historical experience. The recent outcry in Southeast Asia over Japanese attempts to expunge such accounts from their own textbooks are examples of more general collective memories and the reactions of countries to an attempt of a former enemy to rewrite its history.

The Sociocultural Dimension

Foreign-policy formulation may also be influenced by the ethnic, cultural, and religious makeup of a country and its policy makers, or what Kelman calls the norms and values of society at large and the norms and values of the many subgroups to which the policy maker belongs.[23] In the United States it is generally accepted that the presence of an economically powerful and articulate Jewish minority, as well as the common historical origins of Judaism and Christianity, go a long way toward explaining the tilt in American foreign policy toward Israel in disputes with her Muslim neighbors. If Islam were as firmly entrenched in the American system as Judaism, the policy decisions reached in Washington might be considerably different. The "Atlantic Alliance" is built on a shared cultural history, religious affinities, a common language, and kinship connections. For the same reasons the "longest unfortified border in the world," which unites more than it separates Canada and the United States, is politically feasible.

The Economic Dimension

Here several contradictory influences must be considered. Foreign investment creates reciprocal obligations between investor and the host country, and these obligations may influence the content of policies or the manner in which they are carried out. Foreign trade patterns may do the same. On the other hand, both investment and trade may generate feelings of resentment against a partner perceived to be getting the better of the deal. There is also the shady area of corruption fueled by the availability of extensive foreign resources. In most Western writings on policy formulation there is an often unspoken assumption that those officials responsible for policy consider themselves the stewards of the national good as they interpret it. This may not be true anywhere in the world, but certainly in Southeast Asia there are some clear cases of personal, or peer-group, policy making and policy execution calculated to enhance personal or family fortunes. The country may not suffer unduly--or it may even gain--but this is incidental to the intent of the person or persons involved. It is, however, difficult to gather hard facts on corruption, and one is therefore usually left only to speculate on its impact on foreign policy.

COMPLICATING FACTORS

Research complications on this topic can be grouped into two categories: the accessibility and reliability of information, and the usefulness of the insights gained.

Accessibility and Reliability

ASEAN decision makers must be among the most approachable in the world. It is difficult to imagine gaining access to Prime Minister Thatcher for an academic interview, yet in some (but not all) ASEAN countries access to equally high government officials is possible. One could hardly expect to interview Secretary of State George Shultz even with many weeks advance notice, but four ASEAN foreign ministers generously made themselves available to me repeatedly

and often with very little notice. Military leaders
were equally obliging in most of the ASEAN states, and
again these interviews often had to be scheduled on
very short notice. At the working level of the
ministries of foreign affairs I was often able simply
to drop in to talk with those whom I wanted to see,
sometimes even without the courtesy of a preliminary
telephone call. In several ministries senior officials
set up conference sessions for me so that a subject
could be discussed collectively. In short, most ASEAN
leaders are available, generous of their time, and
candid. ASEAN is an ideal and unusual laboratory for
the practicing political scientist.

There are limits, however, to what can be accomplished in interview sessions. Some ASEAN leaders are
willing and even eager to expound on their interpretations of international events, relations with
foreign powers, and the principles of foreign policy.
Not surprisingly, they are not eager to be probed
about the social, psychological, and cultural factors
that have influenced their perceptions of international affairs. Often these insights must be gained
indirectly or by inference. As Holsti has noted,
"whether the investigator relies on interviews,
questionnaires, or documents, the situations for which
he is most likely to incorporate cognitive process
models into his analysis are precisely those in which
access to relevant data is most difficult."[24]

Scholars have tried in various ways to get around
this problem. An imaginative if controversial
approach was that of Llewellyn D. Howell, who chose
"to have students in higher education act as representatives of the broader elite." Howell therefore
interviewed students, to whom he had access, and took
their responses as representative of the policy-making
elite, to whom he did not have access.[25] Margaret G.
Herman used the on-the-record statements and writings
of forty-five world leaders, including four from two
ASEAN states, in her attempt to relate personality
types to foreign policy outcomes.[26] A basic problem
for both Howell and Herman was that the leaders were
not accessible or would not submit to the type of
interview necessary for such research.

In Herman's research public documents were the
only source of information available. In my research
they were not the only source, but they proved to be
crucial supplements. Questions may be raised about the
validity of such public documents--speeches, press
conferences, official statements, etc. As Holsti has
noted these are often intended to convey specific
information, or signals, to specifically targeted
audiences. They may also be intended "to persuade,
justify, threaten, cajole, manipulate, evoke sympathy
and support, or otherwise influence the intended
audience."[27] The same criticisms can be leveled

against many in-person interviews. Is the interviewer being told only what the interviewee wants him to hear, or, in some cases, what the interviewee *thinks* the interviewer wants to hear? Can such written and oral evidence be taken seriously by the scholar (or the journalist)? Unhappily there are no simple answers to these frustrating questions.

There are obviously some world leaders who have earned a very low degree of credibility. Their statements seem usually to be grounded in the immediate situation and are patently tendentious. Probably no serious scholar or journalist would take one of Mohmar Quadaffi's frequent outbursts as a definitive statement of his position or intentions. Such obvious behavior is easy to deal with. Far more difficult to deal with is the leader who has earned a reputation for making credible statements, but who for political, personal, or other reasons shades the emphasis or the content of a given message to fit a particular situation. Of course, what I am describing might be called human nature, but for most of the world's population the problem of credibility does not arise. Credibility becomes an issue only when one deals with the policy-making elite. In the end, the task is essentially the same as that of the historian who is faced with a mountain of questionable and perhaps openly contradictory evidence. Sifting, winnowing, and establishing levels of credibility remain the responsibility of the researchers in both cases.

Utility of Research on Perceptions

Even assuming that all of the other hurdles are cleared, what is the usefulness of research on perceptions? Do policy makers in fact make policy on the basis of their personal perceptions? The answer is again a not very satisfying "sometimes--in certain situations, perhaps--but often no." Certainly perceptions guide a policy maker toward formulation of his personal choices, but these may not coincide with his eventual policy choices. External influences such as domestic considerations, peer pressures, or role expectations may lead to a policy choice that is not entirely compatible with the individual's personal choice. On the other hand, sometimes personal and policy choices coincide.

In cases where personal choice and policy alternatives do not correspond precisely, a policy maker's perceptions may nevertheless predispose him to seek the least incompatible policy alternative available. Alexander George has referred to this as the "bounded rationality" of policy makers--that is, the limits set by the policy maker's "operational . . . beliefs," which "structure and channel the ways in which he deals with the cognitive limits on rationality."

George also argues that such "bounded rationality" may be particularly significant in the perception of threats: "ambiguous situations are perceived as . . . posing latent crises [and] ambiguous information that challenges the existing image . . . is discounted or ignored." Thus, a policy maker's "operational code beliefs introduce diagnostic propensities into his information processing."[28] In other words, individuals matter, and research on perceptions offer more utility than futility.

Indeed, perceptions cannot be ignored in most studies of foreign policy and international relations, and for many such scholarly undertakings the study of perceived threats is particularly relevant. Many nations perceive tigers on their door-steps, and it is important to find out where they think these tigers come from, why they feel the tigers choose these particular front doors, what they think the tigers' intentions are, and what they propose to do about them. The tigers perceived to be roaming the ASEAN region are the objects of this study, and the policy makers of the ASEAN nations are the subjects.

NOTES

1. Opening remarks at a conference on threat perceptions sponsored by the Pacific Forum held in Hawaii in February 1982. These papers, including the opening address of Thanat Khoman, were later published by Pacific Forum. See Morrison, ed., *Threats to Security in Asia-Pacific.* The published version of the Deputy Prime Minister's remarks did not contain a reference to "tigers." The quotation above was taken from the original presentation.

2. Although General Benny Murdani has been the most candid of Indonesia's leaders, his views are not unique. The statement quoted at the beginning of this chapter, which was issued by the Vietnam News Agency from Hanoi, was actually made at the time of General Murdani's low-profile and sparsely reported visit to Vietnamese army outposts along the Chinese border. See *Far Eastern Economic Review,* 7 March 1984, 8.

3. This study does not include the sixth member of ASEAN, Brunei Daresalam. Considerable research for this study had been completed before Brunei joined ASEAN (shortly after severing its last colonial ties with the the United Kingdom on 1 January 1984). Even had Brunei been added at a later stage it is doubtful that research on Brunei's foreign policies would prove very fruitful in view of its very brief history of independence.

4. From the time of a lecture tour through ASEAN in 1980, when I first began to take notes and formu-

late hypotheses about different perceptions of external threats, to a return visit to the Philippines in mid-1986, this and other research has taken me to the ASEAN region on four occasions (1980, 1983, 1985, 1986). I have had opportunities for interviews and informal discussions with two heads-of-governments, four foreign ministers, at least seventy-five senior officials in foreign affairs and defense in the five governments, and at least as many nonofficials who influence or interpret government policies. Many of these were kind enough to talk with with me on several occasions, and some welcomed me to their offices several times during each of my visits. No names have been cited, however, unless the information referred to is also a matter of the public record. I apologize to my readers for not sharing my sources with them, and I realize that I am demanding more of my readers than the canons of good scholarship dictate. However, in almost every case my contacts preferred to talk with me off the record, and I am therefore obliged to respect their anonymity.

5. Ole Holsti, a political scientist who is determined to try to bring some order out of the present chaos, and whose own work is an exception to the generalization I have made, has reviewed the littered landscape. See "Foreign Policy Formulation Viewed Cognitively," esp. 22-30.

6. "The Enemy Beyond."

7. I am indebted to political science colleagues at De La Salle University in Manila, who during my oral presentation of this subject in 1985 argued that my analytical framework was actually complicating my analysis. Later I came to regard the framework as one of inquiry and analysis rather than of structure.

8. Holsti, "Foreign Policy Formation Viewed Cognitively," 26-29, has summarized and documented these and other arguments against the importance of studies of individual policy makers. My position generally agrees with that of Holsti, though we approach our research from different perspectives.

9. Kelman, *International Behavior*, 588-89 makes this point in another context. Kelman is actually focusing on individual policy makers and is simply pointing out various influences on the perceptions and actions of the individuals.

10. Indeed, as it will later be argued, many of these constraints, or influences, provide the keys to understanding the perceptions of the individual policy makers.

11. "Foreign Policy Formation Viewed Cognitively," 29-30.

12. This generalization may be applicable to other nations outside ASEAN. Boulding has noted that "the information gathering apparatus always tends to confirm the existing image of the top decision-maker,

no matter what it is." "The Learning and Reality-Testing Process in the International System," 10.

13.   Boulding, *The Image*, 14.

14.   Fortunately, my own task in this research is easier than that of Sergeant Friday, for I shall be content to accept and report the various interpretations of realities conveyed to me by my informants. Unlike Sergeant Friday I am not obligated to construct a defensible image of "reality."

15.   Steinbruner, *The Cybernetic Theory of Decision*, 95.   All of chapter 4, "The Cognitive Process," 88-139, is particularly relevant to the discussion in this section.

16.   Buchanan and Cantril, *How Nations See Each Other*.

17.   For a good example of the present complexity and sophistication of cognitive mapping see Axelrod, "The Analysis of Cognitive Maps."

18.   Sprout and Sprout, "Environmental Factors in the Study of International Politics," 315.

19.   Steinbruner, *The Cybernetic Theory of Decision*, 95-121 discusses many of the devices we use to achieve consistency.

20.   Except in the Philippines a nuclear threat was rarely mentioned in discussions with political leaders, academics, and media representatives in ASEAN.   Although the nuclear threat was mentioned in the Philippines, this seemed to be connected more with local politics than with a genuine concern about nuclear war. (A Brookings Institution study that listed the Philippines as a possible nuclear target because of the presence of U.S. military bases received considerable media coverage.) The issue rarely surfaced in 1980, but during 1983, while the bases agreement was being renegotiated, the opposition frequently brought up the "nuclear lightning rod" argument. By 1985 and 1986, the doldrums between bases renegotiation talks, there was again little mention of the subject.

21.   Three such studies that proved very helpful, even though they address entirely different problems, are Cohen, *Threat Perceptions in International Crises*; Knorr, "Threat Perception"; and Jervis, *Perceptions and Misperceptions in International Politics*. The "dimensions" framework of this chapter is suggested in the Cohen study, though he might not recognize (or care to claim) the kinship. Jervis, a psychologist by training, offers many theoretical insights that help the scholar understand ASEAN as a framework that has structured individual contacts within the region, but his work is less directly related to the subject of this study.

22.   When my research plans were formulated in 1980 few scholars were concerned with those aspects of the subject that interested me. By the time I was

preparing to return to the field in 1983 the situation had changed somewhat. Bernard K. Gordon of the University of New Hampshire and Rear Admiral (Ret.) L. R. Vasey, Executive Director of the Pacific Forum, conducted a series of interviews with high government officials throughout much of Asia in mid-1981. In a paper for the conference Gordon later wrote: "It quickly became clear . . . that there are indeed important cross-national differences in perceptions of security threats." (In Morrison, ed., *Threats to Security in East Asia-Pacific*, 33.) The Honolulu conference on threat perceptions, where the collection of papers cited above was first presented, grew out of these initial visits by Gordon and Vasey. The various national contributions provide many examples of different perceptions, but in the end the conference poached very little into the research territory I had staked out. The conference had a pronounced policy orientation, with the American side lecturing the Asians on the real dangers that awaited them, and many Asian participants lecturing to the major powers (particularly the Americans) about their misperceptions of the world political environment.

23. *International Behavior*, 588-89.

24. "Foreign Policy Formation Viewed Cognitively," 42.

25. "Looking East, Looking West." Several observations are pertinent. First, Howell recognizes and discusses the problem of equating the attitudes of students to those of policy-making elites, but in the end he rejects the arguments of those scholars who have concluded that they are more dissimilar than similar. Second, despite the title of his article, he uses the students principally as representatives of the Malaysian elite. He specifically recognizes that students could be studied either as "the successor generation" or as representatives of the political elite, and he chooses the latter.

26. "Explaining Foreign Policy Behavior."

27. "Foreign Policy Formation Viewed Cognitively," 43.

28. George, "The Causal Nexus between Cognitive Beliefs and Decision-Making Behavior," 102-4.

2

Southeast Asia and ASEAN: The Setting and the Context

In May, 1943, . . . the British and U.S.
Governments decided to co-ordinate the land and
air forces of the British Commonwealth, the U.S.
land and air forces, and the British Eastern Fleet.
. . . I was entrusted with the formation of the
South-East Asia Command, . . . which was to include
Burma, Malaya, Sumatra, Siam and French Indo-China.
                    The Earl Mountbatten, 1945

Southeast Asia as a geographic term was largely an invention of Europeans. In fact, until the Earl Mountbatten (later Lord Louis Mountbatten) took over an allied command in Burma during World War II, the region was without a designation. The earl's responsibilities extended roughly from China to India and was officially designated the "South-East Asia Command."[1]Although there was initially some inconsistency in the use of the term and disagreement about the precise countries to be included or excluded, the convention and its meaning are now accepted throughout the world.

SOUTHEAST ASIA: THE EVOLUTION OF A REGION

Southeast Asia extends throughout an area bounded by Burma in the northwest corner to West Irian (Indonesia) in the southeast. Within these boundaries lie the mainland states of Burma, Thailand, Laos, Kampuchea, and Vietnam; peninsular West Malaysia; and insular East Malaysia, Singapore, Indonesia, Brunei, and the Philippines. The term Southeast Asia may have been a fabrication of Europeans thousands of miles away, but the area historically has shared some common experiences, and in recent years many of the nations of Southeast Asia have increasingly interacted in a manner that suggests the emergence of a region in fact as well as in name.

From Colonialism to Independence

The Portuguese were the first to settle in Southeast Asia and the last to leave. They captured Malacca
in 1511, and in 1975 they involuntarily yielded Portuguese Timor to Indonesia, but despite their longevity
the Portuguese had little effect on the course of
history in the new nations of Southeast Asia. The
French had much greater impact on Vietnam, Kampuchea,
and Laos; the British, on Burma, Malaysia, and Singapore; the Spanish and Americans on the Philippines;
and the Dutch, on Indonesia.

For the most part the colonial experience defined
the national borders, created the first--but sometimes
only experimental--political and administrative institutions serving the newly independent states, established some basic parameters of the economic systems,
and through the location of administrative centers,
roads, railroads, and telegraph lines charted a course
of internal development that is still apparent today.
Colonial administration of the educational system
usually defined (or reinforced) the distinction
between elites and masses and prescribed (or buttressed) the social distances that separated the
social classes.

The history of Southeast Asia certainly did not
begin with the arrival of the Europeans. However, so
far as the contours of modern Southeast Asia are
concerned, the colonial period was far more important
than its relatively brief length might suggest.

The brief but important Japanese interregnum from
1942 to 1945 also significantly affected developments
in Southeast Asia. Few states experienced the physical
destruction seen in Manila as American and Filipino
troops engaged the Japanese Imperial Army in fierce
street-to-street combat, but many Southeast Asians
suffered physical and emotional hardships and all
witnessed the deterioration of the social, economic,
and political infrastructures constructed by the
colonial powers over the previous decades or centuries. Most important, the myth of European invinci-
bility was destroyed forever. In some six months
Japan, a small, East Asian island nation, almost
totally dismantled colonial empires that had been in
the making for centuries. Decolonization was inevitable eventually, but the Japanese occupation served
as a catalyst that accelerated the process
considerably.

The Japanese interregnum permanently altered
relationships between the colonies and their rulers
and the structure of politics within each of the
countries. The master-servant relationship was destroyed forever, and within each Japanese-administered
state the indigenous peoples got their first taste of

power--often imagined or symbolic, but sometimes real. The impact varied, and the Japanese experience was interpreted and reinterpreted differently in each of the countries of Southeast Asia as they sought political solutions consistent with their own historical experiences. In all countries, however, politics after 1945 would never be the same.

Independence came in many ways in Southeast Asia. In 1945 Thailand, the only state not to have undergone a colonial experience, had only to "correct" its pragmatic decision to accept an alliance with Japan during World War II. In a formal sense Brunei, like Thailand, had never been a colony, but, as a protectorate of Great Britain from 1888 to 1984, this distinction was more legal than practical.

Indonesia and Vietnam were the first of the colonies to proclaim independence (August 1945), but the Netherlands and France abandoned their colonies with great reluctance. It was not until 1949 that the Dutch finally yielded their claims to ultimate sovereignty over all Indonesian territory (except West Irian), but for the hapless Vietnamese the quest for meaningful independence was to be lengthy and bloody. France finally gave up all territorial claims to Vietnam after a disastrous defeat at Dien Bien Phu in 1954, but Vietnam was not unified until the capture of Saigon in April 1975, and today the struggle to achieve an integrated Vietnam continues internally. Elsewhere in Indochina, Laos and Kampuchea, after several false starts, quietly and almost without notice achieved independence from the French in 1954 in the shadow of the much more dramatic events taking place in Vietnam.

The Republic of the Philippines was granted independence from the United States on 4 July 1946, two years after the targeted date set in the Tydings-McDuffie Act of 1934, but President Macapagal in 1963 changed the national day celebrations to June 12 to commemorate the proclamation of independence from Spain made by General Emilo Aguinaldo in 1898. Independence came to Burma in 1948, although the British decision to partition the Indian subcontinent and grant independence to India and Pakistan in 1947 had given the Burmese a clear signal that Britain intended to withdraw from the region.

The absence of a strong nationalist movement and the domestic unrest ravaging parts of the country caused Britain to defer independence for Malaya until 1957. In 1963 the British colonies of Singapore, Sabah, and Sarawak joined Malaya in the new Federation of Malaysia, and in 1965 Singapore withdrew from the two-year-old federation to make its own way as a fully independent state.

With the Indonesian acquisition of West Irian from the Dutch in 1963 and East Timor from Portugal in

1975, the unification of Vietnam in 1975, and the breaking of defense and foreign affairs ties between Britain and the Sultanate of Brunei in January 1984, the process of European decolonization in Southeast Asia was complete.[2]

Beyond Independence

Although the postindependence paths taken by the ten states of Southeast Asia were almost as diverse as their roads to independence, some common issues, themes, and outcomes can be detected.

Internal Dissent. Each state faced internal dissension as contending factions competed for recognition as the legitimate representatives of the people, however ill-defined "the people" might have been. The struggle for recognition took many forms, developed at different times, and still continues today in some parts of Southeast Asia. The governments of Malaya and Burma faced bloody competition from contending elites while bargaining with their colonial masters for the best possible independence arrangements. The government of the Philippines began to battle the contenders almost as soon as independence was granted, and the revolt that appeared to have been quelled resurfaced some forty years later in an even more threatening and virulent form.

Indonesia faced an abortive *coup* attempt and a right-wing Islamic revolt just before the Dutch gave up their colonial claims, and in the early years of independence the government was forced to respond frequently to fissiparous regional demands. In 1965 Indonesia underwent a painful internal struggle that left hundreds or perhaps thousands dead as violence spread through the major islands of the country.

In Laos the battle between contenders, often cloaked in modern ideological garb, was grounded in traditional historical rivalries, and in Kampuchea the competition was muted and largely hidden until Prince Norodom Sihanouk was deposed by Lon Nol in 1970 in a *coup* that set in motion a painful train of events that culminated in a Vietnamese invasion and occupation of that once-peaceful backwater in late 1979.

Vietnam has waged the longest internal political struggle in Southeast Asia. While initially the competition was between the Viet Minh, who controlled the north, and outside powers--first the French and then the Americans--the struggle rapidly became one between the south with its American patron and the north with its several socialist-bloc patrons--first primarily China and later predominantly the USSR. Thirty years of internal struggle ended in April 1975 when the last American helicopter evacuated struggling refugees from the roof of the American Embassy in Saigon, but the political quest for a meaningfully unified Vietnam remains as elusive today as ever.

Colonial Political Models. Relationships between the governing and the governed, and the institutions created to mediate these relationships, were shaped by each nation's colonial experience. Each former colony adopted many of the institutions of its colonial administration, but adapted these to fit its unique history, culture, and political experience. The process of adaptation continues today--sometimes almost unnoticed but occasionally obvious, agonizing, and painful.

Burma, Malaysia, and Singapore were all recipients of the Westminster parliamentary model. Burma was the first Southeast Asian state to inherit this model and the first to abandon it. Except for Burma, Westminster parliaments still exist in the other former British colonies.

In Malaysia, "Malaya" until 1963,[3] the Westminster model slowly gave way to increasing administrative centralization and decreasing parliamentary vitality. In May 1969, when the Kuala Lumpur racial riots triggered some ten months of emergency rule under the National Operations Council, relationships between the governing and the governed were fundamentally altered. They remained changed even when parliamentary rule was restored in 1970.

Singapore retained the Westminster parliamentary system throughout its Malaysian and independence periods. However, the very nature of the ruling party, the People's Action Party (PAP)--its efficiency, effectiveness, discipline, and, when necessary, particularly in Singapore's formative years, its ruthlessness in dealing with an even more ruthless opposition--has transformed the Westminster tradition into something peculiarly Singaporean with roots that go back not only to Britain but also to China and Southeast Asia.

The Philippines began with a political-administrative-judicial model that looked very American but performed in a very Filipino manner. The Philippines had a system of popular representation whereby Filipinos were elected to institutions with familiar American names through processes that were also described in common American terms. Yet the electoral games played were vastly different. The declaration of martial law in 1972 abolished the colonial model, and the People Power Revolution of February 1986 brought in new incumbents and restored openness in government. However, throughout history the Philippine political process has demonstrated more continuities than discontinuities. It has been, and remains, uniquely Filipino.

Indonesia experimented with various Western political models derived from several sources until in 1959 President Sukarno abolished the "winner-take-all-tyranny," as he described Western democracy. In its place he substituted the original revolutionary constitution of 1945, which in Sukarno's view was much more in harmony with the traditions of Indonesia. Although Sukarno's critics later accused him of abusing these traditions for his own purposes, many argued that he had returned the Indonesian polity to the mainstream of Indonesian, or perhaps Javanese, history. For Sukarno and for traditional Java, discussion, below-the-surface political bargaining, circumspection, and on-the-surface consensus were more respected than frontal attacks, polarization, and majority rule. Although Sukarno and the "Old Order" were discredited, the "New Order," no longer new and also increasingly under attack by its opponents, retained many of the Javanese characteristics of the Sukarno era, but without Sukarno's flamboyance, colorful excesses, and mercurial policy gyrations.

If Southeast Asia has experienced any revolutions, in the strictest sense of the term, they have occurred in the states of Indochina. The late Ho Chi Minh greatly admired and respected the French and their culture, and perhaps he even admired French political institutions in their native habitat. He did not, however, accept that institutions appropriate to France were necessarily appropriate for Vietnam. He was a well-travelled and perceptive revolutionary who brought to Vietnam a revolutionary ideology. However, although Ho's philosophies may have been revolutionary, from the beginning in 1945 to the present time, Vietnam's revolutionary movement has been sustained to a great extent by indigenous roots that are grounded in the soils of both Vietnam and China, two countries that have been both longtime lovers and historical enemies.

The revolutions in Laos and Kampuchea were stimulated by events in Vietnam, and today the governments of the two are those installed and sanctioned by Vietnam. When the Vietnamese stationed troops in Laos they met little resistance from the badly divided, administratively ineffective, and politically pressured Laotian regime of Prince Souphanouvong, and today they occupy Laos with few troops and little resistance.

In Kampuchea an already murky situation was complicated by the appearance of a little-understood visionary (or an unfeeling madman, as most would describe Pol Pot), who brutalized the Khmer people in ruthless pursuit of indiscernable goals, but who, to the embarrassment of many nations, constituted the recognized government when Vietnam invaded Kampuchea

in 1978 and replaced Pol Pot with Heng Samrin. The
Khmers have a long and proud history; even with the
albatross of Pol Pot around their necks it seems
unlikely that the last has been heard from the Khmer
nationalists, who today are represented by a coalition
government that includes the old Pol Pot faction but
is at least nominally headed by the former ruler of
Kampuchea, Prince Sihanouk.

Heterogeneous Societies. Colonialism left each country
with a legacy of social pluralism that has made nation
building difficult. Most of the mainland states of
Southeast Asia face tensions generated by highland-
lowland differences, not unlike those found in many
mountainous countries of the world. Many also must
deal with regional unrest, which is reinforced by
cleavages defined by tribal ties, culture, language,
religion, or ethnic origins.
     Every Southeast Asian state also has an eco-
nomically and sometimes numerically significant "overseas Chinese" minority. The Chinese are an important
element in the development of each of the nations of
the region, and often contribute significantly to the
strength of present-day economies. Nevertheless, they
are often suspected and disliked by the indigenous
majorities. The Chinese of Southeast Asia have gone a
long way in adopting and adapting local ways of life,
but their differences often stand out more than their
similarities. Even in Thailand, where the process of
acculturation has proceeded farther than elsewhere in
Southeast Asia, and where Sino-Thais intermingle freely with native Thais, relations sometimes become
strained. Sino-Thais may be virtually indistinguish-
able to an outsider, but they not infrequently retain
their separate identities to their fellow countrymen
and to themselves. Elsewhere in Southeast Asia this
situation is even more common and more apparent.

THE MAKEUP OF ASEAN: FIVE PROFILES

     In world perspective the five original members of
ASEAN are prosperous and open societies with leader-
ships committed to economic modernization, some degree
of popular political participation, and a free-market
system that is integrated into the international
economies of the First World. To these generalizations
I must add some exceptions and caveats, which will
become evident in the country profiles.

Thailand

     Thailand is unique among its ASEAN neighbors for
several reasons. It escaped colonialism because it
served as a useful buffer between French and British

imperial holdings; for more than two centuries it has retained a single monarchial line, an institution that even today is a vital force in Thai political and social life; and it has the longest land borders with the largest number of neighbors of any of the ASEAN states (some two thousand statute miles of borders separating and linking Thailand with Burma, Laos, Kampuchea, and Malaysia).[4] Given its borders and its troubled neighbors, it is not surprising that Thailand often finds itself at the center of international tensions.

Until 1932 the Thai monarchy ruled without significant constitutional restraints, though several modernizing kings set up advisory bodies intended to encourage broader participation in government. Ironically, it was probably the most democratic-minded king, Rama VII,[5] who suffered the indignity of the *coup* that marked the beginning of the constitutional era. Three characteristics of this *coup* were later to be repeated many times in modern Thai political history: the key figures were young army officers, the event was bloodless, and only a small number of elite were involved or apparently even concerned. Rama VII readily accepted the new constitution thrust upon him, and despite many later *coups*, attempted *coups*, and changes in government, the Thai monarchy has not been the controlling force in Thai politics since 1932, although its waxing and waning influence has sometimes been significant.

Today the unifying influence of the monarchy provides one of the most significant counterweights to the forces that strain the fabric of Thai society. The institution of the monarchy is almost universally accepted, and often revered, throughout Thailand, and the present king, Bhumibol Adulyadej (Rama IX), is popular with most segments of society. During the late 1960s and early 1970s the king, who is an accomplished jazz saxaphonist, joined restive university students in impromptu jam sessions on campuses, and generally served as a mediator between them and an often hostile government. Although the king's efforts did not prevent some violent student demonstrations, particularly in 1968 and 1973, he has generally been credited with lowering the level of tensions during a period of worldwide student activism. Moreover, King Bhumibol's influence extends into the upper reaches of government.

On several occasions when Prime Minister Prem was faced with almost certain defeat in a developing *coup*, a symbolic gesture by the king in support of the incumbent was sufficient to discourage the would-be usurpers.[6] Most premiers have discovered that the support of King Bhumibol is crucial at times of political crisis. The king cannot create the government. However, a gesture of support may keep a faltering prime minister in office; a gesture of non-support may topple a government. The king does not make policy, but in some situations he can make or break the policy-makers.

Thailand has always succeeded in coping with internal and external crises by pragmatic ad hoc adjustments to meet new situations. If it can be said that much of Britain's illustrious history must be attributed to its genius for "muddling through," then certainly the same can be said for Thailand. Besides its genius for pragmatic flexibility, Thailand is blessed with many attributes missing in most Third World countries: good agricultural land, a strong administrative infrastructure, a people fairly homogeneous culturally and linguistically, and the unifying force of a long-established monarchy. Although it has often found itself at the vortex of international rivalries, as it is today, Thailand has survived and the Thai people have prospered. Despite current political pressures, Thai history seems on course.

Malaysia

Malaysia is best known for its tin, its rubber, and its ethnic diversity, and the three are related. The British needed labor to support a booming economy based on tin and rubber, and to the British colonial managers and civil servants the Malay community did not seem suitable. Thus Britain turned chiefly to neighboring China, where economic and political pressures in the nineteenth century had created a large pool of potential migrants who were willing and eager to seek better opportunities abroad. Most of these potential recruits had already migrated from the overcrowded farms of southern China to the treaty ports on the South China Sea, and it was thus only a matter of transporting them to Malaya for work in the tin mines and later the rubber plantations.

The Chinese came to Malaya in droves, most of them transported by private entrepreneurs under conditions only slightly better than those found on cattle boats. Very few Chinese who came to Malaya intended to remain in the country, and indeed most had dreams of making enough money to return to China, buy a small plot of land, and raise their family in a traditional Chinese way.

Reality rarely mirrored the dream. Most labor recruits arrived heavily indentured, and those who succeeded in paying off their debts and amassing significant savings were the ones who left the ranks of the common laborers to become economic middlemen. Their genius for "buying and selling" (the Chinese term for "business") created in Malaya a sophisticated network for collecting commodities and distributing finished goods. This system eventually extended to every village in the country. In the process the Chinese who stayed (though until much later the number who returned considerably outstripped those who stayed) moved above their Malay customers on the economic scale, and some, but actually very few, became so manifestly opulent that they created the myth that all Chinese were wealthy, either openly or secretly. Much of the political distrust of the Chinese today can be attributed to these two factors: objectively, the average Chinese is much better off economically than the average Malay, and, subjectively, the myth persists that all Chinese are actually rich whether they show it or not.

The Chinese constitute the dominant ethnic minority of Malaysia, but other ethnic groups were also encouraged to come to Malaya to support the rapid economic development taking place in the peninsula. Most of these came from India, another British colony. Many Indians remained on the rubber plantations, but many gravitated to menial labor on the roads and the national railways, to junior clerical positions, and to low-level positions in the service sector. A fraction of the Indian, Ceylonese, Sikh, and Pakistani community (as the various Indian migrants are now known) moved into the professions of law and medicine, and some were highly successful in business. However, in general, the Indian community did not match the record of the Chinese in upward economic mobility, and have rarely suffered the political and physical attacks vented periodically on the Chinese.

Today the Malays constitute only a slight majority in their own country, and many are very sensitive to this demographic reality. The colonies of Sabah and Sarawak were incorporated into the Malaysia proposal in 1961 to offset the Chinese majority of Singapore (at the time it was hoped that the protectorate of Brunei would also be included to improve the demographic arithmetic) and thereby make the enlarged federation politically acceptable to the Malay leadership.

Leaders of the Malay, Chinese, and Indian communities have learned to work together in a mutually advantageous symbiotic relationship, and cordial personal ties have often developed across communal lines. Nevertheless, the Malaysian political process is still significantly influenced by ethnic considerations, and this is reflected in the very names of the political parties. The dominant voice in Malaysian politics is the United Malays National Organization, and its major partners in the Malayan Alliance since the early 1950s have been the Malayan Chinese Association and the Malayan Indian Congress. The ruling coalition today (Barisan Nasional--National Front) is considerably broader, but even those parties that do

not carry ethnic names clearly identify with particular communities and unhesitatingly represent the ethnic interests of their constituents. Almost no political, social, or economic issue can be decided outside
the ethnic context. This is a simple fact of Malaysian
political life.

Malays are Muslims by convention and legal definition. It is logically and legally impossible to be a
Malay without also being a Muslim. The extent of
one's commitment to Islam is a private matter, however, and in Malaysia all shades of Islam can be
found. Historically, the top political leadership has
been drawn largely from the ranks of upper-class,
Western-educated Malays, and these often seemed more
influenced by their Western experiences than by their
Islamic backgrounds. On the other hand, some of the
most significant opposition leaders have more traditional religious roots, and Malaysia has experienced
a small number of disruptive and sometimes bloody
upheavals that can be attributed to religious extre-
mists who usually profess to be true followers of the
Prophet.

In recent years Malaysian leaders have exhibited
an increased devotion and commitment to the fundamen-
tals of Islam, and some have become strong supporters
of revivalist Islamic movements; but in general, most
have remained moderate in their actions and pronouncements. Even the most militant fringes of Sunni Islam
in Malaysia pale in comparison to their Shi'ite
cousins in Iran and elsewhere.

Just as Malaysia is fragmented socially and culturally so too does it have a history of political
fragmentation. As the Japanese Imperial Army moved
down the Malayan Peninsula it found a bewildering
array of political units between Kelantan in the north
and Singapore in the south. There were four states
that together constituted the Federated Malay States
(FMS), five "fully autonomous" states, known collectively as the Unfederated Malay States (UMS), and the
Crown Colony of the Straits Settlements (Penang,
Malacca, and Singapore). With the exception of the
Straits Settlements, every political unit had its own
Malay ruler (termed a "sultan" in all but one of the
states), and all were under the general supervision or
direction of British officials whose titles varied
more than their responsibilities. Some four hundred
miles across the narrow neck of the South China Sea
from Singapore lay Sarawak, the private domain of the
Brooke family of England, and to the north the Sultanate of Brunei and British North Borneo, owned at
the time by a joint stock company, the British North
Borneo Chartered Company, Ltd. Eventually, all of
these disparate units, except Brunei, were to make up
the Federation of Malaysia in 1963. Except for the
separation of Singapore in 1965 the Federation has

remained intact and viable. However, the central government in Kuala Lumpur has constantly struggled against fissiparous forces created by the diverse nature of its political traditions, the unevenness of economic development, and the heterogeneity of the Malaysian population. In the process the Federation has largely become a "federation" in name only. In the constant tug of war between the center and the periphery, the center has always proved dominant when a crisis has threatened its authority, and now it possesses all the legal and constitutional tools necessary to guarantee its continued domination.[7]

If colonialism presented Malaysia with some of its most difficult political and social problems, it also helped it to develop the resource base that has made solutions to these problems possible. Of course, tin was present in Malaysia when the British arrived, but it was British and Chinese entrepreneurship that extracted and marketed the ore. Even on today's depressed market, tin continues to be one of the mainstays of the Malaysian economy.

Rubber, on the other hand, was not indigenous to Malaysia; it was a British botanist who first successfully grew Brazilian rubber trees in Singapore soil and began an industry that was quickly to transform Malaya from a sleepy colonial backwater to a thriving international supplier. Rubber too has suffered a decline in market value as synthetic substitutes have been developed and as demand wanes in response to industrial downturns anywhere in the world. Yet without rubber Malaysia would not be in the fortunate economic position in which it finds itself today. Rubber is still a prized and reliable export commodity.

Finally, of the five original ASEAN members only Malaysia has undergone orderly constitutional transition from one leader to another. Thai succession has been marked by bloodless *coups*; the single devolution of power in Indonesia was accompanied by mass violence; the Philippine record of orderly succession was broken by the People Power Revolution; and Singapore's processes have yet to be tested. The constitutional machinery in Malaysia has worked on three occasions, and never once has the legitimacy of the new leader been seriously questioned.

Singapore

When Sir Stamford Raffles founded Singapore in 1819 he had visions of a trading center and a naval station whose importance would stem from its strategic location for both commercial and military purposes. Despite the opposition of Raffles's employer, the British East India Company, which was far more interested at the time in its Indian possessions, Singapore grew rapidly into a thriving port and regional distribution center, just as Raffles had envisioned, and today the accuracy of Raffles's vision is apparent.

Singapore's economic development proceeded at a faster pace than its political development; it was not until 1959 that the colony was given most of the powers associated with internal governance. Even then important powers such as internal security were not solely Singapore's responsibility, and powers related to foreign affairs remained exclusively in British hands.

As the electorate grew from an exclusive British "club" to include, first, all landholders regardless of national origins, and, eventually, all permanent residents of legal voting age, the nature of Singapore politics also changed. With the election of the PAP in 1959 it at first appeared that the course of Singapore politics had veered far to the left to reflect the demands of an overwhelmingly Chinese-speaking electorate.[8] In fact, as it later became evident, the PAP was not one but two parties represented by Chinese-educated and English-educated leaders who were bound together in an uneasy coalition by a unifying desire for independence.

The PAP coalition was probably destined to break up quickly because of the widely differing philosophies of the two sets of leaders, but the proposal for a new federation to include Singapore, put forward by the Malayan prime minister in 1961, had a catalytic effect on the fissures already tearing at the coalition. By the time the Federation of Malaysia was created in 1963 the PAP moderate (English-educated) wing was in power, bearing the original name, while the extreme left wing of the original party (the Chinese-educated wing) had broken ranks, created the *Barisan Sosilis* (Socialist Front), was soon to be soundly defeated in general elections, and thereafter was to abandon the constitutional road and disappear underground to continue its revolutionary struggle.

Singapore remained a member of the enlarged Federation of Malaysia for less than two years, and it was a stormy marriage that never enjoyed even a brief honeymoon. The causes of the breakup are numerous, complex, and as yet not fully explained, but the end result was the total independence of the Republic of Singapore on 9 August 1965.

Independence created many new challenges for Singapore, and at the time there was considerable skepticism that a mini state the size of Singapore (227 square miles with a population of 2.5 million) could survive in a highly predatory world environment, and particularly in a setting in which it was surrounded by hostile neighbors. After some very early manifestations of self-doubt the PAP leadership quickly regrouped and began attacking the republic's manifold

problems with the vigor, determination, and rationality that soon became the hallmarks of Singapore's
economic development programs.

Britain's decision to withdraw its forces east of
Suez necessitated new defense arrangements and significant economic readjustments to compensate for the
loss of British bases in Singapore. Despite a Five-
Power Defense Arrangement (Singapore, Malaysia,
Britain, Australia, and New Zealand) Singapore was
quick to accept responsibility for its own defense and
to build a small but highly mobile land force based on
the Israeli model, which is supported by a small air
force equipped with the most modern and technologi-
cally sophisticated equipment available.

In the economic realm Singapore has been equally
successful. At the risk of oversimplifying a very
complex subject, Singapore economic successes can be
explained by five major factors: the PAP concentrated
on those economic ventures for which Singapore is best
suited; the Party maintained a virtually corruption-
free government; the government encouraged and
actively sought foreign investment; it imported the
best technology and the best minds; and, in general,
Singapore was successful in creating a physical,
social, and economic environment that appeals to individuals and corporations.

Of all the ASEAN countries Malaysia and Singapore
probably have the best chances of moving from Third to
First World status within the next quarter- to half-
century. Singapore's economic performance since independence has outstripped that of Malaysia, and it is
predicted to join the club of developed states first.
But Malaysia, in contrast to Singapore, has a solid
base of natural resources that today includes petroleum and natural gas as well as the commodities introduced or developed during the colonial era. Both are
promising candidates for First World status early in
the next century, and some international financial
institutions already regard Singapore as a member of
the club.

Singapore has faced its share of serious problems, particularly in the last few years of international recessions, volatile fuel prices, and fiscal
unpredictability. It has also suffered from some of
its own successes, but these issues can better be
treated elsewhere.[9]

Indonesia

By any measure Indonesia is a very large country.
If a map of Indonesia is superimposed on a map of the
continental United States of the same scale its borders extend into both the Atlantic and the Pacific
oceans. In area Indonesia is larger than Alaska; in
fact, it is only slightly smaller than Alaska and

California combined, and larger than the total area of all members of European Economic Community. In terms of population, Indonesia is the fifth largest nation in the world. Some 40 per cent of the total population of Southeast Asia is Indonesian. Past and present Indonesian leaders have been sensitive to statistical comparisons such as these, and they have often expressed frustration that Indonesia does not get the international attention that its size justifies. Probably the flamboyant rhetoric and international posturing of the late President Sukarno, and the more subtle and reasoned calls today for an "independent and active" foreign policy, are both expressions of this frustration.

Indonesia may be large on all measures, but in terms of its population distribution, culture, and history it is very much a country with a focus on the heartland island of Java. Indonesian theater, art, music, social structure, and nationalism owe far more to Java than to the rest of Indonesia taken together. Although there are no formal barriers to non-Javanese political leadership, in fact it is difficult for a anyone from the "outer islands" (a term coined by the Dutch that includes all Indonesia except Java) to rise to the top. Sumatrans are the only possible exceptions. Historically there has been considerable interaction between Java and Sumatra, but the odds of success for a Javanese are better than those of a Sumatran, and Indonesians born beyond Java and Sumatra are at a great disadvantage.

Part of the distrust of outer islanders is embedded deep in Indonesian history, but the distrust is also very modern. Early in its life the struggling republic was faced with numerous revolts, particularly in the Celebes and South Moluccas, that had to be put down by the republican army at a time when its resources were stretched thin. Moreover, the major revolts were able to look to outsiders for assistance, either the Dutch or the United States, which offered support in the form of covert aid. It was difficult for the republican government to maintain control over an area as vast and diverse as Indonesia, and, although the threats are now more subtle, regional tensions remain a serious problem for the Suharto government. The heartland is secure, but politics in the outer islands must always be watched with care.

Finally, Indonesia is overwhelmingly Muslim, and in fact it has the largest number of Muslims of any country in the world. However, it is not an Islamic country, even in the moderate sense that Malaysia professes to be Islamic. The late President Sukarno often courted and exploited Muslim cultural and political organizations, but he also built an ideological wall insulating Islam from the political process. Ostensibly *Panca Sila* (the Five Principles) was inten-

ded to weld a highly diverse and geographically dispersed population into Indonesians, but, as its Muslim
critics sometimes charged, the practical effect was to
reduce greatly the political leverage that Islam could
be expected to command in a nation populated chiefly
by Muslims. The New Order regime of President Suharto
has renounced most of Sukarno's policies, but *Panca
Sila* has remained a cornerstone of Indonesia's state
ideology. Indeed, the Suharto government has gone even
farther than Sukarno in requiring its acceptance by
all registered organizations. Muslim leaders continue
to complain that *Panca Sila* is intended more to contain the political potential of Islam than to build a
national ideological consensus.

The Philippines

For centuries the Philippines remained aloof from
the rest of Asia, and this situation is only gradually
changing today. In ethnic terms, Filipinos are akin to
Indonesians and Malaysians, and there are many similarities in language that indicate the presence of
historic ties. Yet Filipinos have generally not been
accepted as kinsmen by most Southeast Asians, and even
within ASEAN there have been many doubts expressed
about the real commitment of the Philippines to any
regional undertaking. The origins of this mistrust are
to be found in the two colonial experiences the
Philippines has undergone.

The Spanish conquest of the Philippines was in
part motivated by economics and in part by religion.
The first Spanish expedition to land in the Philippines was led by Ferdinand Magellan, who was trying to
to chart a Pacific passage to the Spice Islands.
Magellan landed in Cebu in the central Philippines in
1521 to take on supplies; he was killed by a Cebu
warrior, Lapu Lapu, when the Spanish intervened in a
local tribal war; and shortly thereafter his fleet
sailed away. However, on the basis of the right of
discovery by Magellan, the Spanish claimed the islands
in 1542, after it had become apparent that the
location would be suitable for transshipping Mexican
silver and Chinese silks. Moreover, there were good
religious reasons for conquest. Islam was continuing
its seemingly relentless expansion northward and east-
ward, and a Christian Philippines would provide a
bulwark against Islam's further expansion.

The colonial conquest was successful, but it cut
the Philippines off from much of the world. Spain was
not successful in its bid to become a major colonial
power in Asia, and, as a Spanish colony, Philippine
ties were mainly with the home country and Spanish
colonies in the New World. As the only Roman Catholic
country in Asia the Philippines had little in common
with its East and Southeast Asian neighbors, most of

whom were Buddhist or Muslim. These differences remain today, and it is not unusual to hear Filipinos speak condescendingly of the superiority of their religious doctrines, just as their Spanish mentors might have done four centuries earlier.

The American colonial experience, which began as a result of the defeat of Spain in the Spanish-American War in 1898, may have realigned the international perspectives of Filipinos, but it did nothing to bring them closer to their neighbors. In fact, American colonialism probably isolated them even more from their ancient history, for the new colonial masters systematically and persistently introduced all the trappings of modern America--the English language; mass American-style education; American political and administrative institutions; and, perhaps most significant, a trans-Pacific orientation that virtually blocked further contacts with Southeast Asian neighbors. In many ways the Philippines was tutored to be an American state, though no responsible American administrator would suggest such a union.

Spanish colonial policies and practices encouraged the growth of a landed aristocracy that has survived to the present day. Moreover, landed families have dominated practically all aspects of Philippine life--education, politics, economics, the media, the arts, etc. If the faces that emerged after the People Power Revolution of February 1986 seem familiar, it is not surprising: most can trace their roots to Spanish agrarian and social practices of three or four centuries earlier.

Two colonial experiences grafted on to the traditional social organizations of a geographically dispersed people have produced a modern Filipino society that is filled with contrasts. At the top is a cosmopolitan, educated, landed elite that can be as comfortable in New York as in Manila. At the bottom is the majority of Filipinos who may exhibit strong vicarious likings for foreign institutions, practices, and customs, but who remain tied to their surroundings by poverty. However, both the elite and the masses have retained much of their uniquely Filipino past. The result is a cellular social structure in which *campadres* are tied to *campadres* even when they come from vastly different social classes; extended family and language ties that define social relationships; and family responsibilities that are expected to take precedence over all others, even if they lead to a violation of a public trust. Absent, at least until the People Power Revolution can prove itself to have been more than a one-time accident, has been an overarching sense of civic responsibility that binds citizens directly to the nation without passing indirectly through the many mediating traditional institutions of Philippine society.

ASEAN: THE ORGANIZATION

ASEAN was created in 1967 following a sputtering four years of the Association of Southeast Asia (ASA-- Malaysia, Thailand, and the Philippines, 1961-65) and a stillborn MAPHILINDO (Malaysia, Philippines, and Indonesia).[10] The former recorded some very modest successes and articulated some useful long-term objectives. MAPHILINDO, however, a by-product of the period of *konfrontasi* (confrontation) between Indonesia and the newly created state of Malaysia over Malaysia's right to exist, recorded no accomplishments worthy of note except to have served as a step in the creation of ASEAN.

From its inception until well toward the end of its first decade, ASEAN showed little promise. Though avowedly economic in nature, it recorded very modest economic achievements. In fact, ASEAN often seemed much more a social club than an economic organization. Literally hundreds of nationals from the five member nations visited each other's home countries, talked in seemingly endless committee and working-group meetings, and dined and socialized together throughout ASEAN Southeast Asia. Such encounters, of course, were dominated by the top elites of the countries, but they were by no means confined to this upper stratum. ASEAN meetings increasingly dipped down to include assistant ministers, parliamentarians, technocrats, bureaucrats, and, later, private businessmen.

Some critics, particularly foreign observers, were quick to describe ASEAN as "all talk and no action." On the surface such criticisms were valid, but they missed the important point that ASEAN, by its very existence, was redirecting the flow of the main channel of Southeast Asian history. A dominant theme of Southeast Asia's history has been the rich variety of differences found from country to country and within the borders of each country, but for the states of ASEAN this seems to be yielding to a second historic theme, adoption and adaptation at an international level of political and social forces emanating from each of the countries individually. The result is an increasing consensus among the leadership of the member nations, and perhaps even "consensus" is an inadequate term to describe the changes that are taking place.

As outside forces exert influence on the states of ASEAN, the elites, in the familiar historical process of coping through selective adoption, experimentation, and adaptation, are gradually beginning to view the world around ASEAN in similar ways. Such would not have been possible two decades ago, when the physical, cultural, and psychological obstacles to meaningful communication within ASEAN were formidable. But because of advances in communications technology,

the increased frequency and dependability of air
travel, and--most important of all--because of a
desire to communicate, ASEAN-member nationals have
seen and heard much of one another in the past decade.
Thirty or forty years ago a telephone conversation
between Singapore and Manila was an exciting, time-
consuming, and sometimes fruitless international
adventure, and cable traffic had to be routed through
London and Washington. Today, one dials direct without
operator assistance, and computers in Manila interact
instantly with computers in Singapore. Moreover, and
again this is the most important point, there are now
persons in Manila who want to communicate with their
counterparts in Singapore. And in their communications
they are increasingly bridging cultural barriers and
understanding each other to an extent unimaginable
even a quarter-century earlier.

What may be emerging in ASEAN is an overarching
identity that could forge a very unhistoric unity
among neighboring states that historically have known
little about each other. This is not to say that a new
superstate is in the process of formation; such is not
likely to develop soon, if ever. However, it does mean
that a regional group of nations with similar economic
philosophies, similar ideas about relations between
the governing and the governed, and similar defini-
tions of "development" and "modernization" are beginning to view the world about them in an increasingly
similar perceptual framework.[11]

ASEAN members have increasingly found themselves
in agreement on what constitutes a threat or an opportunity, a cost or a benefit, a good or an evil. In
this sense an ASEAN identity is emerging. If the
result seems to run counter to the mainstream of
Southeast Asian history, the process by which it is
occurring is very much in the indigenous tradition.
Six disparate nations are coping with forces emanating
from outside the region by adopting and adapting
ideas, philosophies, technologies, and practices that
have not been part of their own traditions. The ideas
and technologies may be new, but the process is not.
Adoption and adaptation have been taking place in
Southeast Asia for centuries. The striking feature
today is that much of the process is taking place
increasingly within a regional framework. ASEAN has
made a difference.

NOTES

    1. Mountbatten's command responsibilities were
not nearly as clearly defined as this simple explanation suggests. There was also the China-Burma-India
Theater (a British and American construct). Generalis-
simo Chiang Kai-shek claimed part of Mountbatten's

South-East Asia Command, and each of the armed services of each of the Allied countries had its own command boundaries. See Mountbatten, *Report to the Combined Chiefs*, 3-21. The opening quotation to this chapter was also taken from this source (p. 3).

2. Indonesia under President Sukarno frequently claimed that the new economic and military colonialism of Japan, Europe, and America in Southeast Asia (what Sukarno and others termed "neo-colonialism") is more subtle but as debilitating as the older and more blatant form. A similar argument is sometimes used by Vietnam. On the other hand, the Vietnamese occupation of Laos and Kampuchea is also considered to be colonialism by some countries of the region. Thus, many arguments can be heard that decolonization has not run its course.

3. The terms "Malaysia" and "Malaya" will be employed as they are appropriate to the time. When the discussion includes events before and after 1963, or when a geographic connotation is intended, "Malaysia" will serve for both.

4. To this list might be added a fourth uniqueness: it was an ally of both Japan and the United States during World War II. When an invasion seemed inevitable Thailand invited Japan to occupy the country as a friend and Japan accepted. At Japan's request Thailand declared war on the Allied powers, but a government in exile in Washington refused to acknowledge the declaration and mobilized Thais abroad to support the Allied cause. After Japan's surrender the Thai Parliament rescinded the declaration retroactively and accepted the policies and pronouncements of the exile government. Thus, in legal terms Thailand was an ally rather than an adversary of the United States.

5. Rama VI, who ascended the throne in 1910, decreed that he and all Chakri Dynasty kings before and after him would take the name "Rama." Thus the founder, Chakri (actually a military title used by the first incumbent whose real name was Thong Duang), became Rama I, and today's ruler, King Bhumibol Adulyadej, is Rama IX. Because of their popularization in story and song the best known Thai kings are probably Mongkut (Rama IV) and Chulalongkorn (Rama V), who together reigned for more than a half-century from 1851 to 1910. Their political biographies were the subject of *The King and I*, the musical comedy taken from Margaret Landon's *Anna and the King of Siam*. Considerable liberties were taken with historical facts, particularly in the musical, but, as reported, both kings were bright, well educated (self-educated in the case of Mongkut), and progressive in their policies. It was Mongkut who opened Thailand to Western influence. Many of the innovations they introduced are dealt with in Riggs, *Thailand*.

6. The deputy army commander-in-chief attempted such a *coup* in April 1981, just a year after Prem had taken office. Prem joined the entire royal family at Korat, northeast of Bangkok, and when it became apparent that the king was backing his prime minister, the *coup* attempt immediately lost momentum. Most of the rebels surrendered the following day without a fight.

7. See Tilman, *In Quest of Unity*.

8. At the time of the the creation of Malaysia, Singapore was 78 percent Chinese and 15 percent Malay. The remainder were Indians, Eurasians, etc. Except for a small English-speaking segment the Chinese overwhelmingly spoke their local Chinese dialects, chiefly Hokkien, and to a much less extent Cantonese, Hakka, Teochiu, etc. The ethnic breakdown has changed little, but today the Chinese are overwhelmingly English educated, usually speak Mandarin to those from the Chinese educational stream who do not share their native dialect, and find their home dialects of decreasing utility.

9. See chapter 8.

10. For the first sixteen years of its existence ASEAN was composed of the four member states of ASA and MAPHILINDO plus Singapore. Brunei was admitted to the Association in 1984. Sri Lanka indicated that it would like to join, but the ASEAN membership discouraged it from making formal application.

11. Of course there is a great gap between the philosophies of political participation of Philippine President Corazon Aquino and Brunei Sultan Hassanal Bolkiah. However, in ASEAN Brunei lies at one extreme on this dimension and the remaining five states are clustered much more closely together.

3

Policy Formulation:
The Policy Makers and
the Policy Setting

*In the end it's the president who makes policy. He
may let ministers and generals make pronouncements,
but he makes policy.*
                              Indonesian journalist
                                   Jakarta, 1983

*It's too soon to say who makes foreign policy here.
I think the president will leave much of it to the
foreign minister and the ministry, but it's too
soon to be sure.*
              Senior official, Ministry of Foreign Affairs
                                   Manila, 1986

*Frankly, I sometimes feel more at ease confronting
the enemy than selling ideas to our own people.*
                                   Arun Panupong
                      Deputy Foreign Minister of Thailand
                                   Bangkok, 1985

        This chapter is concerned with *who* makes policy
in the ASEAN states, *how* policy gets made, and *why* one
policy prevails over another. These questions will
resurface many times later in discussing specific
perceived threats, but the purpose here is to identify
the dominant personalities and describe the processes
in more general terms.

INDONESIA

        The forces shaping Indonesian policy making,
including the making of foreign policy, are subtle,
deeply imbedded in a very complex and sophisticated
Indonesian/Javanese culture, and rarely what they
appear to be on the surface. Fortunately, the policy
makers may more easily be identified, even if the
processes by which they reach their decisions are
obscure.

The Policy Makers

In today's Indonesia the adage, "leaders lead and followers follow" applies; without doubt the principal leader, President Suharto, leads all lesser leaders as well as his followers. The minister for foreign affairs, Dr. Mochtar Kusumaamadja, occasionally makes important policy pronouncements--often concerning relations with Vietnam or the People's Republic of China (PRC)--that seem to signal an impending change of direction in Indonesian foreign policy. Commander of the armed forces, General L. Benny Murdani, apparently holds views not entirely consistent with those of President Suharto on the subject of Kampuchea and Vietnam's national interests in Indochina, and on appropriate occasions he expresses these in a manner that in many countries of the world would be interpreted as portending a shift in national policy. Often the long silence of the president following unexpected statements by his foreign minister or chief of staff suggests to outsiders that Indonesian policy is undergoing a significant reorientation. However, whether it is the normalization of relations with the PRC or a compromise on ASEAN's Kampuchean policies, eventually the president will speak, and after he has spoken it is apparent to all that Indonesian policy has not deviated from its original course.

That President Suharto is the final arbiter of policy differences in the second echelon is not surprising: this is the role that presidents are expected to play in most countries. However, the manner in which the president is influenced by second-echelon leaders and his decision making style are uniquely Indonesian.

It is common in Jakarta to refer to various "power centers" that in the Indonesian political process compete for the attention of the final arbiter. Estimates of the number of such points of access and influence vary, but certainly the Ministry of Foreign Affairs and the army must be included in any tally. Almost every person interviewed in Jakarta mentioned these as power centers, but beyond these two there was little agreement.

Some members of the Dewan Perwakilan Rakyat (the DPR, or Parliament) in discussions in 1983 and 1985 felt that they or their leaders were part of the policy-formulation process in foreign affairs and that the DPR should be regarded as one of the power centers. Some practicing politicians and outsiders close to government argued that the media has had an impact on the formulation of foreign policy by mobilizing support on some issues, either in support of a particular power center or independent of all power centers. Thus, so this argument goes, the media has become a power center in its own right. Perhaps

Parliament and the media should be included in the realm of policy making in general, but in foreign policy matters their influence is not apparent.

The process by which the president chooses from among conflicting policy alternatives is frequently discussed in Jakarta. Three decision-making models are most often posited. The first model posits that the president is forced by domestic political consider- ations to balance one faction against another. In this model the substance of the policy alternative is less important than its source.

The second model is based on simple preference. President Suharto is a man with firm convictions deeply imbedded in his personality. Foreign policy decisions are his decisions, and he makes them because they are consonant with his convictions. Power cen- ters may incrementally affect policy making at the periphery, but the core of the decision is what is desirable to the president.

The third model draws from Javanese culture and is a variant of the first two. Some observers liken the policy making process of the Jakarta foreign- affairs elite to the policy process in a traditional village council. The village headman listens impas- sively and at great length to the conflicting positions of the village elders, and when he feels that he has heard enough he pronounces the consensus of the council. In cases with the potential to be significantly disruptive, this consensus must mollify all major parties and defuse the issue, and here the headman's discretion is not unconstrained. However, even in the most contentious cases the headman enjoys some latitude in choosing the "consensus" that best fits his own predispositions, and in many situations the "village consensus" largely reflects the headman's personal preferences.

Regardless of the model to which one subscribes, it is clear that President Suharto is the dominant foreign-policy voice in Indonesia. Others may suggest alternatives, but the president is the only authorita- tive spokesman on all critical issues. Perhaps, as Girling has concluded, the army has penetrated the bureaucracy, political decisions are made within the bureaucracy, and President Suharto dominates the entire system, including the bureaucracy.[1] Perhaps, as Liddle has observed, "the Indonesian political struc- ture can be described as a steeply ascending pyramid in which the heights are dominated by a single office, the president," and the president "commands the mili- tary which is *primus inter pares* within the bureau- cracy."[2] However one conceptualizes decision making, as a seasoned journalist has concluded, Indonesian foreign policy making may be difficult to understand, but the key role played by President Suharto is apparent.[3]

The Policy Environment

Geography, culture, and history have created the environment of foreign policy making in Indonesia. Some of these influences will be dealt with in the chapters that follow, for they relate to Indonesian perceptions of specific countries. Here I shall attempt to examine those aspects of the policy environment that have more general application to the policy-making process.

Indonesia's strategic location in the middle of several major sea arteries forces the country into the mainstream of international politics even if it should prefer to remain aloof, a preference sometimes wistfully expressed by Indonesian leaders. Indonesia is an island nation with as much territorial water as territorial land.[4]

A senior Indonesian official observed wryly in 1983 that "because we are a country of both land and water you could say that we are very open and porous." On the other hand, he continued, "you could say that we are protected from outside interference by a 'great moat' that surrounds us." As for the effect on policy making of the two contradictory perspectives, "we Indonesians use either argument, depending on which supports the case we are making at the moment." Although these comments were made half jestingly, the insights into the policy-making environment are valid. The effects of the contradictory perceptions of the nature of the world surrounding Indonesia are evident in many aspects of Indonesian foreign policy.

It is not unusual for a single leader in the course of the same conversation to speak proudly of the Indonesian genius for adopting and adapting foreign technology, ideas, and institutions; to lament the chameleonlike tendency of Indonesians to borrow from abroad; and to argue that "Indonesia would be best off if everyone just left us alone like they have done with Burma." The influence of the "porous archipelago" and the "protective moat" perspectives are evident in comments such as these.[5]

A variation of the protective-moat perspective on the world is sometimes called the "Jogja syndrome" in Jakarta intellectual circles. The Jogja syndrome refers to one of the most difficult and glorious periods of the Indonesian Revolution. In December 1948 Dutch forces bottled up the revolutionary army in the city of Jogjakarta and virtually isolated the entire fledgling republic in the confines of this single city in central Java. Lacking outside support, and with almost no contact with the outside world, the revolutionary army had to survive by its own wits. Some important leaders, including the president, experienced the Jogja siege firsthand, and even those who were not present often remembered it as Indo-

nesia's finest hour.[6] National resilience, ZOPFAN
(Zone of Peace, Freedom and Neutrality), and sympathy
for the beleaguered Vietnamese, among other foreign-
policy issues, are likely manifestations of the protective moat perspective, or the Joga syndrome.

Finally, no discussion of the foreign policy
environment in Indonesia can be complete without
recognizing the prime importance of two historical
memories--the Indonesian Revolution, and GESTAPU (or
GESTOK, as it is more frequently called in Indonesia).[7] The former can more appropriately be dealt
with in greater detail in connection with Indonesian
perceptions of the Vietnamese and their revolutionary
struggle (chapter 4), and the latter, in connection
with Indonesian perceptions of China (chapter 5). It
is sufficient here to note that no interpretation of
Indonesian perceptions of the world surrounding it can
ignore these two historical memories.

MALAYSIA

From the birth of the Federation of Malaya in
1957 to the present time, foreign policy formulation
has generally been the domain of a small number of
elite, and the primary architect of a particular
policy often has been a single individual. Even
though the top leadership has been constrained very
little by institutional checks, opposition criticism,
or public opinion, the policy environment has imposed
some restraints on the discretion of Malaysian policy
makers.

The Policy Makers

Malaysia has had only four prime ministers since
independence in 1957, and three of these were very
actively involved in foreign relations. The first
prime minister, Tunku Abdul Rahman, who inherited no
foreign-policy bureaucracy and no precedents, seems
sometimes to have consulted no one before making
foreign-policy pronouncements. The Tunku, as he is
known throughout the world, was a very shrewd politician whose apparent bumbling and naivete were actually
useful political tools that he exploited to the
fullest. He was basically a charismatic, anticommunist, English country gentleman, who intuitively
sensed the problems of the contending ethnic groups in
Malaya and was well respected because of this by most
of the ethnic leaders. Most leaders were content to
leave foreign policy (and many other policies as well)
to the Tunku's discretion.

Tunku Abdul Rahman was both prime minister and
foreign minister, and he was actively involved in
foreign affairs. However, the Tunku did not have a

great capacity for facts, and he became impatient with
details and tedium. There was therefore a small
foreign-policy "team," consisting chiefly of the
recognized heir to the top position, Tun Abdul Razak,
a close political confidante of the Tunku, Tun Ismail,
and the senior civil servant in the Ministry of
Foreign Affairs, Ghazali bin Shafie. Perhaps the key
figure was Ghazali Shafie--his later emergence on the
political scene as a member of Parliament and eventually a long-time foreign minister supports this
view--but it was generally the Tunku who dominated
Malayan (and Malaysian) foreign policy until he turned
over the mantle of leadership to Tun Razak following
the Kuala Lumpur riots of 13 May 1969.[8]

The Tunku's designated and groomed successor, Tun
Abdul Razak, was almost the opposite of Tunku Abdul
Rahman in terms of style and personality. He was
direct in dealing with others, and often brutally
direct in his confrontations with subordinates. He had
a great capacity to retain facts and he did not hesi-
tate to overwhelm his critics by reciting them from
memory. He rarely engaged in small talk, brooked no
nonsense from his subordinates, and did not suffer
fools easily. However, Tun Razak, the architect and
top administrator of Malaysia's successful rural
development scheme, was less concerned with international affairs than with domestic matters. He
retained intact the remainder of the Tunku's team, Tun
Ismail and Ghazali Shafie, though under Razak, Ghazali
Shafie resigned as permanent secretary of the Ministry
of Foreign Affairs, was elected to Parliament, and
eventually joined the cabinet as minister for home
affairs, while Razak, like the Tunku before him,
continued to hold the title of foreign minister.

Few expected that Deputy Prime Minister Hussein
Onn would ever become prime minister. Razak's termi-
nal illness was a well-kept secret, and in the public
mind Hussein Onn, who had suffered a heart attack, was
thought to be the less healthy of the two. In fact, it
was widely speculated that Hussein Onn might retire
from politics after the June 1975 general assembly of
his party, the United Malays National Organization
(UMNO). However, when Razak died Hussein Onn was
still first vice-president of the party, and in this
capacity he was the obvious choice for the prime
ministership.

As prime minister, Hussein Onn kept the Razak
cabinet virtually intact. Ghazali Shafie retained the
home affairs portfolio and apparently remained a member of the foreign-policy team. Less than five months
before his death Razak had surrendered the post of
foreign minister to Tengku Ahmad Rithauddeen, who
retained the post in the first Hussein Onn cabinet.

The politician who became prime minister in July
1981, Mahathir bin Mohamad, came from a background

different from that of the previous three prime ministers. He was the first locally educated prime minister (University of Malaya--in Singapore at the time
but later moved to Kuala Lumpur), the first outspoken
critic of his former colonial mentors, and the first
leader to encourage Islamic political activism. Although he had been trained as a physician, he had
always taken a keen interest in politics, even in his
student days in Singapore. As prime minister he played
an active role in international affairs, and he was
the architect of new policies that were intended to
shift Malaysian foreign policy from the course originally charted by the first prime minister, Tunku Abdul
Rahman. Despite his active interest in foreign affairs, Mahathir assigned the foreign affairs post to
Ghazali Shafie, but Ghazali Shafie was always over-
shadowed by the prime minister in matters dealing with
foreign policy. In fact, until Musa Hitam resigned as
deputy prime minister in 1986, he was almost as
visible in the foreign affairs arena as was the
foreign minister.

The Policy Environment

Three characteristics of the Malaysian policy
environment stand out in bold relief: the presence of
a large ethnic Chinese minority within a multiracial
population and with historic ties to a revolutionary
threat; a politically dominant Islamic majority surrounded by an Islamic world increasingly asserting
itself politically; and increasing economic prosperity
coupled with an unequal distribution of wealth. All of
these, of course, are related, but individually as
well as collectively they have affected perceptions
and created many of the parameters of Malaysian
foreign policy.
The Chinese of Malaysia constitute some 37 percent of the population in the peninsula and 25 percent
in East Malaysia. It is common to hear of the
"bargain" struck at independence by which the Chinese
would retain their hold on the economy and the political realm would be left largely to the Malays.[9] If
there ever was such an understanding it began to break
down immediately as the Malay leadership instituted
programs to bring Malays into the world of finance and
business, often with quotas that worked against the
economic interests of the Chinese, and the Chinese
reacted by demanding more political support from their
own leadership.
The Chinese of Malaysia are far more integrated
than assimilated. They are an integral part of the
social and economic fabric of the country, but they
remain a clearly identifiable minority with unique
cultural characteristics. They are not identical to
the Chinese of China and Taiwan, but in the eyes of

many of their fellow countrymen their similarities are far more apparent than their differences. It is this fact that has significantly affected the perceptions of many non-Chinese Malaysians.

Most of the guerrillas who took to the mountains and jungles during the Emergency (as the attempted communist-led rebellion of 1948-60 is officially termed) to challenge the returning colonial regime and its successor, the government of the newly independent Federation of Malaya, were ethnic Chinese. Even today, though the ranks of the revolutionaries have dwindled to a small band of hardcore dissidents in northern Malaya and southern Thailand, the revolutionary movement is still dominated by ethnic Chinese. These facts have had an impact on Malaysian perceptions of the threats surrounding them.

From independence to the present time all Malaysian prime ministers have been Muslims, but Mahathir bin Mohamad was the first to have been identified at one time as an "ultra," the term used in Malaysia to describe politically active Muslims for whom Islam constitutes the dominant and guiding force shaping their policies and programs. Mahathir came into office about the time that renascent Islam was becoming an important political force in nations with Muslim majorities or large Muslim minorities. Indeed, the "Islamic revolution" apparently sweeping the world was viewed with great expectations or trepidations, depending on one's persuasion. Malaysia, for centuries an Islamic backwater, was caught up in the revolution, and Islamic study groups (*dakwah* movements) sprang up throughout the country, inside and outside the government. Most of these were spiritual or intellectual, but some were committed to the violent overthrow of any government that did not demonstrate adequate concern for the traditional principles of Islam.

After assuming the premiership, Mahathir either moderated his stance or proved himself to be much more moderate than his earlier positions had suggested, but he was faced with the realities of dynamic and growing Islamic political movements that threatened the survival of a moderate government in Malaysia. Mahathir's domestic political response was to coopt the religious right into the larger political coalition, a coalition that had been created by Tun Razak in the aftermath of the racial riots in 1969.

Internationally, Malaysia under Mahathir became much more involved in world Islamic movements. Almost immediately after Mahathir's ascendancy to the premiership Malaysia hosted a meeting of the Regional Islamic Organization for Southeast Asia and the Pacific (RISEAP); put forth former prime minister Tunku Abdul Rahman for the presidency; offered to create a headquarters and training center for RISEAP in Kuala Lumpur;[10] and created an Islamic University.

Malaysia has established formal though not very cordial ties with the Palestine Liberation Organization (PLO), and has been active in the Organization of Islamic Conference, in addition to other efforts to demonstrate that it has taken a renewed interest in the affairs of the Muslim world.

Despite recent economic setbacks, all of the ASEAN states have amassed impressive rates of economic growth in the past several decades, and Malaysia has been one of the economic leaders in ASEAN. Yet not all Malaysians have shared equally in the fruits of economic progress. Of course, such a statement is applicable to virtually every nation in the world, but in Malaysia there are many geographic, cultural, and ethnic divisions that coincide with economic cleavages, and this mutual reinforcement has exacerbated the impact of the unequal distribution of wealth.

Malays are Muslim by definition; they tend to be concentrated outside the major urban centers; they usually speak Malay as their first, and sometimes only, language; they are greatly overrepresented in the agricultural sector and are found in large numbers in other low-income jobs; and they are located predominantly on the lower end of the economic scale. Chinese are on the opposite end of almost every spectrum. They are religious eclectics; they are located disproportionately in cities and regional towns; for them Malay is a second, third, or fourth language no matter how proficient they become; they dominate the service sector and are the major middlemen in the distribution networks for manufactured goods and unprocessed commodities; and they are to be found chiefly at the upper end of the economic scale. International policies must always take into account these domestic realities.

SINGAPORE

In Singapore there is a longitudinal consistency to foreign-policy pronouncements throughout most of the relatively brief lifetime of the republic. Statements made by the leadership last week are generally consistent with positions taken almost two decades ago. In part this is because the seniormost leader, Prime Minister Lee Kuan Yew, has remained in office since independent Singapore began to formulate foreign policies in 1965 and the top leadership cadre has undergone changes only in the past several years. In addition, the basic perceptions of this top leadership have remained consistent over the years.

There is also a latitudinal consistency to foreign-policy pronouncements in Singapore. Elsewhere in ASEAN one finds contending "power centers" within the government that hold different views of the

threats facing their country; as a result each power
center may espouse a different set of foreign policy
priorities. In Singapore the leaders are agreed on the
nature and substance of the threats they face, or at
least they have agreed not to disagree in public, and
the result is a single policy on each major issue.

Finally, the senior leaders with responsibility
for formulating, enunciating, explaining, and imple-
menting foreign policy are able, articulate, and
available. Unlike the situation in many countries of
the world, it is not difficult for foreign journalists
and academics to gain access to Singapore's policy
makers. They also have a history of holding news conferences, giving speeches, attending symposia and
conferences, and making statements before countless
international bodies.

The Policy Makers

The prime minister, Lee Kuan Yew, is a forceful
leader whose perceptions of the world have provided
the framework of Singapore's foreign policy. Indeed,
Singapore's major foreign policies are largely the
products of the prime minister, though they have been
marginally influenced by a small circle of longtime
colleagues.

The former minister for foreign affairs, S. Rajaratnam, clearly played an important role in articulat-
ing Singapore's foreign policy (as he continues to do
today even while slipping into retirement), and as one
of four members of the PAP inner circle he remained in
almost daily contact with the prime minister. Thus, he
had many opportunities to influence the prime minister. However, with both men in general agreement on
the broad outlines of policy (and this seems to have
been the case throughout their association), Rajaratnam's influence probably involved details more than
general principles. In fact, Rajaratnam's major contributions to the development of Singapore's foreign
policy were in the area of communication. The former
foreign minister proved himself to be learned, witty,
warm, and urbane. He also seemed completely at ease
delivering an unpopular address before a hostile
audience. These attributes helped him effectively
publicize Singapore's policies before international
fora.

The remaining two members of the PAP inner
circle, Toh Chin Chye and Goh Keng Swee,[11] probably
had less day-to-day impact on Singapore foreign
policy. Toh Chin Chye often served as the spokesman,
and was sometimes called the "ideologue" because of
the frequency of his pronouncements. Nevertheless, he
was an outsider within the inner circle. He may have
been consulted on major issues, but, particularly in
the later years of his cabinet career, which ended

when he chose to leave the cabinet in 1980, decisions
were sometimes reached, or were in the final stages of
discussion, before he became involved. Goh, on the
other hand, who retired from the cabinet in 1984 but
remains in close personal touch with the prime minister, was the inner-circle leader whose judgment is
most trusted by the prime minister. However, Goh was a
"problem solver," and unless the problem with which he
was dealing had a foreign-policy dimension it was
likely that he was involved more in a reactive than an
active manner.

In policy making the second-generation foreign
Minister, S. Dhanabalan, is, like his predecessor, not
as visible as some of his cabinet colleagues. However, like Rajaratnam, he continues effectively to
play the role of communicator. Moreover, although
Dhanabalan has sometimes sounded more Machiavellian
than either the prime minister or the former foreign
minister, there is little concrete evidence in his
statements or his actions to suggest that his perceptions and prescriptions vary significantly from
those of his seniors. The first deputy prime minister,
Goh Chok Tong, also has begun in the past year to
discuss foreign affairs in public fora, and occasionally the prime minister's son, Lee Hsien Loong, is
well reported in the Singapore media discussing some
aspect of foreign policy.[12] Thus, there are now
several spokesmen on foreign policy, but where important matters are concerned there remains only one
chief architect, the prime minister. Furthermore, all
foreign-policy decisions, major and minor, are clearly
within the domain of the executive arm of government--
the prime minister, several cabinet members, senior-
level civil servants, and their consultants and
advisors. Members of Parliament have had little to
say on the subject.[13]

The Policy Environment

Singaporeans may wish to be left alone but they
cannot, as Foreign Minister Dhanabalan has noted.[14]
The size and location of the republic make isolation-
ism impossible. Singapore is strategically important
to virtually every large and mid-size nation of the
world; unlike Burma, Singapore could not opt out of
the international system even if it were so inclined.
For this geographic reality Singapore pays a high
price in terms of the breadth of policy options available to the political leadership, but its strategic
location also presents Singapore with opportunities
not available to countries languishing in international backwaters. Simply because of its location
Singapore cannot be ignored. Raffles saw this in
1819, and it is even more apparent today. Yet the
island has no natural resources except its physical

location and its people, and these can be assets or
liabilities depending upon how they are utilized and
managed.

The long-term strategy and the short-term tactics
of Singapore's leadership have been to maximize the
benefits of the country's strategic location and minimize the costs of its minuscule size. To do this
requires a careful appraisal of the threats it faces;
the formulation of policies most appropriate for
coping with these threats; and relationships with its
neighbors that at least reduce the threats on its
flanks and at best create an international bloc
stronger than each of members individually.

Chan Heng Chee has recently identified "four
permanent interests" that have shaped Singapore
foreign policy: economic development and prosperity;
security from interstate conflict and tensions;
security from internal subversion and insurrection
manipulated from outside its borders; and avoidance of
embroilment in big-power conflict and rivalries.[15]

In a similar vein Foreign Minister Dhanabalan, in
an address before a National University of Singapore
forum in November 1981, enumerated four "fundamental
precepts" of Singapore's foreign policy: Singapore
must be friends with all nations willing to be
friends; trade with any state regardless of ideology;
avoid alignment with a great-power bloc; and cooperate
closely with its ASEAN neighbors. To these fundamental
precepts Dhanabalan added three practical operating
principles: work with any state regardless of ideology
whose interests parallel those of Singapore; rally
international support for Singapore's causes; and
support all worthy causes espoused by Singapore's
supporters that are not in conflict with Singapore's
interests. Finally, the foreign minister added three
operating strategies by which these precepts and principles will be achieved: focus on specific issues that
most directly affect Singapore's interests; keep well
informed on such issues; and select carefully the
time, place, and forum to make the Singapore case.[16]

Singapore, more than most states, needs international political and economic stability and predictability if it is to prosper, or even survive. Larger
nations may withdraw to within themselves in troubled
times, but a small densely populated island offers
little refuge from a major storm. Disruptive or sub-
versive actions inspired or manipulated by its neighbors or by major powers can destroy Singapore's credibility as a safe haven for foreign capital and
expatriate entrepreneurship. Military skirmishes that
approached Singapore's borders, either between feuding
neighbors acting on their own or as proxies for the
major powers, can similarly damage Singapore's credibility. And a prolonged and severe world recession
can cripple Singapore just as effectively as war or

subversion. In a country in which the volume of international trade is three times that of its gross national product, the free flow of international trade is crucial. This is the situation in which Singapore finds itself, and with its ratio of 3:1 it may be unique in the world.[17]

In brief, Singapore is highly vulnerable to forces over which it has only limited control, and it faces dilemmas that larger states can avoid or minimize. Ironically, its resources are also its potential liabilities. This is the environment of Singapore policy making.

PHILIPPINES

The People Power Revolution of February 1986 swept out most of the personalities previously involved in the formulation of Philippine foreign policy, but as yet it has not altered greatly the course of that policy. The perceptions of the present policy-making elite are very similar to those of the prerevolutionary leaders. In some cases there have been shifts in emphases and modest reinterpretations. However, in terms of perceptions of external threats revolutionary reinterpretations are not yet evident.[18]

The Policy Makers

During the more than two decades of the Marcos regime foreign-affairs policy making, and indeed all policy making, was increasingly the province of the president, his wife, and a few members of the first lady's family. Despite the popular image of Carlos Romulo as a strong foreign minister, his role in policy making under Marcos was minimal. As an elder statesman, Romulo often spoke about international affairs in idealistic terms, and he remained an idealist until his death in December 1985. But under Marcos his pronouncements rarely had much to do with Philippine foreign affairs.

After Romulo's retirement in 1984, the Ministry of Foreign Affairs underwent a series of changes in leadership, but no foreign minister wielded much influence with Malacanang. Arturo Tolentino was named as the replacement for Romulo, but he was sacked shortly thereafter for openly criticizing the president.[19] A career foreign affairs officer, Pacifico Castro, was named as the acting foreign minister, and he continued in this temporary capacity throughout the remainder of the Marcos regime. In the waning years of Romulo's life and after his retirement Philippine foreign ministers were more ornamental than functional. The minister made few important decisions, and he had little influence on the top policy makers.

It was frequently joked in the coffee shops that the "real" foreign minister in the last decade of Marcos' rule was the first lady's brother, Benjamin ("Kokoy") Romualdez. Romualdez was ambassador to the United States during much of this time, but his frequent absences from Washington and visits to Manila provided enough circumstantial evidence to keep the joke alive. In fact, it may not have been a joke at all, and, indeed, his name was one of the two most frequently mentioned as the person most likely to succeed Acting Minister Castro.[20]

The other person frequently mentioned for the post was the first lady, Imelda Marcos, and indeed she too functioned as a roving ambassador and psuedo-foreign minister throughout the Marcos era. The first lady was credited with the first significant break-through in relations with the USSR when she visited the Soviet Union in 1972. She also made foreign-policy pronouncements, often it seemed without much reflection or planning, but rarely did these contradict a Marcos policy in any significant way.

The extent to which the first lady acted independently was frequently debated in Manila. At the Ministry of Foreign Affairs the position consistently taken was that Mrs. Marcos always acted as an agent or representative of the president, that during her foreign travels she talked several times a day with him on a special hot line set up for every trip, and that any so-called policy statements she might have made were actually trial balloons launched at the request of the president. Outside the Ministry of Foreign Affairs, however, the first lady was often regarded as an unofficial diplomat who enjoyed considerable independence, or, for some critics, as the de facto president and foreign minister (in addition to other titles relating to domestic responsibilities).

Despite the influence of the first lady and some of her family, chief of staff of the armed forces General Fabian Ver, and a small group of friends and advisors who had easy access to Malacanang, President Marcos had the final word in major foreign policy decisions. However, except for U.S.-Philippine relations, foreign policy did not enjoy the highest priority with the president, and thus others could be allowed to dabble in it so long as they did not tamper with U.S.-Philippine relations. These were the domain of the president, though he may have been influenced by the arguments of his wife, who also took a keen interest in the U.S.

The Aquino government came to power without the benefit of any transition arrangements. Foreign Minister Salvador Laurel worked out of his bank office for several months because he could not gain access to the offices of the Ministry of Foreign Affairs, and for a time no one knew who held which posts in the ministry hierarchy. Every ambassador was required to submit his resignation, and many resignations were accepted. There were also wholesale changes in staff in many of the embassies throughout the world.

The president has devoted more time to the Philippines' internal problems than to foreign affairs. Even in the sensitive area of Philippine-U.S. relations President Aquino has had considerably less to say in public than did presidential candidate Aquino. Foreign Minister Laurel has made several public statements on foreign affairs, but in general his message was that more detailed policy statements will be forthcoming later. Even in their visits to the United States the President (who made a state visit in September 1986) and the Foreign Minister (who spoke to a meeting in Boston several weeks later) had surprisingly little to say on Philippine foreign affairs.

A statement of a policy is not a policy, and in the first several months of the Aquino administration it was impossible to know which of the few policy statements made were destined eventually to become policy. Similarly, it was difficult to be certain that those who spoke on foreign policy were, in fact, speaking for the Aquino government. In such a situation generalizations about policy making must be regarded as tentative.

Until late 1986 it seemed that President Aquino was content to leave foreign affairs largely in the hands of the foreign minister while concentrating on the legion of domestic problems facing the Philippines, and this delegation of responsibility may continue though it is now less certain. In any case, Foreign Minister Laurel plunged into his new role with great enthusiasm. In the first few months in office he attended two ASEAN ministerial meetings (one of which he hosted), talked with President Reagan, and visited Japan, the PRC, Western Europe, and the United States, among his other travels.

Despite this flurry of activity, the foreign minister is also the vice-president, has a national constituency, and political ambitions of his own. Thus, much of his time is taken up with internal matters, and he is more dependent than many of his counterparts in ASEAN on the senior officials of the ministry. At the top Laurel has staffed the ministry with able, experienced, and committed foreign-service professionals. If the president should remain only minimally involved and if the foreign minister continues to be concerned about the many other endeavors with which he is involved, perhaps the Ministry of Foreign Affairs may regain its relevance in the policy making process.[21] On the other hand, in the currently confused political environment other policy makers may emerge from the ranks of the contenders.

The Policy Environment

Except for issues involving Philippine-U.S. relations, foreign affairs has never been a matter of great concern to the Filipino elite. Following the declaration of martial law in 1972, and especially after the assassination of Benigno Aquino in 1983, Filipinos turned inward even more, and very few foreign-policy topics attracted official or unofficial attention.

Unlike the Indonesians, Filipinos have mixed feelings about colonialism and the colonial experience, and some retained pleasant memories of the colonial period; their past experiences with armed revolt left fewer unpleasant memories than were left to their Malaysian and Indonesian cousins; unlike the other members of ASEAN, most Filipino policy makers were unambivalent in their perceptions of the Japanese occupation; and the Kampuchean crisis was far from Philippine shores. Foreign affairs have rarely been seen as important for Filipinos, certainly not as important as their internal problems.

Philippine-U.S. relations are different. Almost any issue in this area is placed high on the policy agenda and receives considerable attention, both in government and in the media. Almost any person questioned will have an opinion on issues involving the Philippines and the United States, even in the absence of much information.

It is not surprising that Philippine-American relations are the major topics of foreign affairs discussion, for they may in fact more appropriately be viewed as an extension of Philippine domestic concerns. For most of the Filipino elite, relations with the United States are more akin to family relations—complete with family squabbles, emotional reconciliations, and a heightened sensitivity to slights, no matter how petty. Other countries can be dealt with as impersonal outsiders, but family members cannot be depersonalized. Injuries inflicted by members of the family may take much longer to heal, and may leave much uglier scars.

Even for the average Filipino there is also nothing impersonal about the United States. In the most rural barrios very few Filipino families do not have at least one relative living in the United States, and in Manila there are sometimes as many family members living or visiting in the United States as there are members residing in Manila. U.S.-Philippine affairs are very much matters of family concern.

There are other issues that must be considered in discussing the environment of policy making in the Philippines—the Japanese occupation, Filipino experiences with their domestic Chinese minority, and geographic realities, among others—but these will be deferred until later chapters where they can more appropriately be linked to the perceptions of specific external threats.

THAILAND

Explaining Thai policy making presents some unusual difficulties. There is an apparent fluidity in Thai political behavior that is probably only a manifestation of actions and reactions within the complex web of personal and political relationships woven among the top elite. Even Thai scholars and political practitioners profess not to understand fully the dynamics of Thai decision-making.[22] With all of these inherent limitations in mind, an attempt will nevertheless be made to identify some of the principal loci of decisions, the key policy makers, and to describe the general environment within which policy making takes place.

The Policy Makers

The military has historically been one of several factions constantly in contention for political supremacy in Thailand, and with regularity the military has achieved its goal, usually as a result of a bloodless *coup*.[23] In fact, since the constitutional *coup* of 1932, prime ministers drawn from the military have ruled for forty-three years, and civilians, for only eleven.[24] When in power it is not unknown for a military prime minister to bypass completely an unsympathetic Ministry of Foreign Affairs and make highly significant policy decisions without even informing the other organs of government. Although this may be the extreme case, it has happened,[25] but there are other less extreme examples of the way a military prime minister has the advantage over his civilian counterpart.

In the past the Thai Central Intelligence Agency (TCIA) has played an important role in providing information to the architects of Thai foreign policy, and the head of the TCIA is almost always drawn from the top ranks of military intelligence. One recent student of Thai foreign policy has drawn two conclusions from the TCIA's close ties with the military: first, the military has an effective means of setting agendas and priorities by selectively emphasizing or deemphasizing the various bits of information that the TCIA collects and processes; second, the TCIA is likely to feel more comfortable with military prime ministers, who in turn may find it possible to be better informed than their civilian counterparts.[26]

Today the Thai government is again led by a former general and dominated by the military, but the

Thai political process has become more complex than it
was under previous regimes. In previous administrations dominated by the military, other political
constituencies have largely been excluded from the
political process, and the interests of those outside
the military have figured only minimally into policy
making. Thus, previous prime ministers with military
origins have had to respond to only one dominant
constituency. However, General Prem has been faced
with a growing number of increasingly strident political constituencies, and his strength and durability
may be attributed to his success in brokering the
escalating and often conflicting demands of these
shifting coalitions and constituencies,[27] including
multiple demands emanating from within the military
establishment. In the process the influence of the
military seems to have declined, and its inability to
get the transitional constitutional amendments extended in 1983 demonstrated this new weakness.[28] Of
course, as one moves from purely domestic issues to
issues of international security, the hand of the
military is correspondingly strengthened.

Prime Minister Prem's chief contender for the
allegiance of the military has been General Arthit
Kamlang-ek, until June 1986 the commander-in-chief of
the Thai armed forces. However, the prime minister's
abrupt dismissal of Arthit and his replacement by
Prem's longtime supporter, General Chaovalit Yongchaiyut, may have reduced the conflicting demands coming
from within the army, at least for the time being.

Within the Prem government a major architect and
certainly the principal spokesman for foreign policy
is the foreign minister, Air Chief Marshall Siddhi
Savetsila, an engineer by training who holds two
degrees from the Massachusetts Institute of Technology.[29] During the Japanese occupation of Thailand
Siddhi joined the *Seri Thai* (Free Thai) movement,
collected information for the OSS, and was captured
and imprisoned briefly by the Japanese. In 1979 Siddhi
was appointed minister without portfolio attached to
the prime minister's department. A year later he was
made foreign minister. In 1983 he ran for election
from a Bangkok constituency and won handily, and today
his strong position in the Social Action Party has
increased the influence he wields as foreign minister.

Most bureaucrats responsible for collecting,
sifting, and transmitting information to their
superiors, and the superiors who in turn may suggest
policy alternatives to the top leadership, would be
described by John D. Steinbruner as "grooved
thinkers." In simplified terms, these bureaucrats put
new experiences into old bottles and describe them by
the familiar labels. The result is stability and continuity. "Uncertainty, political pressure, heavy work-
loads, [and] potential controversy" can be dealt with

"because of the ready-made, well anchored structure to which new problems can be fitted."[30]   Yet,   as Steinbruner and others well recognize, not all bureaucracies are dominated by grooved thinkers, and not all grooved-thinking bureaucrats have significant impacts on the perceptions and policies of their leaders. However, in the case of Thailand, Steinbruner's concepts seem particularly useful.

Thai scholars have not used the term, but concepts similar to the grooved-thinking model have been used to explain some aspects of Thai foreign policy formulation.[31] Thai bureaucrats and policy advisors are said to see what they expect to see--that is, new experiences are given old labels so that new perceptions will not contradict old beliefs.

Ministries rarely are willing to talk about their work to the public, but on one occasion in 1983 the Thai Ministry of Foreign Affairs opened its doors to the press. Several of the published exchanges reveal clearly the types of thought processes Steinbruner and Sukhumbhand Paribatra each described in his own way. A reporter asked the deputy minister of foreign affairs, Arun Panupong, if the ministry had any inkling that Saigon would fall as quickly as it had in 1975. Arun, who is a career diplomat with considerable first-hand experience in the U.S., replied that he and some of his colleagues had "some vague inklings Saigon was on the verge of collapse," but, he continued, "the government in general insisted that nothing of that sort would happen." He concluded by asking rhetorically, "when the government in Bangkok insisted that Saigon wouldn't fall, what could I have said?"[32] Despite the misgivings of Arun and others, new information had been poured into old bottles to create new perceptions with familiar labels.

In Thailand, Prime Minister Prem is the broker and arbiter of policy, and the Ministry of Foreign Affairs is only one of several sources of influence. The military is another, and on many issues, it is apparently the dominant influence. Prem's style of decision making might best fit the model of the "uncommitted thinker" posited by Steinbruner,[33] and the leading military officials could perhaps be described as "theoretical thinkers" (or, alternatively and perhaps more appropriately, "ideological thinkers").[34] If so, Steinbruner's puzzlement may go far toward explaining the mysteries of Thai policy making: "One cannot say with complete confidence what the consensus will be if an 'uncommitted' thinker with a 'theoretical' staff directs a 'grooved' bureau chief."[35]

The Policy Environment

Many Thai political leaders perceive Thailand to be a "front-line" state, and it is this perception that has moved the locus of some foreign-policy formulation from the Ministry of Foreign Affairs to the military leadership. Yet the military clearly does not speak with a single voice, and factionalism within the army probably provides Prime Minister Prem with as many opportunities as challenges. The factionalism and fluidity of military politics only mirrors the situation in the larger political arena,[36] but certain historical patterns become apparent.

Thai foreign policy has frequently been recognized for its flexibility. When Thailand undergoes major shifts in policy it does so in response to major changes in the policy environment. The Thais have been successful in maintaining their sovereignty and autonomy for centuries by aligning themselves with powers, or coalitions of powers, that were capable of overwhelming their potential adversaries.[37]

The reign of Rama Khambeng (1270-1317) saw the development of close ties with China, and China supported the Sukothai state against the Khmers. Following the Opium War and the decline of Chinese power, Thailand signed a Treaty of Friendship with Great Britain, which was rapidly becoming the dominant force in the region. As French influence grew in Southeast Asia Thailand made territorial concessions in return for French support. During World War II the realities of power dictated Thailand's alignment with Japan, but Japan lost.

After World War II it was apparent that the power of the United States had eclipsed that of all the European nations combined, and Thailand became one of America's most supportive allies.[38] However, with the pronouncement of the Guam Doctrine, the winding down of the Vietnam War, the total withdrawal of American forces from Vietnam, and the quick collapse of South Vietnam, the situation had changed significantly. After a brief period of indecision, which ended when Vietnam invaded Cambodia and Laos, Thailand lined up with a new coalition consisting of the ASEAN states, the PRC, and the United States to confront its newest external threat--Vietnam. Thus was created the front-line-state perception within which current Thai foreign policy is formulated.

To be on the front line means that Foreign Minister Siddhi and other foreign-policy architects are constrained, influenced, and apparently preempted by the army. This situation is the result of what two Thai scholars have referred to as the general acceptance throughout Thai government of the "Vietnam bogey." According to their interpretation, Indochina is not an issue in Thai domestic politics, and foreign policy matters dealing with Indochinese problems are therefore left largely to military bureaucrats. In their view the army is not interested in many foreign-policy issues, and these are left largely to the

Ministry of Foreign Affairs, but when military security on Thai borders is involved, "the Vietnam bogey
has allowed the military to make most of the critical
decisions affecting . . . the directions of foreign
policy. . . . In the name of 'national security,' the
military have been able to monopolize all channels of
information concerning border security and . . . to
implement measures without the MFA's . . . approval."[39]

POLICY MAKERS AND THE POLICY SETTING

At least in ASEAN policy making, individuals
matter. Most ASEAN leaders enjoy considerable latitude in foreign-policy formulation, and many policies
bear the clear imprint of the top leadership of the
countries. That is not to say that the policy setting
is unimportant. However, the setting serves more to
structure or affect the nature of the perceptions of
the leadership than to impose strict "yes" or "no"
choices on the policy options available to leaders. In
the ASEAN environment, if leaders choose to exploit
their positions to the fullest (and some do not) the
top leadership can have a significant impact on the
course of their countries' foreign policies. In ASEAN,
in matters of foreign policy, leaders can lead if they
choose to do so.

NOTES

1. Girling, *The Bureaucratic Polity*, chap. 3.
2. Liddle, "Soeharto's Indonesia," 71.
3. Tasker, *Far Eastern Economic Review*, 20 January 1983, 22.
4. Morrison, "Southeast Asia in a Changing International Environment," frequently makes the point that
the world perspectives of nations vary according to
their physical settings (landlocked nations and island
nations interpret the opportunities and threats surrounding them differently), and that different physical settings lead to different foreign policies.
Morrison's apparently self-evident observation is
imaginatively and usefully applied in his study, but
as he recognizes it has many limitations. In terms of
physical setting the most similar ASEAN nations are
Indonesia and the Philippines, but obviously many
other variables have intervened in the formulation of
their foreign policies.
5. In the course of two-hour interview in 1983 a
young politician with considerable interest (but
admittedly doubtful influence) in foreign affairs
discussed all three of these points with equal conviction. Djiwandono, "An Analysis of the Role of a

Third Party," 55-58, points out some ambivalence in Indonesian foreign policy similar to those I have noted, but he attributes these more to the Indonesian quest for an "independent foreign policy."

6. The Central Java regiment based in Jogjakarta was commanded by Lt. Col. Suharto. Dutch troops took Jogja on 19 December 1948, but Suharto led his troops out of the city and took up positions in the country-side. On the following day President Sukarno, Vice-President Hatta, and most members of the republic's cabinet were arrested in Jogja. For the story from President Suharto's perspective see Roeder, *The Smiling General*, chaps. 14-16.

7. *Gerakan Tiga Puluh September* (GESTAPU--the "30 September Affair") and *Gerakan Satu Oktober* (GESTOK-- the "1 October Affair") refer to the complex series of events that began late in the night of 30 September and early in the morning of 1 October 1965, and culmi-nated in the annihilation of the Communist Party of Indonesia, the massacre of thousands of Indonesians and Indonesian-Chinese, the overthrow of Sukarno's "Old Order," and the emergence of General Suharto and the "New Order."

8. For a discussion of the personalities involved in the formulation of Malayan and Malaysian foreign policy during the regimes of Tunku Abdul Rahman and Tun Razak see Pathmanathan, "Readings in Malaysian Foreign Policy."

9. Probably one of the first authors to discuss the "bargain," as it is usually interpreted today, was R. S. Milne in his early study of the politics of independent Malaysia. See *Government and Politics in Malaysia*, 36-51. Many authors have followed Milne's lead, often without attribution or explanation. The origins of certain features of the "bargain" can be historically documented, but the allocation of eco-nomic power to the Chinese community, a crucial aspect of the bargain as interpreted by Milne, is question-able. In other contexts Milne has referred to this part of the bargain as an "understanding," which is probably a somewhat better description. However, it could even better be described as an "assumption," probably chiefly on the part of Chinese businessmen and British expatriates.

10. See Chin, "A New Assertiveness in Malaysian Foreign Policy," 281.

11. In an essay to appear in a volume published by the Institute of Southeast Asian Studies in 1987 I have described the various circles (or "orbits") of leadership from 1965 to 1986. Throughout this period Lee remained at the center. The first orbit included Rajaratnam, Goh, and, until his strained relations with the others caused his retirement from the cabinet in 1980, Toh Chin Chye. There was greater fluidity in the second and third orbits, and beginning in 1980 the

"second generation" moved into the second orbit and some key old-timers (sometimes referred to by younger politicians as "the long-march generation") moved out. In the cabinet reorganization following the 1984 elections, of the four first-orbit leaders, only Lee remained. Toh is now a senior backbencher and a frequent critic of the government. Initially Goh served in an official capacity and informally he remains the leader whose judgement is most trusted by the prime minister. However, he began winding down after the 1984 elections in preparation for moving totally out of government. Rajaratnam, who has suffered some health problems in the past several years, holds the title of Senior Minister of State, which carries few if any official duties. They hold no official policy-making positions, but Rajaratnam and Goh have easy access to the prime minister. The second-generation leadership (headed by the first deputy prime minister, Goh Chok Tong, and including among the senior three ministers Foreign Minister Dhanabalan) are increasingly permitted and encouraged to speak on behalf of the government, but rarely, if ever, do their pronouncements contradict a view held strongly by the prime minister.

12. Since the formation of the new cabinet there have been several examples of departures from policies formulated by Lee, but these have not involved fundamental changes and have been in the domestic arena. Three salient facts must be kept in mind: the prime minister remains the chief architect of all major policies; there is a basic consensus on all foreign policies; and the second generation of leadership shares this consensus, or at least does not depart from it in public.

13. A recent study shows that between 1965 and 1979 only 2.22 percent of the space in the records of Parliament was devoted to foreign affairs. Topics dealing with China were the most discussed foreign affairs subject, but this accounted for only 0.15 percent of the total space. See Lee, "Singapore and East Asia," 335-38.

14. The foreign minister was replying to a question in Parliament. See Sunday Times (Singapore), 24 March 1985, 10.

15. "The PAP in the Nineties: The Politics of Anticipation," 28.

16. "Why Singapore Needs an Active Foreign Policy," 30, 34, and 38-39.

17. This figure and the uniquness of Singapore's position were noted by Goh Chok Tong in his opening address before the Singapore Institute of International Affairs/National University of Singapore, "Conference on the Security of the Sea Lanes," 2.

18. When talking informally with some senior officials of the Aquino Ministry of Foreign Affairs in

1986 I was asked for my impressions of the differences
in perceptions between the two administrations. When I
responded that in general the continuities were far
more striking than the discontinuities there was
little surprise registered. The comment of one official, to which the others nodded in agreement,
explained the absence of surprise: "We are all Filipinos living in the same country at the same time, and
we are about the same age. Nothing about this has
changed."

19. Tolentino resurfaced as Marcos's vice-presidential candidate in the disputed election that led to
the People Power victory. It was also Tolentino who
briefly seized the Manila Hotel in June 1986 and
proclaimed himself acting president in Marcos's
absence.

20. There were many skeptics in Manila in 1985
who doubted that Ambassador Romualdez would have
accepted the job on any terms. As the reasoning went,
he already had all the power and influence of a
foreign minister without being tied to the office, and
he also held the very prestigious position of ambassador to the United States, the most sought-after plum
in the diplomatic service.

21. Press reports in late 1986 asserted that the
president had taken over policy making in the foreign
arena and that Foreign Minister Laurel, because of his
stand on the draft constitution, had fallen into dis-
favor and was only a figurehead at the ministry. See
New York Times, 30 October 1986, 6. It is difficult,
however, to see any manifestations of this change if
it has occurred.

22. The Institute of Security and International
Studies in Bangkok generously convened an informal and
off-the-record meeting for my benefit in 1985. Some
of Thailand's leading scholars concerned with foreign
policy, policy making, and internal Thai politics were
joined by some senior serving and retired military
officers, politicians, and bureaucrats. The topic for
discussion was "decision and policy making." It was
one of the most stimulating two-hour discussions in
which I have participated, but I departed with no firm
conclusions about my subject. The optimism of an outsider trying to understand Thai policy making was not
bouyed by the final comment of a retired senior official: "after all that has been said today, I admit
that I don't know how policy gets made here."

23. On Thai political factionalism see Riggs,
Thailand, chap. 8.

24. Phuangkasem, p. 3. If the government of
retired General Prem were included the contrast would
be even more striking. However, Prem was technically a
civilian when he accepted the premiership, though he
came from the army and his base of power was, and
remains, within the army.

25. In mid-1964 the prime minister, General Thanom Kittikachorn, secretly agreed to American use of Thai air bases for bombing sorties over Vietnam, and this was formalized in a four-hundred-page "Contingency Plan" in 1965. However, these arrangements were not revealed to the minister of foreign affairs, or any other member of the cabinet, until a year after the plan had been put into operation. See Asadakorn Eksaengsri, *Foreign Policy in Thailand*, 144-50.

26. Ibid., 128, 129.

27. Ramsay, "Thai Domestic Politics and Foreign Policy," 5-9.

28. The issues and the politics were complex. In brief, the transitional arrangements appended to the 1978 Constitution, which enhanced the political power of the military, particularly in Parliament and the cabinet, were scheduled to expire on 21 April 1983. An amendment was introduced in Parliament and supported by most of the army leadership to amend the constitution to retain the transitional amendments. Prime Minister Prem remained publicly aloof and refused to associate himself with either side, and the amendment bill was narrowly defeated in Parliament, thus satisfying the army critics. However, the military's feelings were assuaged when Prem moved the general elections, scheduled for 12 June, to 18 April, thus permitting these elections to take place under the old rules.

29. Most of this information on Siddhi has been taken from a lengthy interview and profile that appeared in the *Straits Times* (Singapore), 2 September 1985, 15.

30. *The Cybernetic Theory of Decision*, 127.

31. One of the most perceptive observers of Thai politics and foreign policy, Sukhumbhand Paribatra, has described several instances of "grooved thinking" in the Thai decision-making process. For examples, see "Irreversible History?" and (with Suchit Bunbongkorn) "Thai Politics and Foreign Policy in the 1980's."

32. A lengthy summary of the day-long meeting at the Ministry of Foreign Affairs was reported in two parts in *The Nation Review* (Bangkok), 16 and 17 February 1983. The quotations in this paragraph have been taken from part one, p. 5.

33. A committed thinker may adopt different belief patterns to fit different situations, and thus he may adopt widely varying policy alternatives depending upon the situation and the proponent with the final access to him. Steinbruner believes that President Franklin Roosevelt was a good example of such a "committed thinker." *Cybernetic Theory of Decision*, 124-36.

34. Steinbruner characterizes a "theoretical thinker" (the terms "ideological" and "theological" are also suggested, and either seems more appropriate)

as a person (or a system) with an abstract, generalized, and extensive set of beliefs to which great commitment has been made." Ibid., 136.

35. Ibid.

36. For a brief summary of the complex and confusing state of Thai politics on the eve of the scheduled 27 July elections see Sukhumbhand Paribatra, "Looking Forward with Cautious Optimism," *Far Eastern Economic Review*, 10 July 1986, 26-27. In conclusion Sukhumbhand notes wryly that "one could with equal accuracy call this article 'Looking Forward with (Cautious) Pessimism.' That is the beauty of Thai politics if not of those who make it tick."

37. A similar analysis, but with less emphasis on "flexibility," is made in Singh, "Thai Foreign Policy." Russell J. Fifield explains Thai foreign policy in terms of five principles: self-reliance, independence, multiplicity, counterweight, and plasticity. *National and Regional Interests in ASEAN*. In a provocative summary of the course of Thai international relations, two Thai scholars have extended to the foreign-policy arena the patron-client relationships observed in Thai domestic politics. The end result is much the same, but the explanation of the emergence of these coalitions is provocative. See Suchit Bunbongkarn and Sukhumbhand Paribatra,"Thai Politics and Foreign Policy in the 1980's," 31-32.

38. Jha, *Foreign Policy of Thailand*, 14, 15, 20-23, 25-31, 33, 34, 157, 158, and chap. 3, passim.

39. Suchit Bunbongkarn and Sukhumbhand Paribatra, "Thai Politics and Foreign Policy in the 1980's," 30-31. The authors report that it took the personal intervention of the king with the commander in chief of the armed forces, General Arthit, to convince the army to withdraw forces sent to enforce a territorial claim against Laos. The Ministry of Foreign Affairs had opposed the army operation on the grounds that it was potentially damaging to longer-range Thai interests, but without the king's direct intervention the MFA's objections apparently would not have been heeded.

4

The USSR and Vietnam:
Perceptions of the Partners
and the Partnership

*Soviet actions and policy have been relentlessly
consistent: to secure the Russian heartland from
attack, to communize the world, and . . . to keep
it under Communist control.*

Lee Kuan Yew
Prime Minister
Singapore, January 1981

*The USSR in Southeast Asia? Why worry about the
Soviets? They represent about 5 percent of the
power of the Americans, and no one worries about
the them.*

Senior official
Ministry of Foreign Affairs
Manila, May 1986

*Vietnam had no choice but to turn to the USSR. It
was rebuffed by America and the West. But sooner or
later it will rediscover its historic independence.*

Senior official
Ministry of Foreign Affairs
Jakarta, 1985

Vietnam has been formally linked to the USSR only
since the two signed a treaty of friendship and Vietnam joined the Council for Mutual Economic Aid (COME-
CON) in 1977. However, cooperation between the two
was not new. Indeed the support, admittedly more ideological than material, given to the revered leader of
the Socialist Republic of Vietnam, Ho Chi Minh, in his
revolutionary days prior to World War II marked the
beginning of an entente that with numerous obstacles
and diversions has continued to the present time. But
just as friends, enemies, and observers disagree on
the extent to which Ho was a communist and the extent
to which he was first and always a Vietnamese nationalist, so too do interpretations differ on the course
being taken by the current Vietnamese leadership.

The sharp differences in the perceptions of this partnership would probably not have emerged had the relationship between Vietnam and the Soviet Union continued to be one of ideology, trade, economic aid, or even modest military assistance. However, after the final U.S. withdrawal from South Vietnam in spring 1975 and all of Southeast Asia except the Philippines shortly thereafter, there followed a series of bilateral agreements between the USSR and Vietnam, after which the Vietnamese invaded Kampuchea (25 December 1978) and occupied Laos. The fifty thousand Vietnamese troops in Laos have not met the opposition faced by the Vietnamese forces in Kampuchea. In the view of most, and probably all, ASEAN leaders the continuing occupations of the countries would not have been possible without Soviet assistance. According to their views, Vietnam's material resources were drained by three decades of war against first the French and then the Americans, which was followed by demands for new commitments of resources occasioned by the process of integrating the south into the new republic.

A recent study estimates that the Soviet Union has provided Vietnam with military assistance valued at more than one billion U.S. dollars since 1980, and that economic aid, much of which is directly or indirectly in support of the Kampuchean undertaking, is running currently at a level of $3-5 million daily. In fact, the same author concludes that of all the aid the Soviet Union is currently providing to its friends throughout the world, Vietnam receives about 25 percent.[1]

SOVIET NATIONAL INTERESTS IN THE REGION

That the USSR has invested heavily in non-ASEAN Southeast Asia is evident; what it hopes to obtain from its investments is not as clear. Perhaps, as the Singapore prime minister noted in the opening quotation, Soviet involvement with Vietnam and Kampuchea is part of a larger strategy to communize the world. Perhaps, as PRC officials believe, the primary Soviet goal is to surround and contain China. Perhaps Soviet foreign policy is responding to internal political pressures in the decision-making process--military leaders may have been pressured for Southeast Asian bases independent of any larger strategic goals of the political leaders.

Whatever the origins of its policies, in Southeast Asia the Soviet Union faces a series of seemingly irreconcilable dilemmas. If the Soviet Union hopes to improve relations with the PRC, its ties with Vietnam will have to be loosened significantly, perhaps broken completely. If the USSR, as it frequently has claimed, desires to move closer to ASEAN and its members, this will be difficult so long as the Soviet Union continues to support Vietnam in Kampuchea. If Premier Gorbachev earnestly desires better relations with the United States, the Soviet-Vietnamese entente (and Afghanistan) present an additional complication so long as ASEAN remains adamant in its stand. Perhaps the Soviet Union perceives opportunities in establishing supportive relationships with indigenous antiregime movements in the ASEAN region, but any advantages derived from these associations will be more than offset by the deterioration of relations with the regimes in power.[2] In short, unless one accepts that the highest Soviet global priority is (1) world domination, or (2) the containment of China, it is difficult to assess Soviet national interests in the ASEAN region. However, at a less cosmic level some pertinent observations are possible.

Despite the costs it has borne in purely military terms, the USSR's return on its investment in Vietnam has been significant, at least in the short run and perhaps in the long run as well. The Soviet Union has acquired the friendship and support of a country with a long history of anti-Chinese sentiment and the use of naval facilities at Cam Ranh Bay that are crucial to the continuing expansion of fleet operations in the Pacific and Indian oceans. How available and how secure this naval base may actually be, and how long this arrangement may last are issues that are subject to different perceptions among the various ASEAN policy-making elites. All are agreed that the USSR is now using Cam Ranh Bay and that Vietnam is useful to any strategy for the containment of China. Beyond this, however, interpretations of motives, long-term developments, and mutual costs and benefits vary throughout ASEAN according to the leaders' perceptions of the two principals involved. Whether the alliance is a "conspiracy of events"[3] or a concurrence of long-term and common national objectives is a matter of perceptions throughout ASEAN.

ASEAN PERCEPTIONS OF THE USSR

Perceptions of the USSR in the context of East-West tensions have been influenced by several factors common to several or all of the ASEAN states. First, philosophically and politically the nations of ASEAN are much closer to the West than to the socialist bloc. All have opted for a free-market economic model, though all, with great variation among themselves, provide--or attempt to provide--some degree of centralized direction to the free-market economy. However, no ASEAN member, with the exceptions of Singapore until 1976 and Indonesia within the context of *Panca Sila*,[4] has professed to be socialist in any

ideological, philosophical, or economic sense. Not
only does this increase the difficulty of conducting
trade with nations in the economic orbit of the USSR,
it also creates an internal guidance mechanism that
makes its difficult to steer a foreign-policy course
near the shores of the communist-bloc countries.

Second, with the exception of Thailand, each
ASEAN country was a former Western European or American colony and this colonial experience left an imprint on the present-day leadership. Except for Indonesia, most of today's leaders were educated in the
language of their country's colonial master. Some were
educated in the mother country and others attended
replicas of Western institutions transplanted to their
home soil; but the educational systems they inherited
were greatly influenced by the institutions and practices of the mother country. Although such educational
experiences do not prevent the growth of nationalist
sentiments, and indeed nationalist leaders have
emerged from the Western educated, such nationalism
was generally founded on ideological and philosophical
principles associated with America and Western Europe.
Many of today's ASEAN leaders explored the thoughts of
Marx and Lenin in their student days, but in the end
those who succeeded the Europeans and Americans, sometimes helped more than hindered by their former
colonial masters, were not inclined to be particularly
sympathetic toward the ideological East. Whatever the
wrongs the West has perpetrated on them or their
countries, today's ASEAN leadership seems to feel much
more comfortable in dealing with friends and adversaries drawn from an ideological and philosophical landscape with which they are familiar.

Indonesia

Many Indonesian leaders recall with some displea-
sure that the USSR was not quick to recognize the new
Indonesian nation and that the two countries did not
exchange missions for more than four years thereafter.[5] Nevertheless, relations, although spotty and
troubled, were sufficiently sound to cause the USSR to
support Indonesia with military assistance and as an
"independent third-party" in confrontation with the
Dutch over West Irian.[6] During confrontation with
Malaysia in the closing years of the Sukarno regime
Indonesia's relations with the USSR deteriorated in
the context of the U.S.A.-USSR *detente*, worsening
Sino-Soviet relations, and increasingly intimate ties
between the Partai Komunis Indonesia (PKI, or Indonesian Communist Party) and the PRC.[7]

Despite frequent assertions that the New Order
would pursue an independent foreign policy relations
improved little under the leadership of General Su-

harto.[8] A systematic survey of Indonesian elite attitudes during 1968-70, which was followed by a less
systematic followup in 1973, found that the generally
negative perceptions of the USSR seemed to be associated with the elites' perceptions of the Indonesian
Communist Party. Moreover, these negative impressions
were only somewhat offset by the USSR's anticolonial
stance, including specifically its support of the
Indonesian positions on West Irian, the Outer Islands
revolts, and "confrontation." Indonesia's perception
of the USSR may have been negative, but at the time
the USSR was not perceived as a threat because there
was no domestic communist party through which any
major communist power could infiltrate, the USSR was
separated from Indonesia by a great distance, and
there was no dependence on Soviet military assistance.[9]

Several years ago a Radio Moscow broadcast laud-
ing the PKI provoked public outbursts, this time by
students and the Parliament;[10] the Jakarta manager of
the Soviet national airline, Aeroflot, was arrested as
a spy after a fist fight at Halim Airport;[11] and later
the government expelled a second Russian official for
spying.[12] Despite these recent manifestation of tensions, foreign ministry officials are quick to argue
that relations are now on a much more even keel.

Officials in the Ministry of Foreign Affairs are
also more charitable than some of their counterparts
elsewhere in ASEAN in interpreting Soviet intentions
and actions in Southeast Asia. The view that the USSR
either wants or will get a permanent naval base in
Vietnam is not widely held in the Ministry of Foreign
Affairs,[13] and MFA officials share little of the concern expressed by Marcos's officials about Russian
submarines thought to be roaming the waters of the
South China Sea.

Some Indonesian military leaders, on the other
hand, have viewed the intentions of the USSR much more
harshly, but even among senior officers the hard line
seems to be softening, and is now more likely to
parallel that of the MFA. On this issue greater consistency between the perceptions of the civilians and
the military was facilitated by the retirement (and
later death from a heart attack) of General Ali Murtopo and his replacement as the top military figure by
General Benny Murdani. Murdani influences, or controls, one of the country's major outlets for political information, but it is not easy to assess the
degree to which his views represent those of the
senior officer corps of the Indonesian army. What is
certain, however, is that when the perceptions of the
military and those of the MFA are not in agreement,
and when the two perceptions may lead to different
policy alternatives, it is usually the military's

interpretation that carries more weight with the president.[14]

Malaysia

In the early years of its existence Malaya was strongly anticommunist despite its often professed desire to remain neutral in the cold war struggle. Although Malaya did not join the Southeast Asia Treaty Organization (SEATO), which the ingenuous Prime Minister Tunku Abdul Rahman said his people "did not like" for reasons he did not fully understand,[15] it was linked closely to Britain, Australia, and New Zealand during the Emergency and thereby indirectly was tied to the United States and the West. The first prime minister was (and remains) an unapologetic Anglophile, and with this disposition went strong anticommunist sentiments that were reflected in Malaysian foreign policy throughout his long tenure in office (1957-69). Although the principal enemy was China, which was viewed as the patron of the Malayan Communist Party rebels in the jungles, in the mind of the Tunku international communism was monolithic. Thus, though not actively involved on the ground, the USSR had to bear a major share of the responsibility for the revolutionary movement in Malaysia.

It was inevitable that relations between the USSR and Malaysia would be placed on formal foundations. The Soviet Union by the mid-1960s had become a significant purchaser of Malaysian rubber, and later it was to become its largest customer. The USSR accounted for only about 4.5 percent of Malaysia's total world trade in 1965, but the balance was strongly in Malaysia's favor, and virtually all of this represented the sale of rubber. Although it was announced with an apparent lack of enthusiasm because the action was unpopular with many Muslim leaders, the acting foreign minister reported in Parliament in June 1966 that Malaysia and the USSR had agreed to establish diplomatic relations. Parliament was told that this "was entirely in keeping with . . . [the] policy . . . [of] fostering . . . friendly relations with all countries irrespective of their social and political systems."[16]

Razak's confrontational style and dogged persistence may have contrasted sharply with the Tunku's cultivated image of intuitive decision-making combined with lucky bumbling, but he was equally suspicious of communist intentions. However, it fell the lot of Razak and his successor Hussein Onn to readjust Malaysian policy toward the socialist bloc to fit the new realities of U.S. withdrawal from the area. Nevertheless, despite the rhetoric of ZOPFAN (Zone of Peace, Freedom, and Neutrality)[17] and "equidistance," it is apparent that Malaysia does not intend to place itself politically too close to the USSR. Prime Minister Mahathir was embarrassed by the discovery that his political secretary during the time of his membership in the Hussein Onn cabinet, Siddiq Mohamed Ghouse, was a Soviet mole; and two aides of a former prime minister, the late Tun Razak, had confessed to communist connections earlier.[18] As a result of the Siddiq revelations three Soviet diplomats were expelled, the first such expulsions for Malaysia, though not an uncommon occurrence elsewhere in ASEAN.

Mahathir on numerous occasions has expressed his concerns about the intentions of the USSR. He chose the inhospitable forum of the New Delhi Nonaligned Conference of 1983 to deliver a stinging rebuke to the USSR for the invasion of "its puny neighbor," Afghanistan, an invasion that the prime minister regarded as "a repetition of the disregard for principles that have been so blatantly demonstrated in Kampuchea." He told the delegates that "the Soviet Union claims to champion the cause of the weak and oppressed, but it had no hesitation about marching into Afghanistan to prop up an unpopular regime" and that if the conference failed "to condemn the Soviet Union, then fear will stalk the little nations situated next to predatory neighbors."[19]

The prime minister has also expressed concern about the probable consequences of a Soviet naval presence at Cam Ranh Bay. Although Mahathir regards Soviet behavior as typical of that of any major foreign power, it is clear that he views the projection of the Soviet Union's naval power into the region as a greater threat to Malaysia than the American presence. According to his statements he remains a strong believer in the efficacy of ZOPFAN, but in his view the concept must apply equally to all major powers.[20]

Philippines

Philippine views of the USSR for the first quarter-century of independence largely paralleled those of its colonial mentor, the United States. In his first term in office (1965-69) President Ferdinand Marcos took several modest steps to nudge Philippine foreign policy away from its pronounced anticommunist stance, though, in fact, it could be argued that in so doing the president was correcting course to keep it on a parallel with the course of U.S. policy. In any case, Marcos relaxed restrictions on Filipino travel to Eastern European countries in 1967 and a year later initiated trade with the socialist bloc.[21] The Philippines and the USSR have never enjoyed close relations, but the Philippine disillusionment that set in following U.S. withdrawal from Vietnam in 1975 and the political bargaining that has accompanied each renegotiation of the bases agreement have combined to produce a new series of mixed and sometimes contradictory signals.

It appeared that a thaw might be in the making when First Lady Imelda Marcos visited Moscow in mid-1982[22] and announced a cement plant agreement between the two countries--the first of its kind and an enterprise not in keeping with earlier presidential comments on the risks of Soviet aid--but relations went quickly back to normal when President Marcos denied a Russian request for ship repair facilities in Zambales.[23] Moreover, the cement deal seems to have been stillborn, and some officials close to Mrs. Marcos privately questioned at the time if it would ever come to fruition.

In early 1983 as the bases renegotiation talks with the United States were approaching, the specter of the Russian menace was raised with increasing frequency. Many Philippine leaders, both civilian and military, expressed concerns about their country's inability to monitor the movement of Soviet submarines in the waters of the southern Philippines, and it seemed clear that surveillance and detection equipment would be given high priority in subsequent aid requests. However, the rediscovery of the growing threat of the New People's Army (NPA) throughout the nation shifted the priorities of the Marcos military establishment to smaller weapons and transport. At the same time USSR-Philippine relations improved dramatically, at least on the surface.

First Lady Imelda Marcos's warm reception in Moscow when she attended the funeral of Konstantin Chernyenko in March 1985 received extensive media coverage in the Philippines, as did Gorbachev's apparently prompt acceptance of her invitation to visit the Philippines[24], a visit that did not take place, however. The Russian diplomatic delegation to Manila is considered to be among the strongest and most capable in Southeast Asia, and the reception they receive, particularly in the universities, must be encouraging.[25] The reception afforded the deputy chairman of the Presidium of the Supreme Soviet when he visited the Philippines in April 1983 was cordial and at times enthusiastic, and I. P. Kalin reciprocated with kind expressions of support for almost every Philippine faction except the NPA.[26] The nature and timing of Marcos's departure also proved to be an embarrassment to the USSR. The Soviet delegation in Manila, perhaps because of bad luck, was the last major embassy to distance itself from President Marcos in the waning days of his administration.[27] Although this lapse seems not to have complicated unduly official relations with the Aquino Ministry of Foreign Affairs, it has left unpleasant impressions with some individual policy makers.

Singapore

When the prime minister of Singapore, in the opening quotation in this chapter, bluntly told two Japanese reporters that the goal of the Soviet Union was the communization of the world[28] he was restating a theme voiced consistently by Singapore's leaders for more than a decade.[29] In the view of the Singapore leadership Russian aims have been unambiguous, clearly signalled, and relentlessly pursued. To Singapore's leaders the Soviet invasions of Hungary and Czechoslovakia were only Eastern European manifestations of what was later to occur in Afghanistan, Kampuchea, and Laos. The appearance and growth of Soviet naval forces in Southeast Asia--according to Prime Minister Lee, beginning with the appearance off Singapore of a single destroyer flying the Russian flag at the time of the Commonwealth Heads of Government meeting in 1971 and progressing through the use of Cam Ranh Bay by the Soviet fleet[30] --are part of a grand scheme. The USSR is intent on world domination, and the invasions of Afghanistan by the the Soviet Union, and Kampuchea and Laos by the Vietnamese, are part of this strategy. Moreover, in the opinion of the former foreign minister, Soviet foreign policy is not driven by Marxism but by "old-fashioned imperialism," and its "ultimate aim is to make the Soviet Union the dominant imperial power in the world."[31]

As the leading figure of the "new generation" of Singapore leadership has also noted, the motivations of the USSR are military and commercial as well as ideological. The Soviet Union is dependent on passage through the Suez Canal and the Straits of Malacca to connect its Black Sea and Pacific fleets. In addition, the USSR's two thousand oceangoing vessels constitute one of the largest merchant-marine fleets in the world, and these also need unimpeded passage through the canal and the straits.[32]

Thailand

Thailand enjoyed good relations with czarist Russia: on one occasion czarist Russia intervened with its ally France to take French pressure off Thailand; and one son of the revered King Chulalongkorn attended school in Russia for eight years. However, the Bolshevik Revolution caused a rupture in relations, which were not restored until the close of World War II.[33]

Regardless of history, today Thailand considers itself to be a front-line state, and it is this perception of its own vulnerable position that most affects Thai perceptions of the USSR. In the rhetorical question of the Thai foreign minister, Air Chief Marshall Siddhi Savetsila: "How does Vietnam, with a *per capita* income of only US$160 support a standing army

72

of three million men while Thailand with a *per capita* income of five times that of Vietnam could only maintain an army of less than one-tenth as big as Vietnam's? . . . How has Vietnam been able to finance its occupation armies in Laos and Kampuchea? The answer, of course, is the Soviet Union."[34]

In the minds of most Thai policy makers the USSR-Vietnam alliance--temporary or long-term, a marriage of convenience or an expression of true love--has cast the Soviet Union in the role of a threat. The USSR may be seen as a threat because they support Vietnamese aggression, encourage political subversion within Southeast Asian countries, or because they are attempting to undermine ASEAN solidarity. But whatever their reasons almost every member of the Thai elite interviewed in a recent survey was convinced that the Soviet Union posed a serious threat.[35]

ASEAN PERCEPTIONS OF VIETNAM

Thailand

In part because of its alliance with the USSR and in part for historic reasons, Vietnam today is viewed as the most serious external threat facing Thailand, and the SRV's occupation of Kampuchea has considerably increased Thai perceptions of the presence of this threat.[36] Again in the words of the foreign minister: "Thailand's eastern boundary has become the frontier of the Free World. . . . Just as Pakistan is a main barrier of the Free World against the control of the strategic Persian Gulf, Thailand is the stronghold against further advance of what Vietnam has euphemistically called 'Socialism's Outpost' in Southeast Asia."[37]

Although Thailand has attempted to avoid implicating Laos in its dispute with Vietnam over Kampuchea, the long common border shared with Laos has in the Thai view brought Vietnam to its doorstep. It is, in fact, this border, and the Thai-Kampuchean border, that makes Thailand the front-line state it frequently calls itself.

Singapore

In its attitude toward Vietnam, Singapore is the strongest and most outspoken critic in ASEAN, including the front-line state of Thailand. Singapore has frequently lectured its ASEAN partners, and the rest of the world as well, to "stay the course," an expression heard frequently in Singapore. Singapore provided the leadership at the United Nations to keep the Pol Pot seat for Kampuchea; it played a major role in engineering the anti-Vietnam Kampuchean coalition

headed by Sihanouk; and it successfully led ASEAN
moves to thwart the efforts of the more radical elements of the Nonaligned Conference in Delhi in March
1983 and to exploit the potential of the conference to
get the ASEAN position on Kampuchea before the delegates. In the minds of Singapore's policy makers today's Vietnam, led by the present leadership, is
clearly a threat to the security of Southeast Asia as
a whole, ASEAN in general, and Singapore specifically.
Yet, behind this hard-line approach to Vietnam there
is some flexibility.

The foreign minister of Vietnam, Ngyuen Co Thach,
is sometimes described as a person with whom Singapore
could "do business," if it were not for the crippling
constraints imposed on him by the old leadership in
Hanoi. In addition, some leaders predict that Vietnam,
as its younger generation tires of the high costs of
constant war, will be a very different country in not
too many more years. Also not far beneath the hard-
line and hardheaded assessments of the political
goals, strategies, and tactics of Vietnam lies a
rarely spoken admiration for the grit and determination of the Vietnamese people, who have been victim-
ized by their own leadership.

Indonesia

Within ASEAN Indonesia is often regarded as the
opposite extreme from Thailand and Singapore in its
perceptions of Vietnamese goals and strategies, and
this position is not new. In the early years of the
Suharto regime it might have been expected that Sukarno's inclination to lean toward the socialist states
of the world would have produced considerable criticism of the Old Order's perception of the continuing
struggle in Vietnam. However, in a study undertaken
shortly after the New Order had become firmly entrenched Franklin Weinstein found that this was not
the case. The hostile reactions of the Sukarno regime
to American military intervention in Vietnam were
exempt from criticism by the New Order government.[38]

Probably it is the memory of the Indonesian Revolution, and the perceived similarities of the Vietnamese struggle for independence, that make Indonesians
the most sympathetic of all ASEAN members toward the
plight of their Vietnamese cousins. The importance of
this historical memory can hardly be over-emphasized.
In fact, if there is a single, most important, historical influence that affects Indonesian policy making
in a all fields, foreign and domestic, it is their
revolutionary experience. Virtually every policy maker
will introduce the subject early in disscussions of
many public-policy issues, and the Indonesian Revolution commands a degree of respect and awe reserved for
important national symbols.

Only two countries in Southeast Asia had to fight
for their independence--Indonesia and Vietnam. For the
rest independence came without a struggle. In this
respect Indonesians and Vietnamese are kindred souls
who understand the meaning of struggle against the
powerful forces of colonialism.

Elsewhere in ASEAN, Indonesia is often criticized
for its insensitivity to Vietnam's aggressive ambitions, and journalists have sometimes pointed to the
Indonesian sympathy for Vietnam as a highly vulnerable
chink in the ASEAN armor.[39] Certainly the sympathetic
expressions for Vietnam's current problems heard in
the Ministry of Foreign Affairs, at the Centre for
Strategic and international Studies (CSIS) in Jakarta,
from several military leaders, and occasionally in the
press are rarely repeated elsewhere in ASEAN. However, few of these institutions speak with a single
voice on this issue. Some of the military, although
much less strident than the generals in Thailand, tend
to parallel official policy, which is supportive of
the ASEAN hard line against Vietnam, and the media,
understandably, usually emphasize the official position. One can hear from various important officials
that Vietnam has been "duped" by the USSR, that it had
no choice but to turn to Russia after it had been
rebuffed by America and the West, and that it has
strayed from the correct path--temporarily, many would
add. Most persons reflecting these views continue the
argument by asserting that sooner or later Vietnam
will reassert its historic independence. Ultimately,
so this line of argument goes, Vietnam will play the
role of friendly buffer against a hostile and threatening China,[40] but in the meantime, their potential
friend is travelling the wrong path and cannot be
supported.

Malaysia

Malaysia's perceptions of Vietnam roughly parallel those of Indonesia, but they are not identical,
and, historically, Malaysia has been an indirect adversary of North Vietnam. Although Malaya, and later
Malaysia, did not follow the lead of the Philippines
in sending forces to Vietnam in support of the American and South Vietnamese effort, Tunku Abdul Rahman
was unabashedly supportive. South Vietnamese troops
were schooled in jungle warfare tactics in peninsular
Malaya, and the Tunku voiced his own feelings about
the correctness of the South Vietnamese cause on almost every possible occasion. For the Tunku, caught up
in Malaya's struggle against communist guerrillas in
the jungles, the war in Vietnam seemed very familiar,
and he responded accordingly. The corrective measures
taken by the Tunku's successors generally were intended to distance Malaysia from American policy

during the period between U.S. withdrawal from Vietnam
and the invasion of Kampuchea by Vietnam in 1978. Yet
these corrective measures have not not resulted in
major policy shifts.

Malaysia does not enjoy the Indonesian luxury of
being far removed from the site of the conflict, and
this geographic proximity to the front-line state of
Thailand has forced it to take a less ideological view
of Vietnam and the Vietnamese threat. And, unlike the
Indonesians, Malaysian policy makers have no historical reason for identifying themselves with the Vietnamese revolution. When Indonesians read the history of
the independence movement in Vietnam they are struck
by the many parallels and similarities of their own
experience; Malaysians are much more likely to be
struck by the dissimilarities.

This is not to say, however, that in general
Malaysian contacts with the Vietnamese have not been
somewhat more cordial than those of Thailand, Singapore, and the Philippines. A former Malaysian foreign
minister, who is again serving in that post, Tengku
Ahmad Rithauddeen, apparently made several efforts to
initiate meaningful dialogues with his Vietnamese
counterpart, Ngyuen Co Thach, just as the Indonesian
minister of foreign affairs, Mochtar Kusumaamadja, has
done, and Ngyuen is often met with less hostility in
Kuala Lumpur (and Jakarta) than in the other ASEAN
capitals. It is often heard in Kuala Lumpur (but said
with less conviction than in Jakarta) that Vietnam
ultimately will reassert its historic autonomy and
divest itself of its Soviet albatross. However, Malaysia, though often identified with the "second track"
in ASEAN's two-track diplomacy, is strongly committed
to support of the Thai position in the Kampuchean
dispute, and in the practical application of international politics the perception of a nearby threat
has generally prevailed over the innate desire for
Malay-Indonesian political unity.

Philippines

The Philippines is far removed from Vietnam and
the impact of the Kampuchean issue is almost nonexis-
tent. When Filipino policy makers under President
Marcos were provoked to discuss Vietnam they were
likely to employ cold-war rhetoric that would surely
have startled their Indonesian and Malaysian colleagues in ASEAN meetings, if the Filipinos chose to
express themselves in a similar manner. One senior
Foreign Ministry official commented in March 1985 that
"Vietnam would drive through Thailand to Singapore if
it were not for the U.S. bases at Subic and Clark,"
and he seemed to imply that this might occur with or
without the support of the USSR.[41] At the same time he
was mildly critical of ASEAN for inadequately con-

sulting Kampucheans on the fate of their country and for being unwilling to recognize "the realities that exist." A year later a very candid Aquino government official smilingly repeated the domino analogy, but promptly conceded in follow-up questions that such a scenario seemed highly unlikely. In both 1985 and 1986 such conversations in Manila were rare, however. The Philippines turned inward as it was caught up in its own domestic problems. In 1985 questions about foreign policy were likely to be deflected to a discussion of the names of possible candidates for the position of foreign minister,[42] to counterquestions about American policies regarding the Philippines or Marcos, or to a general discussion of the economic, political, and internal-security problems facing the Philippines. In 1986 the only topic not still under discussion was the identity of the foreign minister. For the past several years foreign policy has not been an important topic in the Philippines.

ASEAN PERCEPTIONS OF THE PARTNERS AND THE PARTNERSHIP: DIVERSITY, UNITY, AND IMPLICATIONS

Beneath the obvious diversity of ASEAN perceptions of the USSR and Vietnam lies a significant level of agreement. All ASEAN leaders are wary of the Soviet naval buildup in the region, but all have come to accept it. On the one hand, the increased Soviet presence in Southeast Asia violates the spirit of ZOPFAN, but, on the other, in creating the conditions for a big-power standoff it may contribute to the practical application of the doctrine. Indonesia and sometimes Malaysia view the Vietnam-USSR partnership as a logical, understandable, and even anticipatable historical development, but it is an historical development that these same leaders view as unfortunate, even if they accept the logic. Most other leaders in ASEAN agree that the partnership represents an unfortunate turn of events, but they do not accept its historic logic or inevitability. And throughout ASEAN the partnership is rarely perceived as a permanent or even a long-term arrangement. A Soviet presence in Southeast Asia is now accepted as inevitable, but a permanent alliance between Vietnam and the USSR is not.

Underlying this skepticism about the permanency of the partnership lies an open and clearly articulated, in the case of Indonesia, or veiled and muted, in the case of Singapore, admiration of the Vietnamese people and the revolution in which they were engaged for three decades. The Philippines has taken much less note of Vietnam, but even there it is not unusual to hear thoughtful leaders speak with feeling about the struggles of the Vietnamese people. Only Thailand demurs. Historically Vietnam has always constituted a latent or manifest threat to Thailand, and today the front-line-state mentality, buttressed by historical memories of concrete examples, dominates Thai political thinking. Intellectuals have begun to question the degree of parallelism between these historical memories and the current situation, but as yet they have not had any apparent impact on the policy makers.

In varying degrees, the leadership of every ASEAN state distinguishes between the Vietnamese people and the government of Vietnam. Even in Indonesia, where contacts with Vietnamese officials are commonplace, highly negative comments may be heard about the the ideological rigidity or political inflexibility of the the aging Hanoi leadership. In Singapore, which unequivocally supports the hard-line Thai position on Vietnam, it is not unusual to hear favorable assessments of a Vietnamese leader such as Ngyuen Co Thach, who in the view of at least one high official "is sensibly flexible but hopelessly constrained by the old men in Hanoi."

Because of the different perceptions of the role and designs of Vietnam in Southeast Asia there has emerged a practice of "dual-track diplomacy" within ASEAN. On one track is ASEAN as an institution, and all of the members of ASEAN, individually and collectively. In ASEAN, Vietnam is dealt with collectively, most commonly through the appointed "dialogue partner," or individually through regular diplomatic channels in a manner agreed to by all ASEAN members. Vietnam has often tried to crack the solidarity of track-one diplomacy, usually by having its foreign minister visit the more hospitable of the ASEAN capitals while bypassing the less, but every time Vietnam has verged on success with this strategy, ASEAN has closed ranks to ward off the threat. Two-track diplomacy, which emerged when some Indonesian leaders created the second-track, is practiced even within Indonesia. The president and the Ministry of Foreign Affairs follow track one, and individuals--coming from the army, CSIS, the press, and the universities--are on track two. The second track, which is direct and uniquely Indonesian (in contrast to ASEAN), represents the historic but often frustrated Indonesian desire to play a leadership role in Southeast Asia. The second track is direct because important individuals speak as Indonesians directly to their counterparts in Vietnam. It is uniquely Indonesian because their sentiments embody and reflect their perceptions of Indonesia and the world that surrounds it. They do not speak as members of ASEAN; they speak as Indonesians.

It may seem curious that this two-track system, which seems to have great disruptive potential for the unity of ASEAN, has been accepted and absorbed by the organization and its members. Yet contradictions are frequently accepted by Southeast Asians in a manner sometimes bewildering to others. ASEAN itself is constructed on a foundation that includes many glaring contradictions, and dual-track diplomacy has only added one more. Some leaders have commented that there is a practical value to dual-track diplomacy and that only Indonesia was in a position to create the second track. But perhaps there is another aspect to dual-track diplomacy that has not been adequately recognized.

Dual-track diplomacy arose because of perceptual disagreements about Vietnam within ASEAN, but its subsequent acceptance and workability may be a product of a deeper underlying agreement. Even the most hardline critics of Vietnam often perceive the Vietnamese people to be basically good but yoked by bad leadership. These critics may find the second track acceptable because it provides the opportunity to bypass much of the aging and inept leadership in Hanoi and reach the leaders of the future. This suggests a high degree of consensus on the nature of the Vietnamese threat.

NOTES

1. Rose, "The Soviet Union and Southeast Asia," 10.

2. Rose describes and elaborates on some of the longer-term dilemmas that the USSR may face if it wants to, or can, continue its alliance with Vietnam well into the future. In the end Rose feels that Moscow is more dependent on Hanoi than Hanoi on Moscow, and thus in the long-term the Russian position is more vulnerable. Ibid., 2-7 and throughout.

3. The term is used by a Singapore scholar, who posits the two extremes and concludes that this term best describes the alliance. See Seah, "Soviet Interest in Southeast Asia," esp. 200-201.

4. The PAP, accused of "undemocratic practices" and faced with probable expulsion, withdrew from the Socialist International at the SI's Thirteenth Conference in Geneva in November 1976. *Panca Sila* (the five Principles) is the national ideology of Indonesia. Socialism is one of these five principles, but it has never achieved a dominant position.

5. *De facto* recognition was given in January 1950, but formal diplomatic relations did not begin until September 1954.

6. Djiwandono, "An Analysis," uses this term to describe the USSR's role in the West Irian dispute. Michael Leifer describes this period as the "highpoint of Indonesian-Soviet *entente.*" *Indonesia's Foreign Policy*, 125.

7. Djiwandono, "An Analysis," 255ff.

8. Leifer, *Indonesia's Foreign Policy*, 125-26, points out that the willingness of the USSR to shelter some exiled PKI leaders led to additional tensions.

9. Weinstein, *Indonesian Foreign Policy*, 82-88.

10. *Straits Times*, 16 January 1982.

11. *New Straits Times*, 6 February 1982.

12. *Straits Times*, 11 February 1982.

13. Rose, "The Soviet Union and Southeast Asia," 7-8, has cited evidence that seems to support the Indonesian view that the Russians do not expect to remain at Cam Ranh Bay indefinitely. Rose has noted that the Russians have installed primarily mobile facilities in Vietnam and that this is in sharp contrast to their usual practice of using cement for virtually every overseas construction project.

14. See the statements of the then chief of national security, Admiral Sudomo (*New Straits Times*, 15 February 1982), and the then information minister, the late Ali Murtopo (*New Straits Times*, 7 July 1982). More recently the head of the department of international relations at the Centre for Strategic and International Studies in Jakarta (CSIS), which has always maintained close ties with the army, has played down the Soviet threat to Southeast Asia by arguing that some Western observers tend to confuse "Soviet military capabilities with Soviet intentions." He points out that "U.S. . . . bases in the Philippines are no less capable of doing the same thing." Djiwandono, "The Soviet Presence," 429. It is common practice for observers, despite *pro forma* disclaimers, to identify policy statements emanating from the CSIS as the likely positions of the army because of the close connections of the two. The first patron of CSIS was General Ali Murtopo when he was at the peak of his career, and as his influence waned he was replaced as chairman of the CSIS board of directors by General Benny Murdani. Although I have sometimes fallen into the same trap because of the absence of a practical alternative strategy for assessing opinions, all observers should be concerned about the extent to which any institution, individual, or information outlet can represent a group as diverse as the senior officer corps of the Indonesian army. It is unlikely that current CSIS policy statements and the views of General Murdani are in sharp conflict, but this does not address the question of the extent to which Murdani's views are representative of the army.

15. In the course of an interview in Canberra, Australia, in 1959 the Tunku responded to a question from a reporter about Malaya's reason for not joining SEATO. His response was typical of his style but unusually candid for most practicing politicians. He admitted that he could see some value to SEATO, but added, "I don't count, you know. As the representative of my people I have to do what they want, and SEATO is

rather unpopular among my people. I don't know for
what reason." Quoted in Tilman, *Malaysian Foreign
Policy*, 22.

16. Quoted in Tilman, *Malaysian Foreign Policy*,
48.

17. ZOPFAN as a regional concept intended to
insulate the area from big-power interference was
first put forward by Malaysia in 1970, and it was
accepted as a guiding principle by ASEAN in the Kuala
Lumpur Declaration of 1972.

18. On the Siddiq arrest and expulsion of the
three Russian diplomats see *New Straits Times*, 14 July
1981. On the earlier spy cases, see Milne and Mauzy,
Politics and Government in Malaysia, 218; and *Far
Eastern Economic Review, Asia 1977 Yearbook*, 227-28.

19. Mahathir, Address to the Seventh Conference
of Heads of States and Governments of the Non-Aligned
Countries, New Delhi, March 1, 1983, in Pathmanathan
and Lazarus, eds., *Winds of Change*, 210.

20. Personal interview, Kuala Lumpur, 3 April
1983. By request of the Prime Minister this interview
was taped and was to be treated as on-the-record.
Unlike all other interviews it will therefore be cited
as appropriate.

21. Hernandez, "Domestic Politics and Foreign
Policy," 20.

22. Mrs. Marcos's first visit to Moscow occurred
in 1972, and this is sometimes mentioned by Filipino
policy makers as the beginning of the improvement in
USSR-Philippine relations. However, the cement agreement was the first tangible manifestation of improved
relations.

23. The president indicated in denying the
request that he believed the Soviet vessels would spy
on the Philippines. See *New Straits Times*, 22 July
1982. This was not the first mention of spying.
Earlier there had been similar charges levelled
against Russian commercial vessels by the Ministry of
Foreign Affairs (see *New Straits Times*, 16 September
1981), and Soviet "spy flights" over the Philippines
had been protested in 1980 (*Straits Times*, 25 April
1980). For a discussion of the Philippine-USSR cement
agreement see *Asiaweek*, 23 July 1982, 14; and *Far
Eastern Economic Review*, 3 September 1982, 98-99.
Officials have commented privately that the cement
deal was economically unsound because the Philippines
was overproducing cement even before the first lady
went to the USSR.

24. *Business Times* (Manila), 23 March 1985, 1,
16. The same article quoted the acting foreign minister, Pacifico Castro, who accompanied Mrs. Marcos, on
his assessment of the impact of the visit: "It just
shows how warm the new leaders are to the First Lady
and the Philippines--a friendship started by the First
Lady in 1972." At the same time similar comments, even

stronger in some cases, were made to me by senior MFA
officials in Manila. In addition to extensive daily
press coverage, Channel 4 on March 23 carried a long
documentary on Mrs. Marcos's visit. The well produced
videotape emphasized the first lady's cordial reception, the preferential treatment she received from
her Russian hosts, and the warm relations that now
exist between the two countries. Channel 4, Manila,
was the quasi-official voice of the Marcos government,
and the "Peoples' Station" now devotes most of its
newscasts to the activities of Aquino government
officials.

25. At a university-sponsored seminar on U.S.-
Philippine relations I attended in 1985, the one U.S.
official present and the three Russian officials in
attendance engaged in good-natured but pointed exchanges stating their respective official positions on
several contentious international issues. The very
articulate American was frequently greeted with deri-
sive laughter from the predominantly young Filipino
audience of students and faculty, but his equally
articulate Russian counterpart received resounding
applause. A high official in Marcos's Ministry of
Foreign Affairs described a similar experience he had
had at Santo Tomas University. "Imagine," he said,
"when I tried to defend the bases I was booed--at the
bedrock of political conservatism in the Philippines I
was booed."

26. Rose, "The Soviet Union and Southeast Asia,"
17-19, discusses the Kalin visit and the dilemmas the
USSR faces in trying to be on friendly terms with all
political factions in the Philippines. Rose believes
that the NPA may be receiving a modicum of support
from the USSR and that if so this too creates a
serious dilemma for the Soviet Union. This is one of
the few suggestions on record of the possibility that
the NPA is receiving support from sources outside the
Philippines.

27. The newly appointed Soviet ambassador presented his credentials to the president immediately
after the elections. He took the opportunity to con-
gratulate Marcos on his victory at the polls, and an
administration groping for evidence of international
support interpreted the remarks as evidence of USSR
support for the government. It was reported several
times that the Soviet Ambassador attended the last
Marcos inauguration, but this was denied by senior
officials in the present Ministry of Foreign Affairs.

28. Lee, Interview with *Asahi Shimbun*, 5 January
1981. At about the same time the then second deputy
prime minister (foreign affairs), Rajaratnam, was
making a similarly strong statement about Soviet intentions. However, his theme was that the Soviet Union
must act quickly to defeat capitalism before capitalism gathers sufficient momentum to enter its second

golden age. See his speech before the 17th Annual
Chief Executive Officers' Roundtable, 30-37. Rajaratnam repeated this theme in his address to the Far
East-American Council Seminar in New York in October
1981, 25-33. Some of Lee's speeches and interviews in
the mid-1960s, at the zenith of the Vietnam debate in
the United States, emphasized much the same theme. The
prime minister believed that the Americans, if they
had better understood the Vietnamese, would not have
chosen to "put their pilings into the soggy ground in
South Vietnam," but once there had no choice but to
stay to thwart the intentions of the Communists. Television interview with foreign journalists, Singapore,
8 November 1966. Lee later lectured the American
community of Singapore on a similar theme. Address to
the American Association of Singapore, 10 November
1967. On 1 October 1981 Lee opened his address to the
Commonwealth Heads of Government meeting in Melbourne
with the statement: "The most significant development
since the American withdrawal from Vietnam in April
1975 has been the swift and confident moves by the
Soviet Union into strategic areas vacated by the de-
parting Americans" (p. 1).

29. "Afro-Asian solidarity" took first priority
in Singapore foreign policy at the time of independence, and the rhetoric reflected this priority until
late 1966 or early 1967. The British announcement of
their intentions to withdraw east of Suez, together
with a rapid maturing of the leadership as it faced
the problems of international politics, produced a
redirection of Singapore's foreign policy that has
since been consistent.

30. Comment made by Prime Minister Lee in an
interview with the managing editor of *US News and
World Report*, 7 December 1981, 4.

31. Rajaratnam, Address to the NUS Democratic
Socialist Club, 21 December 1981, 25.

32. Goh, Opening Address before the Singapore
Institute of International Affairs/National University
of Singapore, 4.

33. Jha, *Foreign Policy of Thailand*, 31-33.

34. Siddhi, Address before the Asia Society, 13-
14.

35. In an extensive and systematic survey of
threat perceptions among the Thai elite undertaken by
the Institute of Security and International Studies
(ISIS) at Chulalongkorn University, 96 percent of the
respondents reportedly regarded the USSR as a threat
for one or more of the reasons stated above. This
survey has not yet been published, but some of its
findings are reported in Suchit Bunbongkarn and Sukhumbhand Paribatra, "Thai Politics and Foreign Policy
in the 1980's," 27-28.

36. In the ISIS elite survey cited above and
referred to in Suchit Bunbongkarn and Sukhumbhand

Paribatra, "Thai Politics and Foreign Policy," 27-28, 97.9 percent of the Thai elite regarded Vietnam as a threat to Thai security and 98 percent felt that the invasion of Kampuchea had made Thailand even more vulnerable.

37. Foreign Minister of Thailand to U.S. Deputy Secretary of State Kenneth Dan, February 1984, quoted in Suchit Bunbongkarn and Sukhumbhand Paribatra, "Thai Politics and Foreign Policy," 25.

38. See Weinstein, *Indonesian Foreign Policy*, 131-32. The research was actually conducted in 1969-70.

39. See Tasker, "A Conflict of Interests," *Far Eastern Economic Review*, 20 January 1983, 22-23. In some ways the Tasker article is not representative because it displays more balance and understanding of the complexities of the issues than many journalistic reports. However, in my view it too errs in over-stating the depth of the differences dividing the membership of ASEAN.

40. To this should be added the occasionally expressed view that Vietnam and ASEAN may be able to form a bloc of sufficient proportions to resist Chinese advances in Southeast Asia. This view is not uncommonly heard in Indonesia, and the most optimistic commentators view Vietnam as a potential member of ASEAN.

41. It is impossible to escape the feeling, however, that for this particular ministry official, and others as well, Vietnam is distant and not very important and that the views expressed do not represent deeply held convictions. These views might have been intended to satisfy an American interviewer, and different views might be forthcoming in a different setting.

42. With such luminaries involved as Kokoy Romualdez and Imelda Marcos it was not surprising that most Filipino officials preferred to discuss personalities rather than substantive policy issues.

5

China: Ally or Adversary?

*If history teaches us anything it is that China is
Indonesia's number one enemy.*

Member of Parliament
Jakarta, 1983

*With us it is not an academic question, it is a
matter of survival. China is on our side, and that
is all that matters.*

Senior Official
Ministry of Foreign Affairs
Bangkok, 1983

In the Kampuchean crisis China is an ally of
ASEAN in their dispute with Vietnam and the USSR.
China has been particularly supportive of front-line
Thailand and the Kampuchean coalition, headed by
Prince Norodom Sihanouk but still dominated by the old
Pol Pot faction, the Khmer Rouge. However, just as
not all ASEAN members share Thailand's and Singapore's
enthusiasm for the Democratic Coalition, so too all do
not agree on the blessings of a Chinese alliance.

CHINESE NATIONAL INTERESTS IN THE ASEAN REGION

China seems convinced that Russian strategy in
Asia is directed toward encircling the PRC, and Soviet
naval bases in Southeast Asia are one more link in the
chain of encirclement. Vietnam, a traditional enemy
that is also now viewed by China as the surrogate of
the USSR in Southeast Asia, not only can provide the
Soviet Union with ideal sites for such bases, it can
also harass its traditional enemy and divert their
attention from the more serious threat emanating from
the USSR. In this strategically crucial area lies
ASEAN.

China wants and needs a stable ASEAN region made
up of governments that, at best, are friendly or, at
worst, are not hostile.[1] If China cannot have a Viet-

namese government that is friendly, then at least the PRC needs a Vietnam that is not in a position to threaten its southern flank. The chances of getting a friendly Hanoi government anytime soon are remote, and the alternative, in Chinese thinking, is to bleed Vietnam until it is too weak to undertake any serious adventures. Regardless of the misgivings of some of its members, ASEAN has lined up collectively against Vietnam on the Kampuchean issue, and the U.S. and Japan have followed the ASEAN lead. Thus, the PRC finds its own immediate national interests in Southeast Asia dictating policies that parallel those of ASEAN.

In the longer term, however, the PRC faces a dilemma. The more Vietnam bleeds, the more dependent the Socialist Republic of Vietnam (SRV) will become on Soviet assistance. And the stronger the dependency, the better will be the USSR's bargaining position in regard to expanding and consolidating its basing privileges in Vietnam.

So long as ASEAN remains firmly opposed to the Vietnamese occupation of Kampuchea the members will probably find themselves on a parallel course with the PRC. However, despite the present good or even cordial relations between China and most of the ASEAN membership, many ASEAN leaders have nagging doubts that such a situation is permanent. They are delighted with the present entente, but they consider this happy situation to have emerged from a series of historical accidents outside the mainstream of traditional Sino-Southeast Asian relations. Many leaders fear that eventually Chinese relations with the region will revert to a more familiar pattern.[2]

PERCEPTIONS AND MEMORIES

In every ASEAN capital one will eventually be reminded by a key policy maker that in ancient times Southeast Asia was composed of a series of vassal states paying tribute to a powerful Chinese emperor, who in turn saw to it that order in the region was preserved. This was the *Nanyang*, a Chinese term meaning the "Southern Ocean," which itself suggests the China-centric nature of the relationship.[3] Almost all educated Southeast Asians share this historic image of China, but its implications are vague and rarely articulated.[4]

As educated Southeast Asians also know, China exerted influence in Southeast Asia when the Empire was strong, but a strong China capable of dominating Southeast Asia does not now exist. However, many Southeast Asians fear that if Chinese modernization succeeds a "new China" may eventually prove to be capable of resuming its historic role in the region.

Another concern involves the "overseas Chinese." Every ASEAN state has a significant number of domestic Chinese, but in every country except Singapore policies affecting this minority are made largely by policy makers drawn from the politically dominant indigenous majority. The loyalties of the local Chinese are often questioned.

From the beginning of the republican era (1911) until recently official Chinese policy has been to maintain close political ties with the overseas Chinese. Sun Yat Sen relied heavily on the financial support of the *Nanyang* Chinese, and all overseas Chinese were given special recognition and attention in the republican government.[5] Despite a revolution that was intended to sweep aside everything associated with the discredited Chiang Kai Shek government, the new communist regime found it difficult to sever the cords between Beijing and the *Nanyang*. The first PRC ambassador to Jakarta was soundly criticized and eventually withdrawn because of the missionary zeal with which he sought converts among the local Chinese.[6] It was only in the spirit of the upcoming Bandung Conference that the PRC finally negotiated a Dual Nationality Treaty in April 1955, and it was actually several years later before any concrete manifestations of policy changes in Beijing became evident.[7]

The PRC has also maintained political ties with Maoist revolutionary parties throughout Southeast Asia, some but not all of which have been dominated by indigenous Chinese leadership. Although the PRC frequently reiterates that party-to-party policies must not be confused for state-to-state relations, Southeast Asians are often unconvinced that the same leaders can separate their government and party. For its part the PRC in recent years has taken pains to put greater distance between the PRC government and these revolutionary movements, but to the chagrin of many Southeast Asian leaders Beijing has never disavowed all connections with them. In Manila in August 1981 the then foreign minister of the PRC, Zhao Zhiyang, repeated an explanation that has been heard frequently throughout ASEAN: "The relations between China and communist parties [abroad] are only confined to political and moral relations. . . . China will not interfere [in the internal affairs of these countries], nor will China interfere in the internal affairs of those parties. China has done its utmost to try to solve the problems left over from history."[8]

General memories of past Chinese policies and a tendency to perceive the Chinese of China through lenses colored by experiences with their own domestic Chinese populations have affected PRC relations with every ASEAN member. However, these historical memories vary throughout the region, as have the experiences of individual nations with their domestic Chinese.

Indonesia

Indonesia demonstrates the potential for linkages between a country's perceptions of its local Chinese population and attitudes and policies toward the People's Republic of China. One well-respected Indonesian scholar in 1978 explicitly examined the policy implications of the perceived linkages between the two Chinese populations,[9] and as recently as 1983 a lengthy news dispatch filed from Jakarta was headlined "Fifth Column Fear Still Persists in Indonesia."[10] The linkage thesis was certainly appropriate when it was advanced in 1978, but the 1983 headline probably was outdated.

In Jakarta today the "fifth-column" allegation is almost never heard unless it is brought up by an outsider, and even then little genuine concern is likely to be expressed. This is certainly in marked contrast to the situation of a decade or more ago when the "Chinese problem" dominated most discussions. Perhaps the threat posed by the local Chinese is perceived differently outside Jakarta,[11] but the fact is that Indonesian foreign policiy is made principally in the capital city. Thus, so far as foreign policy is concerned, what is being thought and said in Jakarta is much more relevant than what is going on in the countryside. And in Jakarta it seems that Indonesian perceptions of the PRC are shaped chiefly by memories of the 30 September affair (GESTAPU) and only indirectly by Indonesian images of its own Chinese community.

The memory of GESTAPU probably ranks only behind the Indonesian Revolution in the influence it has exerted on foreign policy.[12] The origins and goals of the movement, the identities and motivations of the conspirators, and other details may be open to continuing debate outside Indonesia, but Indonesian policy makers in office today are very certain that they know the answers. In their view the indigenous communist party, the Partai Komunis Indonesia (PKI), received massive support from the PRC. Some officials will go even farther in asserting that GESTAPU was conceived in Beijing, orders to proceed originated in Beijing, the logistical support came from Beijing, and when the *coup* failed those who could escape were given refuge in Beijing.[13] Almost every discussion of the PRC with Indonesian officials includes a quick and certain assertion of Beijing's involvement in GESTAPU followed by an unqualified condemnation of the PRC.

The current political course of the PRC has reduced the immediacy of the Chinese threat, but it has not eliminated it. The People's Republic of China is often described by Indonesian officials as the most serious external threat facing Indonesia, and China's role in GESTAPU proves this to most Indonesian policy makers beyond a shadow of doubt.[14] Moreover, the Chinese threat, as a survey of Indonesian elites found, stems more from the national character of the Chinese people than from their communist ideology. All the big powers are expansionist, so the respondents feel, but China is more dangerous than the others because China is a "hungry giant," the Chinese people are expansionists by nature, and there is the Indonesian Trojan horse waiting to assist their mainland cousins.[15]

In the euphoria of the thirtieth anniversary celebrations of the Bandung Conference of April 1955 it seemed that a breakthrough in Sino-Indonesian relations might be imminent. The PRC had entertained the president's half-brother during a visit of Indonesian businessmen just prior to the Bandung meeting. Indonesia invited the PRC to the Bandung ceremonies, and the PRC accepted. Sino-Indonesian relations seemed destined to take a marked turn toward improvement though the many optimistic predictions of the past had always proved unwarranted.[16]

When Foreign Minister Wu Xueqian accepted the Indonesian invitation to the Bandung celebrations he became the first senior PRC official to visit Indonesia since GESTAPU, some two decades earlier. It was anticipated that Wu would meet privately with President Suharto following the formal ceremonies in Bandung and that this meeting would produce concrete evidence of the desire of both parties to improve relations. However, the expected meeting did not take place, and Wu left Jakarta, having spoken only casually to Suharto in the receiving line at the closing ceremonies in Bandung. Rather than improving the climate of Sino-Indonesian relations, Wu's visit seems to have reopened the old wound left by the memories of GESTAPU. Indeed, if published reports are correct it was this specific historical memory that again disrupted rapprochement.[17]

The foreign minister and many others in Jakarta seem genuinely to favor a rapprochement with the PRC. The often- stated reason was to eliminate the middleman profit on Sino-Indonesian trade, which for many years had passed through Hongkong or Singapore, but there seems to be a general feeling, at least among some key officials in the Ministry of Foreign Affairs, that it is now time to bury the GESTAPU hatchet. However, it seems apparent that many Indonesians, including the president, do not agree.

Singapore

The People's Republic of China enjoys cordial but informal relations with Singapore. The top leadership of the two countries have exchanged visits on several occasions,[18] and a high level of mutual respect and admiration seems to have developed between Singapore's

Lee Kuan Yew and the PRC's Deng Xiao Ping. In his
visit to Singapore in 1978 Deng seems to have been
impressed by the startling economic and social advances made in Singapore, and Lee by Deng's pragmatism
and willingness to tamper with the ideological tenets
of Marx and Mao. Yet questions persist. Whether China
can or will stay the present course is not certain,
and, if it does not, any new course chosen, probably
by new leadership, is likely to be more threatening to
the future of Singapore than the course on which Deng
has embarked. Even if Deng's efforts gain enough
momentum to survive his passage from the political
scene, in the eyes of many Singapore political leaders
China constitutes a long-term threat to the region.

In Singapore's view the PRC's support for ASEAN
in its disputes with the communist world stems from
the realities of the Sino-Soviet confrontation, not
from the conviction that the ASEAN stand is fundamentally correct. In the view of some top Singaporeans,
Chinese foreign policy toward the nations of Southeast
Asia stems from a hardheaded assessment of its crucial
national interests and is devoid of sentimentality. As
one important Singapore leader describes China: "They
know what they want and their policies are calculated
to get it. If you think China is doing something
because they like you, you're going to be fooled."

Singapore is one of the ASEAN states least affected by past Chinese attempts to export its own
revolution. More than a decade ago a senior leader
dismissed the "Voice of the Malayan Revolution"
(VOMR), a clandestine radio station supporting the
communist movement and at the time thought to be
broadcasting from southern China, as a "small bunch of
fanatics preaching to the converted with a message
that is so dull no one else will listen." Even in
1975 there seemed to be no concern that Singaporeans
might tune in to hear these "dull messages,"[19] and
this lack of concern continues to the present day.
However, in Singapore, uneasiness remains about the
impact of the such messages on Singapore's neighbors
to the north, the Malaysians, and to the south, the
Indonesians.[20]

There has also been a concern expressed by the
prime minister that the PRC is showing restraint in
its relations with fraternal communist parties because
it wants ASEAN support for its anti-Soviet position.
According to Lee, "if a country in Southeast Asia
decides to accept the Soviet presence in Vietnam and a
Vietnamese *de facto* occupation of Cambodia I think the
Chinese might stir up trouble for that country."[21]

Despite its good informal relations with the PRC,
and the respect, admiration, and even affection for
China's leadership that is often expressed in Singapore, the two countries do not have formal diplomatic
relations. It seems clear that the reluctance to

establish such relations emanates from Singapore, not
from the PRC. During the first decade of Singapore's
independence this reluctance was related to two
factors. First, there was concern about the "Third
China" image of Singapore held by some of the neighboring leaders, who feared that Singapore might serve
as a springboard for the spread of Maoism or Chinese
chauvinism.[22] Second, the PAP leadership felt that
the Singapore Chinese needed more time to distance
themselves from their Chinese roots and gain a
stronger sense of Singapore identity before being
afforded opportunities to renew their cultural ties
with the ancestral homeland. As time has passed, the
influence of these factors has diminished. China's
foreign posture has changed, most of Singapore's
neighbors have opened embassies in Beijing, Singapore's leaders have gained considerable trust among
their neighboring counterparts, and the PAP leadership
seems to feel that a threshold has been crossed at
home.[23] At present the teaching of some traditional
Chinese beliefs, traits, and skills is not only acceptable but is even a matter of conscious government
policy.[24] And Singapore has reached a tourism agreement with the PRC that will advertise Singapore as the
"gateway to China."

Officially, Singapore has indicated that it will
delay resumption of formal relations with the PRC
until every other ASEAN state has established or resumed diplomatic ties. This understanding was originally part of a bargain struck between Singapore and
Indonesia. In view of Indonesia's obvious reluctance
to resume ties with the PRC it is therefore likely to
be some time before Singapore and the PRC enjoy full
relations.

Whatever the reasons underlying the Singapore-
Indonesia agreement,[25] the republic and the PRC do not
enjoy formal diplomatic relations and a question of
"why" put to a senior government official evoked
only another question in response: "What would we get
out of formal ties? As it is we have no problems
dealing them on all important matters, and we have all
the machinery in place for trading with them. Why do
we need anything more formal?"

Malaysia

Official Malaysian attitudes towards the People's
Republic of China have softened greatly since independence in 1957. In 1974 Malaysia became the first ASEAN
state to establish formal ties with the PRC, and today
it is one of three ASEAN members with PRC embassies,
but suspicions about China remain to the present time.
The media event staged in Kuala Lumpur on the occasion
of the return of the chairman of the Communist Party
of Malaya (CPM), Musa bin Ahmad, showed that Malaysia

remained convinced that the PRC constitutes a long-term threat to Malaysia.[26] The Kuala Lumpur visit of Zhao Zhiyang in August 1981 ended indecisively with both sides making reference to continuing historic problems that had not yet been resolved.[27]

The deep-seated mistrust of the PRC voiced by some Malay leaders seems related to the memory of the Emergency and the historical fact that the communist guerrillas were overwhelmingly Chinese. One recent study has suggested that "'China' has ceased to be an issue" for Malaysia since formal rapprochement between the two countries in 1974,[28] but there is considerable evidence that this conclusion is not shared by all Malay leaders. One articulate and still-influential Malay, a former government official, illustrated his serious concerns about the loyalty of Malaysia's Chinese minority in two anecdotes about sporting events in Kuala Lumpur. Both of these involved the behavior of Malaysian-Chinese spectators at matches pitting PRC teams against non-Chinese opponents, and both served to demonstrate to the satisfaction of the speaker that the Malaysian-Chinese still owed great loyalty to their ancestral homeland.[29] When I asked the same person "Why is China your most serious external threat?" (he had already asserted that it was), he replied with no hesitation: "Because of proximity, history, the Emergency, PRC support for the CPM, and our racial makeup." In one terse reply he summed up well the perception of the Chinese threat held by many Malaysian leaders.

In two studies of Malaysia's "successor genera-tion" of leaders done one decade apart, Llewellyn D. Howell has recently demonstrated that the perceptions of elite policy makers of an earlier generation can also be found in the younger generation of Malaysian students. In a survey of some five hundred students aged seventeen to twenty-one polled in 1971 and 1981 Howell found that his Malay respondents held striking-ly negative views of China and the Chinese. Presumably the perceptions of Malay youth are influenced by much the same memories as those of their elders, although they have not personally experienced the events.[30]

The Emergency is now history but the memory of it remains, and concerns about continuing PRC ties with the Communist Party of Malaya frequently resurface. The prime minister and a recent foreign minister have both roundly criticized the PRC for the support it gave the communists during the 1948-60 period and the continuing party-to-party ties it maintains today.[31] A quarter-century after the Emergency was officially declared to be over, its memory continues to influence the thinking of Malaysian leaders.

Another concern of the Malaysian leadership has been the frequent about-faces of Chinese policy. Prime Minister Mahathir, in a press interview at the Commonwealth Heads of Government Conference in Nassau in October 1985 warned Americans that weapons sold to China now may someday be turned on Southeast Asians. He cautioned that "adventurers in the Chinese leadership" might be tempted "to take over and move toward expansion" because they have already made a 180-degree turnabout. "If . . . . someone comes along and tries to get them to go the other way again, we can't be sure they won't."[32]

One month after the Nassau talks Prime Minister Mahathir reciprocated Zhao's 1981 Malaysian visit. The major topic of discussion was trade, and apparently by mutual agreement more contentious issues were generally avoided.[33] However, Mahathir was reported to believe that the government of the PRC still had not changed its attitude toward party-to-party relations between fraternal communist parties and he commented that Malaysia "is still not happy about it."[34] In a lecture to students and faculty at Qinghua University, Mahathir remarked that "we welcome the many assurances that China . . . will never do anything to harm us," but he added that "trust does not come easily . . . in view of our past experiences."[35] On his return he told newsmen that the PRC and Malaysia have different ideologies, but this difference alone should not interfere with good relations between the two so long as neither interferes in the other's internal affairs.[36]

As a result of the Emergency and its Chinese character, perceptions of China held by Malay political leaders are not greatly different from those held by Indonesians. It seems, however, that Malaysian fears of the disruptive potential of the PRC are considerably less intense than those encountered in Indonesia, probably because of the differences between GESTAPU and the Emergency. GESTAPU was more recent, more traumatic, and more dramatically concentrated into one brief and violent episode.

Philippines

The newly independent Philippines, following the lead of the United States, was profoundly distrustful of anything with the label of communism, and it particularly feared the effect of the Chinese revolution on its own Chinese minority. Many Filipino politicians distrusted all Chinese, and until the mid-1960s official government policy toward the Philippine-Chinese was based on two assumptions: first, most Philippine-Chinese would owe their primary loyalties not to the Philippines but to one China or the other; and, second, loyalty to the Kuomintang (KMT, or Nationalist Party) was "safer" than loyalty to the PRC. Thus, relations with Taiwan were close, and indeed by the terms of of two international agreements the Republic of China (ROC) virtually administered Chinese education in private schools throughout the Philippines.[37] Supervision of these schools was the responsibility of the General Association of Chinese Schools of the Philippines (GACSP), which was dominated by KMT leaders who maintained ties to the Chinese embassy in Manila that were so close as to make the GACSP a quasi-official arm of the embassy and the party. Textbooks were imported from Taiwan, from a private outlet in Hong Kong managed by a retired member of the Overseas Chinese Affairs Commission in Taipei, or written in the Philippines by Chinese teachers screened and recruited by the GACSP.[38]

It was not until about 1965 that the Philippine government began to have some serious second thoughts about the domestic political risks of its policies. The immigration of new teachers from Taiwan, a common practice earlier, was proscribed, and a "Filipinization" scheme proposed by several Roman Catholic Chinese schools in 1964 was accepted as official policy. Chinese education, the last major lifeline of the Philippine-Chinese to their cultural past, ended with the abolition of all Chinese-language education in the early years of martial law.

Filipinization of the Chinese schools, and their eventual closing, was part of a more general movement away from the Republic of China and toward the establishment of official ties with the PRC. The Nixon visit to the PRC and the American withdrawal from mainland Southeast Asia made this sometimes confusing and sometimes painful shift from the ROC to the PRC more feasible.[39] Formal diplomatic relations were established in 1975 and Taiwan was described in the agreement as an "inalienable part" of Chinese territory.[40]

Today Sino-Philippine relations are the warmest they have been since Philippine independence following World War II. Imelda Marcos, at the time a force in her own right in Philippine domestic and international politics, visited the People's Republic of China on four occasions; Foreign Minister Huang Hua visited Manila in 1980; Premier Zhao Zhiyang visited in 1981; in 1981 President Marcos lifted the ban on Chinese visits to the Philippines by permitting the relatives of Philippine-Chinese to remain in the country for a maximum of one year; in 1984 the first lady toasted the Chinese Ambassador with the statement that "we are inspired by the example of the People's Republic of China in coming out of the dark world of colonization into the bright new world of modernity"; the Aquino government chose a respected Philippine-Chinese businessman as its first ambassador to the PRC; and Foreign Minister Laurel returned to the PRC in June 1986.[41]

Despite these warm public expressions of friendship Philippine policy makers in private have often revealed considerable concern about China's long-term intentions toward the region and the PRC's strategy of remaining on friendly terms with fraternal communist parties in Southeast Asia. In the past some of these policy makers were convinced that the Chinese minority, despite apparently successful attempts at Filipinization, continued to constitute a fifth column, but it is not certain that this constitutes a concern of the present government.[42] In the minds of some previous leaders, the Philippine-Chinese, willingly or unwillingly, are waiting to serve the ends of the PRC, just as they previously demonstrated their loyalty to the ROC. Although the present foreign policies of the PRC, including their repeated calls to the overseas Chinese to become part of their adopted countries, or at least to obey their laws, have been welcomed by most Filipino officials, many regard such appeals as mere products of Chinese expediency--that is, as pragmatic adjustments to meet the Soviet threat--rather than as policies derived from historical and philosophical reorientations.

On the other hand, few responsible observers in the Philippines have suggested that the PRC bears any responsibility for the the rapidly growing strength of the New People's Army (NPA).[43] Similarly, PRC or domestic-Chinese support for the Muslim secessionist movement in the southern Philippines has not been suggested.

Considerable concern has been expressed privately about the domestic threat to the Philippine economy posed by the Chinese minority, but few are prepared to relate this to a threat from the PRC. Filipinos seem concerned chiefly that Philippine-Chinese capital will cascade from the country if the future looks ominous, but this threat of the flight of capital is not linked to the PRC. Besides, as one ranking Foreign Ministry official under the Marcos regime commented, "our Chinese are capitalists-- they like China less than we do." He may or may not be correct, but his perception is not unique in either the Marcos or the Aquino administrations.

The various views of policy makers regarding Sino-Philippine relations are inconsistently scattered throughout the government, and the intensity with which they are voiced is much lower than elsewhere in ASEAN. The fact is that at the present time only one foreign-policy issue is frequently discussed and only one elicits strong feelings--U.S.-Philippine relations. Thus, the issue of Philippine-Chinese relations presently is not high on the foreign-policy agenda.

Thailand

In Thailand the presence of a domestic Chinese minority also seems to have had little negative impact

on Thai perceptions of the PRC, but the history of
relations between the domestic Chinese minority and
the indigenous majority is considerably different in
Thailand. The clear distinction between "native" Thai
and "foreign" Chinese has been less precisely maintained in Thailand than in any other ASEAN country, or
anywhere in Asia for that matter. The absence of an
upper layer of colonial overlords may have made it
more profitable for the Thai-Chinese to establish
their linkages to Thais rather than distancing themselves from the natives by identifying with the European colonists;[44] perhaps religion presented fewer
obstacles to intermarriage;[45] or perhaps it was a
combination of these and other factors.

Whatever the historical causes, it is not always
easy to identify a Chinese in Thailand, and even those
who are identifiable are better integrated into the
indigenous society than elsewhere in Southeast Asia.
One prominent Thai official remarked that "we may not
always trust the Chinese [of the PRC] but because of
our familiarity with Thai Chinese we feel more comfortable around them."

As long as the United States was the dominant
force in Southeast Asia and China was an American
enemy, the PRC was also an enemy of Thailand. And,
indeed, the PRC behaved like an enemy by encouraging
Thai communists to rebel against the Bangkok government and by operating a clandestine radio station in
southern China beaming antigovernment messages in the
Thai language to members of the Communist Party of
Thailand (CPT) and other interested listeners.

Many Thai officials remain wary of China, but in
the words of the deputy prime minister, spoken before
a security seminar in Hawaii and quoted on the opening
chapter of this study, one must take account of where
the tigers are at a particular time. "Vietnam is
obviously a tiger . . . squatting at our doorsteps
backed by another tiger not far behind, while the
other . . . tiger still lies hidden in the woods."[46] A
tiger in the woods represents only a potential threat;
the tiger at the door must be dealt with first.

In Thailand the Chinese tiger is most often
viewed as an indispensable ally against a very threatening Vietnamese tiger. Thus, in the view of some high
officials Thailand's relations with China must be
placed realistically in the current political context.
Thailand needs the support of China if it is to survive in the face of the Vietnamese threat.

Despite the support of China in the present political setting there are important Thai policy makers
who believe that China has not abandoned permanently
its support for the Communist Party of Thailand (CPT)
and that its present practice of minimizing party-to-
party relations is for China a "matter of necessity"
and not a basic change of philosophy. China, in the

concrete, may now be an ally, but, in the abstract, it remains a threat.[47]

PERCEPTIONS AND PRAGMATISM

The pragmatic adjustments to China of Thai policy makers are not unique. Every member of ASEAN, to some degree, has succeeded in making similarly pragmatic adjustments in its foreign-policy thinking. Every ASEAN country trades with China, whether it has formal diplomatic relations or not. The trade is not significantly large, and in relative terms it is not growing (see table 5.1), but its potential is regarded as far more important than the present volume.

Table 5.1

ASEAN Trade with China, 1978 and 1983*
by Percentage of Total Volume
(Value in Million U.S. dollars)

	PRC Share of ASEAN State's Total World Trade		PRC Share of ASEAN State's Total World Trade	
	Exports		Imports	
	1978	1983	1978	1983
Indonesia	0	0.1	1.8	0.3
Malaysia	1.5	1.5	3.7	2.2
Philippines	1.4	0.5	2.3	1.0
Singapore	0.6	1.0	2.6	2.9
Thailand	1.9	1.7	1.6	2.2
ASEAN Total	0.8	0.8	2.5	2.0

*Source: International Monetary Fund, *Directions of Trade, 1984 Annual*.

Singapore has been the most successful ASEAN nation in trading with the PRC, in part because of the Chinese connection, but in part because of a Singapore philosophy that trade and politics are separable. Foreign Minister Dhanabalan, in an address before a National University of Singapore forum in November 1981, enumerated four "fundamental precepts" of Singapore's foreign policy, of which the second was "we will trade with any state for mutual benefit, regardless of ideology or system of government."[48] Thus Singapore has had a more productive trade relationship with the PRC than have the other members of ASEAN, just as Singapore has been the major ASEAN trading partner of Vietnam. However, given the Singapore philosophy of trading with anyone that will trade with them, such statistics are much less significant as indicators, causes, or manifestations of political perceptions.

China, ally or adversary? For most leaders in the ASEAN countries the PRC is both an ally and an adversary. Today it serves as a major source of support for ASEAN in the dispute with Vietnam over Kampuchea. The PRC openly supports the Kampuchean coalition and provides a refuge in exile for its leader, Prince Norodom Sihanouk, and other coalition members; it provides material assistance for the rebels in the field; it champions the cause of the coalition at international fora; and it has been willing to downplay its enthusiasm for the Pol Pot faction in deference to ASEAN and world sensitivities. This is China today, but what of the China of the future?

Political leaders throughout ASEAN, with varying degrees of emotion and conviction, fear the China of the future. There is little agreement on what the China of the future may look like, but in the minds of most it will still be China, and this is ground enough for concern. Although said in various ways, one can frequently hear the argument that if China succeeds in its ambitious modernization plans it will be just as threatening to Southeast Asia as if fails. There is, however, little agreement on when China will become a serious threat to the ASEAN region. For many Indonesians, it already is. For other leaders elsewhere in ASEAN the threshold that China must cross before it becomes a serious threat is obscured by the haze of the future and can be only dimly seen, if at all. Yet, most seem in agreement that this threshold exists. It is not a question of "if" it will happen; rather, it is a question of "when."

NOTES

1. An Indonesian scholar has put the proposition in a similar manner: "smaller neighbors should not, *minimally*, be allied with her main enemy and *ideally or maximally*, should be within her sphere of influence." Lie, "China's Policy Toward Southeast Asia," 1.

2. Sheldon Simon argues that China today is behaving in a very traditional and expected manner. China insists on playing a significant role in determining regional relationships and denies access to the

region to those whom it wants to exclude. Vietnam has refused to play by the rules of the game, and China hopes to punish Vietnam for this refusal. See "China and Southeast Asia," 1.

3. However, for the bearers such tribute may have been seen less as a symbol of subservience than as an opportunistic acknowledgment of political realities given in the interest of improving trade relations with the mainland. Feurwerker, "Chinese History and the Foreign Relations of Contemporary China," 4. A Thai scholar has convincingly demonstrated the practical linkages between tribute and trade during a two-century period. See Sarasin Viraphol, *Tribute and Profit*. Wang, "Early Ming Relations with Southeast Asia," discusses tribute, trade, and other topics in the period immediately preceding the Sarasin Viraphol study. Wang shows that during the early Ming period insular Southeast Asia was treated much differently from neighboring Annam and that the strategic importance of the Malacca Straits was as well recognized then as it is today.

4. In an unusual reference to the history of Chinese relations with Southeast Asia, Indonesian Foreign Minister Mochtar responded to a reporter's question at a news conference in Oslo about Indonesian fears of a militarily strong China with the comment: "We used to pay tribute to China every year in the past." *Straits Times*, 25 April 1985, 8.

5. Overseas Chinese were granted representation in the Legislative Assembly in addition to representation in the "Overseas Chinese Affairs Commission" (*Hua Ch'iao Wei Yuan Hui*), which had broad educational, cultural, and record-keeping responsibilities.

6. Lie, "Indonesia in China's Foreign Policy," 332.

7. Fitzgerald, *China and the Overseas Chinese*, 116–61.

8. *New Straits Times*, 10 August 1981.

9. Suryadinata, *Pribumi Indonesians, the Chinese Minority, and China*. Suryadinata is a very well respected authority on the Indonesian Chinese. I may question the validity of his argument today, almost a decade after the research was undertaken, but this does not detract from an excellent study. Suryadinata has argued in personal conversations that his thesis still applies, but on this point he and I are in disagreement.

10. *Bangkok Post*, 27 February 1983.

11. Suryadinata has made this point in informal conversations.

12. Because of its relevance to Indonesian perceptions of Vietnam, the importance of the Revolution was discussed in chapter 4.

13. The Indonesian attorney-general was recently quoted as saying, however, that Beijing no longer

harbors any PKI members. The deputy attorney-general
added that all were thought to be in Eastern Europe
after having been expelled from the PRC. *Straits
Times*, 25 July 1985, 6.
14. The only exception encountered in the course
of my interviews was a high-ranking military officer
who placed China second and the Soviet Union first in
his hierarchy of external threats, but as our discussions progressed he made a very significant distinction between the two. The USSR constituted a temporary
threat that would eventually recede; China was a permanent threat that would never disappear.
15. Weinstein, *Indonesian Foreign Policy*, 118-21.
These interviews were conducted in the early years of
the Suharto government. It is interesting and significant that in this era of militant anticommunism the
elite interviewed viewed the Chinese threat as more
nationalistic than ideological. This suggests that
this perception of the PRC will not change regardless
of the ideology of the incumbent regime in China.
16. Since the early 1970s, and particularly after
Malaysia, the Philippines, and Thailand established or
normalized relations in 1974 and 1975, the restoration
of Indonesian ties with the PRC has been predicted
almost annually by every foreign minister. In 1973
"top army and foreign ministry officials" told Weinstein that because China had softened its criticism
"ties would be restored in the not too far distant
future." Foreign Minister Malik repeated such a prediction to Weinstein in 1975. *Indonesian Foreign Policy*, 122-23. I heard the same predictions in the course
of conversations in 1980, 1983, and 1985. Foreign
Minister Mochtar was scheduled to visit China in 1984,
but he reported that his trip was vetoed by President
Suharto. *Straits Times*, 15 May 1984. The president
seems to have been the key figure in delaying the
resumption of diplomatic relations.
17. The *Far Eastern Economic Review* reported that
Wu had been asked to bring with him a letter from
Premier Zhao Zhiyang acknowledging the PRC's role in
GESTAPU and making the appropriate apologies. Because
the PRC has steadfastly refused to admit that it had
any involvement, Wu arrived without the letter. According to the same report Suharto compromised on the
conflicting positions of the Ministry of Foreign Affairs (who favored a meeting anyway) and the military
(who opposed it) by setting aside "the only available
time," which was the day following Wu's scheduled
departure. Wu declined "with regret" and left on
schedule. Thereafter each side publicly blamed the
other for having "missed an historic opportunity."
See *Far Eastern Economic Review*, 23 May 1985, 27 and
28. Foreign Minister Mochtar has denied the accuracy
of the report so far as the apology is concerned.
According to the foreign minister, Indonesia expects a

statement that the PRC no longer supports movements opposing legitimate governments in Southeast Asia, but Indonesia does not expect China to apologize. See Mochtar's statement to newsmen following his meeting with President Suharto on 25 May as reported in *FBIS: APS*, IV, 102 (28 May 1985), N-1. Foreign Minister Wu continued to deny that the PRC was involved in GESTA-PU, but he stopped short of meeting Mochtar's expectations when he added to his denial a remark about the necessary "moral link" with communist organizations throughout the world. *Straits Times*, 1 June 1985, 9.

18. The most recent was a twelve-day visit by Prime Minister Lee and some of the younger generation of Singapore leaders in September 1985. According to press reports from both Singapore and China the delegation was very cordially received.

19. The high point of the VOMR broadcasts was the theme song, a march with a distinctive and lilting tune that was easy to remember and difficult to forget. The same senior official was greatly amused when I related to him that I had recently heard the tune being whistled by a young Singaporean waiting at a bus stop. His response ("Poor chap; he should have better things to do with his time!") showed no concern for the political implications of my discovery.

20. See the comments by Prime Minister Lee to the effect that Beijing is "keeping a foot in the door" by maintaining friendly relations with indigenous communist parties while exercising restraint in exploiting the relationship because the PRC needs "ASEAN . . . support . . . in keeping out . . . Soviet influence in the area." See interview with Lester Tanzer, 7 December 1981, 7-8. During his 1980 visit to the PRC the prime minister prepared a banquet speech that included criticisms of China's party-to-party relations. He was told that if he made such comments Premier Zhao would have to respond publicly, and Singapore-Chinese relations might be strained. Rather than excising this portion, he chose not to make a speech at all, but he felt that he succeeded in making the point to the PRC leadership on behalf of Singapore's neighbors. Interview with Singapore journalists, 23 November 1980, 16-17.

21. Interview with Lester Tanzer, 7 December 1981, 7.

22. This explanation for not establishing diplomatic relations with Beijing was given in the first session of the first Parliament by Lee Khoon Choy, Minister of State for Culture. See Lee Lai To, "Singapore and East Asia," 345-46. Singapore nevertheless voted for the admission of the PRC into the United Nations in 1965 and 1971 (having abstained in the years in between).

23. The turning point in Lee's mind seems to have been his first visit to the PRC in May 1976, and this

change was fully confirmed during his second visit
four years later. Only shortly before his 1976 visit
he seemed doubtful that the process of transforming
Singapore-Chinese into Singaporeans had progressed far
enough to cross the point of no return. In the course
of his second visit in November 1980 he related in an
interview with Singapore journalists accompanying his
party how "Singaporean" he felt in China in 1976 and
how "our life experience, our perception of the world,
and our national interests make us think, feel and act
differently from the China Chinese." Interview with
Singapore journalists, 23 November 1980, 13-14. This
interview makes it clear that Prime Minister Lee no
longer retained his earlier doubts about the existence
of a Singapore identity.

    24. A government-sponsored movement to return to
the principles of Confucianism began in 1980 but has
not received enthusiastic support from most Singaporeans. As is found elsewhere, Singapore's younger
generation seems more interested in motorbikes, break-
dancing, and McDonald's hamburgers than Confucian
ethics. The government also launched a "Speak Mandarin" campaign in the early 1980s with large banners
strung across shopping center corridors and signs in
taxis. Most of the banners had disappeared two years
later and the taxicab signs were often faded and half-
torn away. However, the "Speak Mandarin" campaign
fared better than the back-to-Confucius campaign because Mandarin is very useful in multi-lingual Singapore. The television service of the Singapore Broadcasting Corporation carries many Mandarin-speaking
programs, and many Singapore taxi drivers keep their
stereo radios tuned to the Chinese service of Radio
Singapore. But "listen" might describe the results
better than "speak" because many Singaporeans seem
embarrassed by their skills in the spoken language.
Some well-informed Singaporeans argue that both the
Mandarin and the Confucius campaigns were launched to
placate that segment of the Singapore electorate--and
their leaders in the ruling party--who felt that Singapore was moving too rapidly toward becoming a Western, English-speaking country. Others have pointed
out that Confucianism, with its emphasis on respect
for one's elders and personal responsibility for the
well-being of one's parents, could have significant
social, political, and economic implications for Singapore. Beyond this, however, it is apparent that some
thoughtful PAP leaders have genuine concerns about the
unintended, and unwanted, absorption of values and
beliefs that have accompanied the transfer of technology, and for them a return to basic Confucian
values is seen as an effective counterpoise. The
reactions have varied, but this concern is almost
universal throughout ASEAN and constitutes one of the
major themes of the final chapter of this study.

25. High officials in Singapore and Jakarta are not in agreement on the origin and purpose of the agreement to delay recognition. The accepted version in Singapore is that it was an unwritten arrangement intended to take the pressure off Indonesia in the wake of the chill in Sino-Indonesian relations following GESTAPU. In Jakarta's view the agreement was reached in order to buy time for the PAP. The PAP needed time for the local Chinese population to develop a Singapore identity without the embarrassment of admitting that Singapore feared the cultural magnetism of the ancestral homeland. Regardless of the rationale of the agreement it has usefully served to hide more contentious issues in both countries.

26. Musa bin Ahmad spent twenty-five years in China before returning to Malaysia in January 1981. He was put on national television where he pointed an accusing finger at the PRC, saying that the PRC still controls the Communist Party of Malaya (CPM) and hopes to make Malaysia a Chinese satellite. It is not entirely clear how Musa got out of China, but the assertion of one official that he was smuggled out (*New Straits Times*, 12 January 1981) seems unlikely. The timing and intent of the sensational television confession are also suspect. The government had to make the arrangements for Musa's appearance on state television, and officials must have realized that his confession would limit the opportunities for improving Sino-Malaysian relations as a result of Zhao's visit scheduled for later in the year. Prime Minister Mahathir was understandably reluctant to discuss the Musa affair with me in an on-the-record interview in 1983.

27. See Chin, "A New Assertiveness in Malaysia Foreign Policy," 276. The strains caused by the Musa affair some seven months earlier are clearly evident in press reports of the visit. See the many articles in *New Straits Times*, 9-11 August 1981.

28. Saravanamuttu, "Malaysia-China Ties," 44.

29. Neither match, however, pitted a Chinese team against a Malaysian team, which undoubtedly would have been a better test. According to my informant the coach of Middle Eastern team was heard to comment bitterly that he had not been aware the match was to be "played in Beijing."

30. Howell did not attempt to explain the perceptions he reported, but he expressed his belief that the attitudes of older students probably paralleled closely those of their leaders. Thus, for his purposes he was willing to accept that student respondents "represented" the policy-making elite, whom it is impossible to survey in the same manner. See "Looking East, Looking West." Howell included two sets of questions on twenty-six nations and nationalities and arrived at two scales, one measuring social distance and the other political distance. On a scale of 1-5

(one being the sense of being closest, or having the warmest feelings for persons of another nation or nationality) for his Malay respondents China scored 3.76 and 4.07 (1971 and 1981) and the Chinese of China, 3.85 and 4.05. For comparison, Indonesia and the Indonesians scored 1.48/1.38 and 1.58/1.79. See tables 1 and 2.

31. See the candid interview of Foreign Minister Ghazali Shafie with U.S. Senator S. I. Hayakawa reported in detail in *Sunday Star*, 16 August 1981. At the United Nations, Ghazali later likened the conduct of the PRC to "sweet and sour rotten fish" (*Straits Times*, 25 September 1981). Prime Minister Mahathir has several times been reported to have said that any PRC support for the CPM, whether moral or military, would be an obstacle to the improvement of Malaysian-Chinese relations. One such statement was made before Premier Zhao at a state dinner in his honor. See *New Straits Times*, 10 August 1981.

32. *Straits Times*, 22 October 1985, 36.

33. Prior to the prime minister's visit a joint delegation from the Malay and Chinese chambers of commerce and industry visited the PRC for eight days and reached an agreement intended to promote two-way bilateral trade. This agreement set the tone for the visit that followed. See *Straits Times*, 2 October 1985, 7 and 17 October 1985, 9. This was reported to be the first joint mission of the two chambers.

34. The prime minister's news conference at Kuala Lumpur airport on his return from Beijing was reported in *FBIS: APS*, IV, 230 (29 November 1985), 0-1.

35. *Far Eastern Economic Review*, 5 December 1985, 30.

36. *FBIS: APS*, IV, 230 (29 November 1985), 0-1.

37. The two agreements were the China-Philippines Treaty of Amity and Friendship (1947) and the understanding appended to the treaty in 1955.

38. Information in this paragraph and the one that follows has been drawn from my largely unpublished research on the role of education in political socialization of minority Chinese students, principally in the Philippines. Research throughout Southeast Asia, Taiwan, and Hong Kong was conducted under the auspices of a National Defense Education Act summer grant in 1967, and the research in the Philippines was supported by the National Science Foundation in 1969 and 1970. The results are summarized in Tilman, "Philippine-Chinese Youth."

39. The confusion and lack of direction in the slow shift from the ROC to the PRC was evident in the case of two Philippine-Chinese journalists who, in their columns, had frequently encouraged Philippine-Chinese to divest themselves of their KMT loyalties and become true Filipinos. Despite what on the surface appeared to be laudable advice from the government's

perspective, they were accused by the Marcos administration of communist motivations and were deported to
Taiwan (late at night and on a Philippine Air Force
transport) for political reeducation. All of this took
place in 1970, just a few years before their advice
became official government policy.

40. Salvador H. Laurel, then a senator and now
vice-president and minister for foreign affairs, at
the request of the Philippine Senate, visited the PRC
immediately following the visit of President Nixon to
gather information and make recommendations on future
Philippine-PRC relations. His report to the Senate,
Laurel Report: Mission to China, contains some interesting contemporary observations, especially in view
of his present responsibilities.

41. On the first lady's visit see *New Straits
Times*, 10 June 1982. On the Huang Hua visit see
Straits Times, 13 March 1980. On the Zhao visit see
New Straits Times, 10 August 1981. On the lifting of
restrictions against the visits of relatives from the
PRC see *Straits Times*, 16 March 1981. On the first
lady's toast see *Bulletin Today*, 10 June 1984, 1. On
the appointment of Philippine Ambassador Alfonso T.
Yuchengco see *Manila Bulletin*, 27 May 1986, 8.

42. One senior member of the Ministry of Foreign
Affairs of the present government responded to my
question about a possible Chinese fifth column with
the comment, "Well, once a Chinese, always a Chinese,"
but none of the four officials around the table seemed
to take this as more than a simple cultural statement.
Not one of the officials was prepared to attribute any
political significance to such an observation.

43. China has flatly denied that it maintains any
ties with the Communist Party of the Philippines or
the NPA. See the statement of the PRC ambassador to
the Philippines, Mo Yan-zhong in *Bulletin Today*, 2 May
1984, 28. In May 1986 officials of the Ministry of
Foreign Affairs in Manila were humorously evasive
about possible external assistance to the NPA and
suggested that I should ask this question at the
Ministry of Defense and come back and tell them the
answer I got. However, in the context of the discussions it was apparent that the external assistance, if
indeed any was suspected, was not coming from the PRC.
A senior military official at the Ministry of Defense
felt certain that "for the present" the NPA was not
receiving material support from abroad. However, the
Muslim movement in the south was "an entirely different matter."

44. This is the argument put forward by the Dutch
sociologist Wertheim in *East-West Parallels*, 46-49 and
chap. 3.

45. This is a common argument made by many scholars, who usually employ it in conjunction with other

explanations. For example, see Coughlin, *Double Identity*, and Skinner, *Chinese Society in Thailand*.

46. Thanat Khoman, "National Threat Perceptions in East Asia--Pacific." Also see chap. 1, n. 1.

47. In a major but unpublished Thai-language study of the perceptions of the Thai elite conducted by the Institute of Strategic and International Studies at Chulalongkorn University in 1982, China was perceived as a threat on an abstract question, but in a concrete hypothetical situation it emerged as an ally.

48. Dhanabalan, "Why Singapore Needs an Active Foreign Policy," 30, 34, and 38-39.

6

Japan: Ambivalence Toward a Partnership

We had a very bad experience with the Japanese and can't easily forget it. Naturally it makes us suspicious.

Senior Official
Ministry of Foreign Affairs
Manila, May 1986

Lately I have been exhorting Malaysians to emulate the Japanese. . . . We have for a long time been looking West, . . . but the West is no longer a suitable model.

Mahathir bin Mohamad
Prime Minister of Malaysia
Kuala Lumpur, February 1982

Japan is a major trading nation. It is inevitable that a major trading nation will have a strong navy. In this sense Japanese rearmament is inevitable.

Senior official
Singapore, 1985

Japan is important to the ASEAN member nations, and they are important to Japan. Despite the obvious benefits for all parties, relations have often been strained. Some ASEAN leaders are quick to note that Japan has achieved economically what she failed to gain militarily and that the resulting relationships are disproportionately beneficial to Japan. Yet it is also understood that Japanese economic prosperity, political stability, and military security are vital if the ASEAN members are to prosper. Within ASEAN only Malaysia has openly espoused a policy of emulating Japan as a model for development,[1] but for all of the Associations's leaders Japan and ASEAN must be partners. Nevertheless, in the view of most, their relationship sometimes seems to be an unequal and uneasy partnership.

JAPANESE NATIONAL INTERESTS IN THE ASEAN REGION

Every day of the year more than 700,000 tons of crude oil and 110,000 tons of iron ore are put ashore in Japanese ports.[2] Some 90 percent of each of these vital raw materials pass through the Straits of Malacca and the Lombok Straits. In fact, of Japan's total world imports of all commodities 40 percent pass through ASEAN waters.[3] Many of these imports come from the ASEAN countries. Between 1981 and 1983 Japan took between 87 and 89 percent of Indonesia's oil exports, 33 to 38 percent of Malaysia's, and absorbed 74 to 80 percent of the output of Singapore's refineries.[4] Overall, Japan takes about 30 percent of ASEAN's total exports.[5] Japan lives, or dies, on raw-material imports, and thus the stability and predictability of the ASEAN region is a national interest of high priority to the Japanese.

The Japanese have invested heavily in the ASEAN region. Asia as a whole represents the second-largest area of foreign investment for Japan, immediately behind North America, and of the total Japanese direct investment in Asia 71 percent is in the countries of the ASEAN region.[6] In recognition of the importance of the ASEAN region approximately 35 percent of all the Official Development Act (ODA) provided by Japan throughout the world has been channelled into ASEAN countries.[7]

The peace and stability of the ASEAN region are essential to Japan. It has often been argued that Japan is more important to ASEAN than is ASEAN to Japan, and in purely economic terms there is much evidence to support such a conclusion. Most of the raw materials produced in the ASEAN area are available elsewhere, and although ASEAN residents have proven to be voracious consumers of Japanese manufactured goods the loss of this market would not be devastating to the Japanese economy.[8] Yet, whether Japan imports its petroleum products from Indonesia or Saudi Arabia, the tankers must transit through ASEAN straits. Even if markets in the European Economic Community (EEC), or perhaps Eastern Europe, could pick up the slack caused by the loss of the ASEAN market, the freighters carrying Japanese autos, televisions, and computers would have to pass through several maritime "choke points" within the ASEAN region. Even if trade were not a factor, Japan's national interests require a peaceful, stable, friendly (or, at least, not hostile) ASEAN.

PERCEPTIONS AND MEMORIES

The Japanese "interregnum," as historian Harry J. Benda termed the Japanese occupation of Southeast Asia during World War II,[9] left vivid memories in the minds of most of the current generation of ASEAN political leaders. These memories, most of which were unpleasant, have in turn influenced these leaders' perceptions of Japan and Japanese motives. Of course, not all ASEAN leaders were equally influenced by the Japanese interregnum.

The Philippines

In the Philippines memories of the occupation are vivid and periodically rekindled.[10] Although his claims were questioned late in his term of office, President Marcos took apparent pride in his wartime record as a guerrilla fighter against the Japanese.[11] At a lower level a senior official in the Ministry of Foreign Affairs several times recounted to me the circumstances surrounding the death of his father at the hands of Japanese soldiers. The very distinguished former foreign minister, the late Carlos J. Romulo, in a "guest editorial" written while accompanying General MacArthur in the struggle to retake the Philippines, wrote emotionally at the height of the fighting to capture Manila that "our sufferings are indescribable. As a nation we have quaffed of sorrow to its bitterest dregs. Some . . . have lost all their worldly goods. Others have known the loss of loved ones. All the loyal carry scars in their hearts. But we have shown the world that . . . those . . . fit to live in freedom . . . are not afraid to die for it.[12]

The wartime experience of the present foreign minister (and vice-president), Salvador H. Laurel, is unique in ASEAN. As the son of Dr. Jose P. Laurel, the president of the Philippine republic that was granted nominal independence under the Japanese in 1943, Salvador Laurel lived a life-style different from those of his colleagues elsewhere in ASEAN. His father was admired by the Japanese and was awarded an honorary degree from the Imperial University in Tokyo in 1937. An elder brother, Jose P. Laurel III (the eldest brother was Jose P. Laurel, Jr.) graduated fourth in his class from the Imperial Military Academy, was awarded an Emperor's Sword for his achievements, observed the Sino-Japanese war in Manchuria, and returned to a special commission as aide-de-campe to President Quezon. While in Japan the elder Laurel brother attained considerable fluency in spoken and written Japanese, and during the Japanese occupation he tutored Salvador in the language.

Salvador Laurel visited his elder brother in Japan for some six weeks in 1937, and at age seventeen he and the entire Laurel family were sent to live in Nara for the remainder of the war. He was there when the atomic bombs were dropped and when the war ended on 15 August 1945. President Laurel was imprisoned in

Japan for collaboration for almost a year, but the remaining members of his family were flown back to Manila in November 1945 after some five months in Nara and Tokyo.[13]

What impact such experiences will have on Philippine relations with Japan is not yet apparent. The foreign minister's initial visit to Japan some three months after having taken office, seems to have been only modestly successful, and no particular significance was attached to the choice of Japan early on his travel agenda.[14] Below the level of the foreign minister, senior officials in the ministry generally seem to have perceptions of Japan very similar to those of their predecessors in the Marcos government. Thus, until concrete evidence demonstrates a significant change, it seems likely that the generally unpleasant wartime experiences of the senior policy makers will continue to influence Philippine perceptions of Japan, as the opening quotation has suggested.

Malaysia

Malays who today dominate foreign policy met the Japanese under circumstances considerably different from those in the Philippines. Many of today's Filipino policy makers pride themselves on their guerrilla skirmishes with the Japanese, but few Malays took up arms in the jungles to fight the Japanese.[15] The anti-Japanese rebels were almost exclusively Chinese--the same guerrillas who fought the British and Malaysian forces later. The Malay community suffered many hardships during the Japanese occupation, but it was generally the Chinese community--most of whom supported either the Nationalists or the Communists on the mainland, both of whom were at war with Japan--that bore the brunt of the Japanese wrath.

Prime Minister Mahathir, who operated a food stall and sold fried bananas in relatively peaceful Alor Star in the northeastern state of Kedah during the Japanese occupation, apparently lived a fairly normal and not totally unprofitable life during this period.[16] Although the outspoken prime minister has levelled considerable criticism at the Japanese on various occasions, his comments rarely if ever reveal the bitterness of some leaders with much more unpleasant memories of the Japanese occupation. Certainly for Mahathir and most Malays the situation was not ideal, but the times were not as difficult as they were for some of their ASEAN neighbors.

Indonesia

Indonesians view the Japanese interregnum with mixed feelings, despite a not uncommon description of life under the Japanese as "worse than life under

Dutch colonialism"--probably the ultimate damnation in the eyes of most Indonesians. The Japanese occupation had a catalytic effect on the Indonesian Revolution, and the revolution is the single most important historical force shaping Indonesian foreign policy.

The Japanese broke the back of colonialism in the East Indies far more effectively and efficiently than could have been accomplished by the small bands of Indonesian revolutionaries, most of whom had been jailed or exiled by the Dutch. The Japanese freed the Indonesian nationalist leadership, and although they were kept on a very short leash, they enjoyed far greater access to their followers than the colonial government had permitted.

In addition, the Japanese gave many Indonesians their first taste of administrative responsibility, either as civilian bureaucrats or in the Japanese-organized military forces.[17] Thus the Japanese occupation of Indonesia is remembered with mixed feelings. Few have forgotten harsh treatment at the hands of individual Japanese, but most realize that these same troops presented them with opportunities that otherwise might not have come for decades or longer.

Singapore

In Singapore, as in the other countries of Southeast Asia, attitudes toward Japan in the abstract and toward concrete Japanese policies must be seen in the perspective of their World War II experiences. A Singapore scholar has recently observed that Singapore's wounds might not have been as deep as those suffered by others,[18] but it is apparent that even in Singapore the legacy of the Japanese occupation has affected perceptions of Japanese intentions.

The Japanese were particularly hostile toward Singapore Chinese whose names appeared on seized records revealing contributions to the anti-Japanese war efforts of Chiang Kai-shek and the Kuomintang or Mao Tse-tung and the Communists. These records, not surprisingly, were voluminous and contained the names of some of the best-known Chinese residents of Singapore, particularly the records kept by the KMT. Although such memories have not been allowed to influence significantly the formulation of policy toward Japan because too much is at stake, they surface frequently, and occasionally at the highest levels of government.[19]

Thailand

The World War II alliance of Thailand and Japan was effected under the threat of invasion, but the Japanese were nevertheless invited to occupy Thailand. Under these circumstances the occupation may have been an inconvenience, and without doubt it produced many individual hardships, but it was not the traumatic experience undergone by those ASEAN nations whose colonial overlords chose to resist the Japanese in their colonies. There are some severe misgivings about Japanese economic policies, and pent-up feelings among youth have occasionally erupted in violent demonstrations, but the absence of bitter memories of Japan in Southeast Asia is apparent in the foreign-policy thinking of Thais today.

REACTIONS TO THE SEA LANES ISSUE

The defense of the international sea lanes is a vital national interest of Japan. Thus, the American proposal in 1982 that Japan should ultimately assume responsibility for the defense of these maritime arteries seemed reasonable in Washington.[20] Yet many ASEAN leaders clearly regarded the transfer of responsibility from the United States to Japan as inimical to their own national interests, and, in some cases, as a new external threat. Reactions to the sea lanes issue provides a useful indicator to elite perceptions of Japan as an external threat.

The United States proposed a 1,000 nautical mile sealane zone to be protected by Japan. This zone comes to within 200 nautical miles of the northernmost boundary of the Philippines, but it is another 1,200 nautical miles to Singapore. All of the ASEAN states except the Philippines are physically removed from the sea lanes to be protected by Japan, but the proposal triggered general concerns throughout the region. And the intensity of the emotional response to the original American proposal seemed to vary according to the geographic proximity or distance of each country from the shores of Japan.

The Philippines

There are many Filipino leaders who hide their suspicions of Japanese motives neither in public nor in private. For most of his two decades in office President Marcos was outspoken in voicing his doubts about the probable behavior of a rearmed Japan, and he was not a lone voice in the Philippines.[21] In private, many of Marcos's foreign-policy advisors revealed even stronger sentiments, and the public seemed eager to watch and listen as films, videotapes, and public exhibits rekindled bitterly pleasant memories of World War II in the Philippines.[22]

Thus it is not surprising that the American suggestion that Japan take responsibility for patrolling its vital sea lanes provoked widespread and often highly emotional reactions in the Philippines. President Marcos may have been guilty of using the issue for domestic political purposes. This seems possible since he had apparently reached an agreement while on an official visit to Washington several months earlier that the Japanese responsibility would not extend as far south as the Philippines.[23] More significant, however, is the fact that the president could generate such popular sentiment on an issue that most observers consider to be moot, at least in the present setting of Japanese politics, and complicated by technicalities that at best will take years to resolve. Although the Philippine leadership has now changed, these underlying sentiments of the Filipino people probably have not.

Singapore

As a result of their global view of Japan's security imperatives, Singapore officials have publicly supported the Japanese and American position that Japan assume responsibility for the defense of its sea lanes. Prime Minister Lee has often been quoted in Japan and elsewhere as a supporter of the 1,000 nautical mile defense concept even when other ASEAN leaders were expressing considerable concern. But, even in Singapore, one can hear many qualifications and reservations expressed.

Singapore prides itself on its practicality and rationality in the formulation of policies, foreign and domestic, and sees the sea lanes issues as no exception. As one senior leader commented, "we have to be hardheaded about it. The United States cannot continue to shoulder full responsibility for Japan's defense so someone will have to take over." And, he added, "Japan will have to do it for itself." But the same leader went on to say that although the rearmament of Japan was "necessary and inevitable" this did not mean that it would not produce problems for Southeast Asia.

As it is sometimes said in Singapore, the very act of rearming to protect the sea lanes makes it politically easier to take additional measures. If rearming should lead Japan to an eventual decision to adopt nuclear weapons, which is not considered impossible by some thoughtful Singaporeans, or if Japan should decide to concentrate on development of a submarine fleet, which is also regarded as a possibility, then, as one senior official put it, "we are in trouble."[24] However, these are problems for succeeding generations; for this generation of leaders the Japanese defense of its sea lanes is "necessary and inevitable," even if there are some nagging and unpleasant memories of past Japanese behavior when it enjoyed military superiority in the region.[25]

Indonesia

It is not unusual in the Indonesian Ministry of Foreign Affairs to hear concerns expressed about probable Japanese behavior once they again command dominant political positions internationally, and the Indonesian military has expressed concern about the nature of the hardware Japan may acquire to carry out its new defense responsibilities. As a high-ranking military figure commented privately, "Japanese rearmament must be watched with great care in Southeast Asia, and particular attention should be given to the kinds of armaments they choose and what they regard as the limits of their responsibilities." As another distinguished and influential official commented, if allowed to "get on top" the Japanese could become "domineering and brutal," but if the United States would keep them "under their thumb" they would continue to be "meek and mild mannered." Some members of the Ministry of Foreign Affairs and parliament are also on record in strong opposition to Japanese rearmament.[26]

Despite these misgivings, in recent years Premier Nakasone's attentive concern for Southeast Asia, his reassuring statements about Japan's awareness of ASEAN's legitimate fears of Japanese rearmament, and the genuine rapport that he seems to have established with many ASEAN leaders have gone a long way toward reducing anxieties, particularly in Indonesia, but elsewhere as well. By 1985 the fear of Japan as an external threat lurked only slightly below the surface, but thanks largely to the higher level of trust generated by Premier Nakasone it had become much more abstract.

Malaysia

Prime Minister Mahathir's "look east" policy is principally a "look-toward-Japan" policy, although on occasion it has included Korea.[27] Malaysia has looked toward Japan for many years as a source of investment, imports, and technology, and Japan is a major customer for Malaysian exports. But looking east therefore involves more than this. The prime minister has frequently described the policy as a long-overdue counterweight to previously unquestioned policies of looking west, and as an attempt to import from Japan and East Asia some of the cultural values and practices that have contributed significantly to Japanese successes in applied technology and marketing. What change looking east has brought to Malaysian foreign policy is not clear, but the prime minister's statements have improved the climate for Malaysian-Japanese relations. In this context it is not surprising that

Malaysia came to accept the right and obligation of Japan to protect its vital sea lanes. However, Prime Minister Mahathir first had to be convinced that a rearmed Japan would not pose a threat to Malaysia.

The prime minister first presumed that the Japanese defense zone would extend to the Straits of Malacca, and, if so, he expressed considerable concern about a new Japanese military presence. Later he was reassured by Premier Nakasone that Japan had no intention of extending its defense perimeter beyond the 1,000 mile limit, and with this reassurance the prime minister became a public supporter of the Washington proposal.[28]

Thailand

Thai leaders today are preoccupied with problems on their borders stemming from the Vietnamese invasion of Kampuchea in 1979. They are therefore rarely provoked to comment on issues involving Japan, except those that touch on Thai-Japanese economic relations.

On a rare occasion when Prime Minister Prem agreed to respond to a reporter's questions on Japanese rearmament he described it as "conceivable that Japan have a greater role in the security of the region," and he accepted as "reasonable" the principle that Japan should accept responsibility for defending its sea lanes as part of the enlarged role. However, he also acknowledged that Thailand "would definitely view . . . with apprehension" the prospect of an "expanded military role . . . that goes beyond . . . the stated purpose." Finally, he remarked that "memories of the Japanese . . . during World War II are still alive," and he could see "no justification or need for Japanese warships on patrol in our region."[29]

PERCEPTIONS AND ECONOMIC RELATIONS

Forty years after total defeat Japan is the dominant economic power in Southeast Asia. Japan is respected for its achievements, but it also pays a price in terms of images and perceptions. A systematic study of Indonesian elites in 1970, which was partially replicated in 1973, revealed overwhelmingly negative perceptions of Japan and the Japanese on the part of Indonesians of all ages. Older respondents often referred to their memories of World War II, but many negative impressions apparently stemmed from postwar relations. Japanese were described as "crude, aggressive, and inscrutable," not only by the older generation who had experienced the occupation, but also by the younger generation who felt frustrated because Japan's economic might was so overwhelming that it left them with little control over their own desti nies.[30] The importance of Japanese economic assistance to Indonesia was recognized, but in the view of these elite such aid was intended by Japan to subjugate them.[31] Japan, in their view, needed and wanted a colonial relationship with Indonesia to assure a reliable source of raw materials and markets for Japanese finished products. According to the elite surveyed, exploitation, not industrial development in Indonesia, was the purpose behind Japanese assistance and investment.[32]

Although systematic studies similar to the one cited for Indonesia are not available for the other states of ASEAN, the sentiments expressed by the Indonesian respondents are frequently heard throughout the region. Thai Minister for Industry Ob Vasuratna publicly threatened "to retaliate" against Japan for its unfair trade and investment practices, and Prime Minister Mahathir, despite the friendly environment of his look east policy, told a Malaysia-Japan Colloquia in 1984 that Japan must "rectify" its trade practices or face "turmoil."[33]

Off-the-record comments by high officials are often even sharper in their condemnation of Japanese trade, investment, and assistance policies and practices. The Fukuda Doctrine has been described to me as a "smokescreen behind which Japan could continue to do business as usual."[34] Or as I have heard in Indonesia, "the Japanese wanted our timber, but they wouldn't give us the technology to make plywood that could compete with theirs."

These, of course, are subjective perceptions, and, as the author of the Indonesian elite survey commented in another context, the Japanese are in a no-win situation. The greater their aid and investment, the more they will be criticized for creating dependency relationships; the less they contribute, the more they will be criticized for being selfish and uncaring.[35] Yet, there is objective evidence to support the subjective perception that the Japanese are intent on perpetuating these colonial relationships.

As table 6.1 indicates, in 1983 Japan was a major trading partner of each of the ASEAN states. The percentage of total world exports was highest for Indonesia (46 percent) and lowest for Singapore (9 percent). On the other hand Japan provides between 17 percent (in the case of the Philippines) and 27 percent (Thailand) of each ASEAN country's total world imports.

The trading relationships between Japan and the ASEAN region are important to all parties. However, some of the disparities that contribute to political and social frictions between the trading partners are more evident when these gross world figures are examined in greater detail. The most obvious issue is the question of trade balances, which are examined in

table 6.2. Japan often discusses its trading relationship with ASEAN in collective terms, and collectively
ASEAN annually shows a large surplus. However, ASEAN
deals collectively with Japan, and with its other
trading partners, only when involved in discussions or
negotiations of major issues such as tariffs or non-
tariff barriers. Usually, however, trade is a national

Table 6.1

Two-Way Trade Between ASEAN and Japan, 1983
(Expressed as percentages of each state's world total)

	Exports	Imports
Indonesia	45.8	23.1
Malaysia	19.4	25.4
Philippines	19.9	17.1
Singapore	9.2	18.1
Thailand	15.5	27.3

Source: Derived from International Monetary Fund,
Directions of Trade Statistics Yearbook, 1984.

Table 6.2

ASEAN-Japan Trade Balances, 1980-1984
(In Millions US Dollars)

	1980	1981	1982	1983	1984	1980-84
Indonesia	9,709	9,182	7,744	6,880	8,102	41,617
Malaysia	1,410	503	508	360	1,537	4,318
Philippines	268	(197)	(227)	(437)	338	(255)
Singapore	(2,404)	(2,524)	(2,547)	(2,981)	(2,835)	(13,291)
Thailand	(797)	(1,189)	(966)	(1,488)	(1,385)	(5,825)
ASEAN	8,186	5,775	4,512	2,334	5,757	26,564

Source: Adapted from Japan Economic Institute
(JEI), *Report 27A*, table 1. There are often dis-
parities in trade figures for ASEAN and Japan.
The JEI report used figures provided by the Japan
Tariff Association. (Parentheses indicate nega-
tive balances.)

matter dealt with on a bilateral basis with minimal or no involvement of the other members of ASEAN. Thus, the national surpluses and deficits illustrated in table 6.2 are more significant than the ASEAN totals.

During the five years reported between 1980 and 1984 only Indonesia and Malaysia consistently ran trade surpluses with Japan, and together they have accounted for every ASEAN surplus. Thailand and Singapore did not enjoy a single annual trade surplus during this period, and the Philippines experienced a deficit in three of the five years. The Singapore case is somewhat less significant because many of these imports were destined for export to other parts of the world, but the figures for Thailand and the Philippines cannot be similarly explained. Neither in the developed nor in the underdeveloped world do such figures create a hospitable environment for the conduct of relations in other spheres. However, in the underdeveloped world the situation is worsened by the makeup of the goods that flow in each direction.

With the exception of Singapore, which has no raw materials, Japan takes few finished materials from the ASEAN countries. On the other hand, virtually every

Table 6.3

ASEAN Exports to Japan, by Category, 1984
(In millions of US dollars)

	Raw or Unfinished*	Finished or Partially Finished**	Percentage Finished
Indonesia	1,050.00	312.20	22.92
Malaysia	1,744.60	450.60	20.53
Philippines	1,103.60	268.20	19.55
Singapore	92.10	442.50	82.77
Thailand	802.90	236.60	22.76
ASEAN	4,793.20	1,710.10	26.30

*Food (some of which may be tinned and other finished goods, but the bulk of which is not), ores and scrap metal, raw materials.
**Textile materials, chemicals, machinery and transport equipment, other manufactured items.
Note: Mineral fuels have not been included because the available statistics do not distinguish between processed and unprocessed fuels.
Source: Adapted from JEI, *Report 27A*, table 2.

item that is imported into the ASEAN region from Japan
is finished or processed. As the Malaysian prime minister said with some apparent bitterness, "Japan
bought practically nothing of our manufactured goods.
The biggest single category--thermionic and cathode
valves, tubes, photocells and diodes--amounted to only
$170 million. . . . We in fact bought more of those
things from Japan than we sold to Japan."[36] There is
clearly some empirical basis for the perceptions of
many ASEAN leaders that Japan benefits significantly
from the existing colonial relationship.

Japanese direct investment in the ASEAN member
states has been significant throughout the past decade. Although the largest investments have flowed
into Indonesia, all countries have benefited significantly from the availability of Japanese capital, as
table 6.4 demonstrates.

Foreign investment is often viewed, however, as a
mixed blessing. On the one hand it is a *sine qua non*
for development, but on the other it creates a dependency syndrome that influences indigenous perceptions
of a colonial relationship. It serves to bind two
nations together with shared common interests in
order, stability, and economic progress, but it often
commits the investing nation to the *status quo*. Investment fuels the engine of development and contrib-
utes to the growth of the gross national product, but
rarely do all persons benefit equally from a growing
GNP. It is not unusual for families or cronies with
good connections to the government to benefit disproportionately from the availability of foreign investment. Even in cases where corruption or collusion is
not a significant factor, those who derive the greatest benefits are likely to be those in the best position to make use of foreign capital. The resulting
economic development may in fact widen the gap between
haves and have-nots and contribute to a heightened
sense of relative deprivation.

Imbalances in foreign trade, the colonial nature
of Japanese-ASEAN trading relations, and the unintended consequences of Japanese investment in ASEAN
have all contributed to perceptions of Japan as an
external economic threat. Yet, the political impact of
these economic influences are vague, imprecise, and
almost subliminal. When Indonesian students took to
the streets to protest the presence of Japanese Premier Tanaka in 1974 there were probably few, if any,
who could have recited the amount of Japanese direct
investment in Indonesia in fiscal year 1973 or the
makeup of Indonesian exports to Japan. Yet, a sense
of uneasiness about the commercial relations of Japan
and Indonesia surely contributed to the bloody riots
in Jakarta more than a decade ago, and today such
uneasiness continues to color Indonesian thinking
about its relations with Japan. Of course, Indonesia

Table 6.4

Japanese Foreign Direct Investment in ASEAN, 1979-1983
(Millions US Dollars)
(Percentages of Total ASEAN Investment in Parentheses)

	1979	1980	1981	1982	1983	Total, 1979-1983
Indonesia	150 (25.2)	529 (57.1)	2,434 (85.9)	440 (52.9)	374 (38.4)	3,927 (63.8)
Malaysia	33 (5.5)	146 (15.8)	31 (1.1)	83 (10.0)	140 (14.4)	433 (7.0)
Philippines	102 (17.1)	78 (8.4)	72 (2.5)	34 (4.1)	65 (6.7)	351 (5.7)
Singapore	255 (42.9)	140 (15.1)	266 (9.4)	180 (21.7)	322 (33.1)	1,163 (18.9)
Thailand	55 (9.2)	33 (3.6)	31 (1.1)	94 (11.3)	72 (7.4)	285 (4.6)
ASEAN	595	926	2,834	831	973	6,159

Source: Adapted from JEI, Report, 27A, table 4.

is not unique. A sense of uneasiness pervades the
thinking of many ASEAN policy makers.

JAPAN AND ASEAN: AMBIVALENCE TOWARD IMPORTANT PARTNERS

The ASEAN region is almost as important to Japan
as Japan is to ASEAN, and most ASEAN leaders well
recognize this reality. Yet many misgivings about
Japanese strategies, tactics, and motives persist.
The demands of geopolitical and economic interdepen-
dence may be a reality, but historical memories color
perceptions. Few, even in the Philippines, expect
Japanese warships to steam into their harbors or Japanese dive-bombers to drop from the sky. Yet, for many
the Japanese threat is no less real because it does
not emanate from the military. In fact, in the minds
of some leaders the threat is all the more ominous
because it is seductive, incremental, long-term, and
not amenable to any permanent solution. Wars are fi-
nite in duration, and in the end one wins, loses, or
reaches a draw. ASEAN's peaceful partnership with
Japan is open-ended, uncertain in terms of costs and
benefits, and fraught with ill-defined risks for future generations if not for now.

NOTES

1. For a significant comment on his look east
policy, see the prime minister's opening remarks at a
conference of the Malaysian-Japanese Economic Association. The opening quotation in this chapter is also
taken from this source.
2. Eto, "Japanese Perceptions of National
Threats," 13.
3. Lim, "Japan in ASEAN," 117, 130.
4. Ibid., 118.
5. Japan Economic Institute, *Report*, *27A*, 3.
6. Ibid., 4 and table 5, p. 12. Note, however,
that in relative (but not absolute) terms, Japanese
investment in Asia is declining. It was only recently
that Japan's investments in Asia fell behind its investments in the United States and Canada. According
to another source, ASEAN accounts for about 20 percent
of Japan's total world investments. See Elsbree and
Khong, "Japan and ASEAN," 124.
7. Elsbree and Khong, 125. However, as the authors point out, Official Development Act (ODA) funds
have gone disproportionately to Indonesia in ASEAN,
and there is a present tendency in Japan to regard the
ASEAN countries as sufficiently developed to attract
investments on their own without ODA support. Japan
reportedly promised increased ODA funds for the

Philippines at the time of Foreign Minister Laurel's visit in May 1986.

8. Two examples of this argument, the first with profuse documentation, are Lim, "Japan in ASEAN,' 115-35, and Elsbree and Khong, "Japan and ASEAN."

9. This now commonly used description of the occupation period was coined by the late Harry Benda as part of his periodization of Southeast Asian history. It was his argument that the interregnum represented a temporary deviation from the main channels of Southeast Asian history. See "The Structure of Southeast Asian History."

10. In February 1983 during the height of the Philippine reaction to the proposed surveillance perimeter (discussed in the following section) the Jefferson Cultural Center in Makati (Metro Manila) opened an exhibition on the liberation of Manila. Included in the exhibit were contemporary photographs, memorabilia, models of weapons, and a videotape (with many contemporary film clips) that detailed the retaking of Manila from beginning to end. On the two occasions when I visited the display the small hall was filled with Filipinos of all ages, but the younger seemed to outnumber the older by a large margin. The reoccupation of the Philippines by U.S. forces is commonly described as the "liberation" by most Filipinos, but a growing number of younger nationalists take exception to the use of this term. The larger-than-life statue of General MacArthur standing in Intramuros has had a question mark chiseled after the word "liberator."

11. President Marcos closed the magazine *We Forum* and in January 1983 sued its editors for libel. The magazine had questioned the president's bravery in guerrilla actions against Japanese forces and raised doubts that he deserved the medals he had won. In the trial that followed, the president's attorney produced American ex-servicemen who attested to his bravery. The same issue surfaced later in the United States.

12. *Free Philippines*, 22 February 1945, 2.

13. *Doy Laurel in Profile*, 11-91. This is probably an autobiographical account, but it is written largely in the third-person.

14. Foreign Minister Laurel attended the ASEAN foreign ministers' meeting in Bali in April (where he also held discussions with President Reagan), but this meeting had been scheduled before the People Power Revolution in February. His trip to Tokyo in search of financial assistance in May was his first diplomatic initiative scheduled after he became the minister.

15. There are several notable exceptions to this generalization, but none are currently influential in making foreign policy. Ghazali Shafie, who served as foreign minister until 1984, according to the autobiographical preface to his published speeches, served as

an intelligence officer connected with the best known anti-Japanese guerrilla movement in the peninsula, Force 136. Two previous prime ministers, Tun Razak (who died in office in January 1976) and Hussein Onn (who retired in July 1981) also served with Force 136. Despite these important exceptions, very few of today's Malay policy makers took part in the anti-Japanese resistance.

16. A lengthy and good biographical account of Mahathir and the Mahathir family appeared on consecutive weeks in *Sunday Mail* (Malaysian edition), 2 and 9 April 1972. According to this account: "For Mahathir the Occupation years were profitable. Refusing to work for the Japanese he jointly ran a banana stall in Alor Star's Pekan Rebu. He sold them fresh and served them in the coffee shop he had nearby. True to his promise he had made himself, Mahathir, who was then in his twenties, was better off than any of his friends."

17. The Japanese trained some ninety thousand Indonesians as auxiliary troops, and many of today's generals (including President Suharto) owe their beginnings to this experience.

18. Chan, "The PAP in the Nineties," 30. The author of this paper certainly knows Singapore well, but it has been my experience that only in the Philippines, of the five original ASEAN countries, is one more likely to hear unsolicited stories about the unpleasantries of the Japanese occupation. An exhibit of memorabilia and photographs of the occupation in 1985, similar to the exhibit described in the Philippines but not as elaborate, also drew large crowds in Singapore. As in Manila, there were many young people among the attendees at the time of my visit, but unlike the exhibit in Manila most of these seem to have been accompanied by their parents, and, in some cases, by grandparents.

19. In a candid and almost conversational address to Parliament in March 1985 Prime Minister Lee described the slap delivered to him by a Japanese soldier, before whom he had failed to bow, as the blow that sent him into politics. See *Straits Times*, 23 March 1985, 14.

20. The issues involving the defense of the sea lanes are numerous, and the question sometimes evokes highly emotional reactions. For a good objective summary of the issues see Michael Leifer, "The Security of the Sea Lanes in Southeast Asia," 16-23.

21. President Marcos was on record many times expressing his concern about Japan and possible Japanese rearmament. In November 1979 in a nationally televised meeting with a Hawaiian trade delegation, and just a month prior to the visit of Japanese Prime Minister Ohira, President Marcos remarked that Japanese officials could not go into remote areas of the Philippines because the residents, at worst, would

decapitate them, or, at best, throw them out. *New Nation*, 29 November 1979. In 1982 he advised Americans that if Japan were sold U.S. arms "see that they are not for predatory purposes." *Straits Times*, 20 September 1982. Prime Minister Cesar Virata, although not usually involved in matters of foreign policy, also voiced his concern about Japan on several occasions. Policy makers, often those involved in dealing with Japan, are usually not reluctant to express concerns about their perceptions of Japan's intentions toward Southeast Asia.

22. "Bitterly pleasant" is used intentionally. Memories of the Japanese occupation and the American liberation of the Philippines are both bitter and pleasant. Many family members and friends were killed or wounded and the populace suffered severe material deprivation. The devastation occasioned by the recapture of Manila, as revealed in contemporary photographs, must have been traumatic. Yet many Filipinos proudly recall this difficult time as a golden age. They suffered alongside Americans for a cause that both peoples supported with few doubts. Many who saw these scenes as children delight in recounting their stories to anyone who wants to hear them. For future generations this golden age may be replaced by memories of another event--perhaps memories of the February 1986 People Power Revolution--but for the present generation of policy makers the memories of the Japanese occupation are still vivid.

23. Initial confusion stemmed from lack of clarity about the starting point of the 1,000 mile limit. Was it to begin at Tokyo Bay or at the southernmost limits of Japan? American officials felt that this issue had been settled earlier in Washington and that Marcos both understood and accepted that the starting point was Tokyo Bay.

24. The prime minister is reported to have told visiting Japanese journalists that "there is no fear of a revival of militarism if Japan does not build nuclear weapons, but, instead, continues under the US nuclear umbrella." After prodding from the newsmen about the possible "rolling stone" effect of a decision to rearm, the prime minister responded that if they meant rearmament would eventually lead Japan to "go nuclear," then "it's better not to start" the process. See interview with *Asahi Shimbun*, 5 January 1981. The same concern was expressed in the interview with Lester Tanzer, 7 December 1981, 7.

25. The issue, of course, is larger than the defense of the sea lanes, for it actually involves the balance of power in East and Southeast Asia. In a provocative address to the Commonwealth Heads of Government on 1 October 1981 Prime Minister Lee seemed to say that under some circumstances a strong China *or* a strong Japan would be inevitable. He asked his col-

leagues which "would it be better to have . . . to
help hold the balance in East Asia?" His answer was
less direct than his question, but he implied a preference for a strong Japan. Melbourne interview, 17. To
this he later added the caveat that "a strong Japan"
does not mean that Japan should become "the protector
of Southeast Asia." *Asahi Shimbun* interview, 30 October 1982, 4.

26. On the opposition of some DPR members, see
New Straits Times, 30 November 1982. Foreign Minister
Mochtar has publicly stated his opposition as well.
See *Straits Times*, 23 March 1981.

27. There are numerous press reports on the look
east policy beginning in late 1981 some six months
after Mahathir took office. For a good summary see
Asiaweek, 5 November 1982, 31.

28. Tilman interview, 3 April 1985.

29. *Asiaweek*, 11 February 1983, 49. This was one
of a series of four interviews in which similar questions were put to each interviewee. The only other
ASEAN leader interviewed was President Marcos, who was
characteristically candid in his opposition to the
presence of Japanese naval vessels near Philippine
waters.

30. Weinstein, *Indonesian Foreign Policy*, 95-103.

31. Ibid., 262-63.

32. Ibid., 266-67.

33. Lim, "Japan in ASEAN," 132.

34. The Japanese government was stunned by the
frequency and intensity of the anti-Japanese rioting
that occurred during Prime Minister Tanaka's tour of
Southeast Asia in 1974. One of several steps taken by
the successor to Tanaka was the pledge to Southeast
Asians that now bears the name of the Fukuda Doctrine.
In summary, it pledges that Japan will contribute to
the peace and stability of Southeast Asia but will not
assume a military role; that Japan will cooperate more
fully with the ASEAN states in the economic sphere;
and that Japan will seek "heart-to-heart understanding" with the people of the region. Succeeding Japanese governments have periodically reaffirmed their
support for the spirit of the Fukuda Doctrine.

35. Weinstein, "Japan and Southeast Asia," 189-
91.

36. The prime minister's address to the First
Malaysia-Japan Colloquium in August 1984 was delivered
in his absence by Minister of Trade and Industry
Tengku Razaleigh Hamzah. Quoted in Lim, "Japan in
ASEAN," 132.

7

The United States:
The Risks of Friendship

*Indirectly the U.S. is a threat. The bases may
attract Soviet missiles. You have a President
willing to fight a limited nuclear war, and this
probably means that the USSR and America will
survive but their allies won't. The U.S. encourages
Japanese rearmament, and this is a threat to us.
And American interests are shifting to the PRC--
another threat to us.*

Foreign policy advisor to the Marcos government
Manila, May 1983

*We would like to be left alone, but we have to be
realistic. . . . A U.S. presence is needed to keep
the balance of power.*

S. Dhanabalan
Foreign Minister
Singapore, March 1985

*America, a threat to us? No, not a threat, but a
danger--yes, very much a danger.*

Senior official
Ministry of Foreign Affairs
Jakarta, 1983

In the harsh world of international politics the
United States is often viewed in the ASEAN countries
as well intentioned, but naive, immature, inconsistent, and driven by domestic political considerations.
Most ASEAN leaders accept that a United States interest and presence in the region is crucial; yet they
liken the American presence to a loose cannon on a
rolling deck. The words of an Indonesian scholar whose
views often parallel those of the top Army leadership
reveal some of the ambivalence of a younger generation
of leadership. Addressing himself to the perceptions
of the next generation of leaders he commented that
"on the one hand they recognize the importance of the
U.S. presence in the region. . . . On the other hand
the U.S. as a superpower has always created an uneasy

feeling."[1] Although he was speaking specifically of younger Indonesian leaders, this perception is not confined to a single ASEAN country.

U.S. INTERESTS IN THE ASEAN REGION

There is little agreement on the nature of U.S. interests in Southeast Asia beyond a sometimes vague concern for "stability" and a "secure military balance,"[2] principles that permeate American policy throughout the world. One scholar-diplomat has posited three areas of American national interest in Indonesia and the Philippines that seem to have more general applicability throughout Southeast Asia:[3]

1. Security--no hostile power should be permitted to dominate the region or to exclude the United States from it;

2. Economy--markets, investment opportunities, trade, and resources must be kept open and accessible;

3. Ideology--it is in the best interests of the United States to encourage the development of governments whose policies are compatible with an American sense of human rights and political freedoms.

A distinguished American argued during the height of the Vietnam debate that the national interest of the United States was to make certain that Southeast Asia was a place where no superpower--including the United States--had a vital national interest.[4] This probably overstates the argument, but it is evident that U.S. policy is driven largely by a desire to deny the USSR uninhibited access to the region. Or, put in the context of the original 1947 policy statement by U.S. Sovietologist George F. Kennan, Southeast Asia is important to the United States because it is one of the areas where the Soviet Union is attempting to break out of Western "containment": "It will be clearly seen that the Soviet pressure against the free institutions of the western world is something that can be contained by the adroit and vigilant application of counter-force at a series of constantly shifting geographical and political points, corresponding to the shifts and maneuvers of Soviet policy."[5] Beyond these general and related principles--stability and the perceived Russian threat to stability--the importance of the ASEAN region, as seen from Washington, stems largely from America's perceived interests in East Asia, an area that in American terminology often includes Southeast Asia.[6]

Although it may not be comforting to America's
ASEAN friends the East Asia that is of concern to the
United States is dominated by Japan and by America's
Japanese interests. As an earlier chapter has noted,
Japan is the United States's second largest trading
partner, just behind Canada, and Japan's continuing
success and friendship enjoys a very high priority on
the American foreign-policy agenda. Perhaps in the
future the PRC will compete for American attention,
but if this happens it will only serve to reinforce
the eastern domination of the East Asia policies of
the United States. It is therefore not surprising that
American security policies take on a decidedly East
Asian flavor. In fact, American military forces operating in Southeast Asia--principally units of the
Seventh Fleet and the Thirteenth Air Force--may be
there chiefly to defend U.S. interests in eastern East
Asia and only secondarily to protect American direct
interests in East Asia's southeastern appendage.[7]

The principal American military presence in the
ASEAN region emanates from the Philippines, where
Subic Bay Naval Base and Clark Air Force Base represent America's largest military installations outside
the United States. By any standard these facilities
are immense.

Subic Bay Naval Base is a natural deep-water port
covering 55,000 acres, more than half of which is land
area. Major ship repair facilities provide more than
two-thirds of the repairs needed by the entire Seventh
Fleet, and these facilities can handle twenty to
twenty-five ships simultaneously, including aircraft
carriers and Polaris ballistic-missile submarines. The
base houses the world's largest naval supply depot,
which handles annually 2.5 million barrels of petroleum products and one million tons of other supplies.
An associated Naval Air Station at Cubi Point provides
support for carrier based aircraft when in port and
also serves as the home base for a squadron of P3
Orion antisubmarine aircraft. Eight separate naval
commands are based at Subic Bay.

Only some forty miles from Subic Bay is Clark Air
Force Base, the home of the U.S. Thirteenth Air Force
since 1946. Prior to a 1979 agreement to reduce the
size of the base by returning large tracts of land to
the Philippine government, Clark covered some 131,000
acres, an area larger than the District of Columbia.
Today the base sprawls over 30,000 acres of Central
Luzon about fifty miles north of Manila. In addition
to serving as a major communications and transit hub
for all Air Force activities in the western Pacific
and Indian oceans the base has a 10,500 foot, all-
weather runway that takes about 12,000 traffic movements per month and some 3,500 passengers per day.
Crow Gunnery Range, which includes firing ranges,
gunnery practice fields, and an electronic warfare

range, is the most sophisticated Air Force training facility in Asia and frequently hosts training programs from friendly countries in the region. Clark Air Base also serves as a supply depot in support of bases in Japan and Korea and is the main support base for Diego Garcia in the Indian Ocean.

Minor facilities in the Philippines include San Miguel Naval Communications Station, which serves as the communications center for the entire Seventh Fleet and provides direction-finding radio service for surveillance operations throughout the region; Camp John Hay, which houses recreational services for military personnel on leave, a Voice of America transmitter, and conference facilities; and Wallace Air Station, which provides radar control for the Philippines air defense system, tactical communications for the Thirteenth Air Force, and a drone facility for training purposes.[8]

Although Southeast Asia is most important to the United States as an extension of East Asia, both East and Southeast Asia are parts of a larger geographic entity that is growing rapidly in importance to the United States. In fact, in the future the Pacific Basin may replace Europe at the top of America's global agenda.

The Pacific Basin has already replaced Western Europe as America's largest trading partner, and in the half-decade since that milestone was passed in 1980 the gap between the two partners has widened significantly. American is increasingly involved in Asia, and trade is both a cause and an effect of this redirection of American global thinking. Whether it is a historic trend or a temporary diversion in the broader sweep of history, the statistics are revealing.

Table 7.1

Patterns of Trade:
U.S., Pacific Basin, and Western Europe
(In Billion U.S. Dollars)

Year	Pacific Basin	Western Europe
1979	91.8	92.9
1980	112.0	110.0
1981	125.9	112.0
1982	123.9	106.9
1983	133.8	104.9

Source: *The Washington Post National Weekly Edition*, 7 May 1984, 19.

In the ASEAN area of the Pacific Basin the growth in trade has been correspondingly dramatic. When ASEAN was created in 1977 U.S. trade with those countries that constituted the Association totalled $945 million. In 1984 the figure reached $26 billion.[9] Although ASEAN leaders are sensitive to their treatment by Washington as an appendage of East Asia it is nevertheless clear that the United States has increasingly larger stakes in the region--as an appendage of East Asia, as a part of the Pacific Basin, and as a unique part of the globe. Or, as Secretary of State Shultz put it in Kuala Lumpur in mid-1985, ASEAN and the United States share many common interests that today keep them on a parallel course in foreign affairs.[10]

ASEAN PERCEPTIONS OF THE UNITED STATES

ASEAN leaders seem in almost total agreement that the friendship of the United States is important if not crucial to their economic progress and perhaps to their physical security as well. However, many, and perhaps most, perceive that this friendship also entails certain risks. As one distinguished leader commented, "this is just the cost of doing business with America." Perceptions of these costs vary from one country to another, but in the end several common themes emerge.

Indonesia

In the early 1970s an American scholar reported that the older generation of Indonesian elites tended to perceive the United States in generally favorable terms.[11] The oldest of the nationalist elites had been impressed by Wilsonian idealism, American reluctance to support colonialism, and the American colonial record in the Philippines. The "Generation of '45" (the veterans of the revolutionary struggle against the Dutch) appreciated President Roosevelt's reluctance to permit some (but not all) of the European powers to reestablish their colonial empires, and they harbored generally favorable perceptions of the United States. Some disillusionment set in when the United States did not unequivocally support the Indonesian Revolution, but on balance most of the Generation of '45 leadership seemed to accept that America supported Indonesia more than it supported the Dutch.

American-Indonesian relations soured rapidly during the late 1950s and early 1960s, and presumably Indonesian elite perceptions of the United States suffered accordingly. In general, the souring of Indonesian-U.S. relations can be attributed to what was seen as an American attempt to draw Indonesia into

the cold war in the late 1950s, U.S. support for the
rebellions in the outer islands in 1958, and America's
belated and unenthusiastic support for Indonesia's
claim to West Irian. Indonesians visiting the United
States at the time were reported to have returned with
very negative impressions of a decaying America that
had lost its sense of direction. At the same time
Americans were seen as arrogant and uninformed on
Indonesia.[12] In short, by mid-1965 the United States
was perceived by Indonesians to be contributing significantly to Indonesia's problems.

American-Indonesian relations improved rapidly
after GESTAPU and the political changes that followed.
Post-Sukarno Indonesia regained its lost friendship
with the United States as America resumed arms ship-
ments, joined in the rescheduling of the crushing
Indonesian debt, and generally treated the country as
a strayed ally returning to the fold. The United
States seemed to feel comfortable doing business with
General Suharto and the technocrats he gathered around
him, many of whom were American educated.

Today the United States is regarded by many Indonesians as being somewhat immature or naive in foreign
policy. Others, often found in the Ministry of Foreign
Affairs, argue that the United States does not have
coherent and long-term foreign policies and is generally content passively to follow the ASEAN lead. Some
thoughtful Indonesians regard the United States and
the USSR as similar threats who should "cease and
desist and take their quarrels elsewhere."[13]

There is a general feeling among many Indonesian
political and intellectual leaders that the United
States fails to accept the regional importance of
Indonesia. In fact, it is not unusual to hear com-
plaints that the United States slights Indonesia in
favor of other ASEAN powers, all of which are smaller,
and in Indonesian eyes, less significant regionally
than is Indonesia. The country most frequently mentioned as having disproportionate influence on the
United States is Singapore, a fact that is particularly offensive to Indonesian national pride in view of
the vast disparity in size between the two neighbors.

Although the Reagan administration was initially
greeted as a welcome change after the problems of the
preceding Carter administration, it did not get off to
a good beginning with the Indonesian leadership. Indonesia was left without an American ambassador following the public debate over the appointment of Abraham
Abramowitz, and Washington, much to the irritation of
most Indonesian leaders, seemed in no hurry to fill
the position. To many Indonesians this only confirmed
the suspicions they had long harbored about the relative unimportance of Jakarta in Washington's overall
view of East and Southeast Asia.[14] However, the eventual appointment of John Holderidge, a senior career

officer who was then serving as assistant secretary
for East Asia and the Pacific, and a decision in
Washington to sell top-of-the-line F16's to Jakarta
seem to have gone far in assuaging Indonesian feelings. Holderidge's successor as ambassador to Jakarta
has been drawn from the same influential policy-making
position, and the person selected is probably viewed
by Indonesia as a choice befitting a major regional
power.[15]

The United States is viewed as a potential danger
in the context of U.S.-PRC-Japanese relations. Particularly in the case of the PRC some Indonesian leaders
are greatly concerned about American goals and strategies in East Asia and the potentially adverse impact
these might have on Indonesia. When President Suharto
visited the United States in 1982 he reportedly received a pledge from Washington officials that the
United States would not help China modernize at the
expense of America's friends in Southeast Asia.[16] U.S.
officials visiting Jakarta are repeatedly asked for
similar reassurances, and there is a nagging suspicion
that the improvement of U.S.-PRC relations enjoys a
higher priority on the American agenda than does the
continuation of good relations with Indonesia.[17] In
fact, the Indonesian foreign minister has stated candidly that in his view American policies toward
Vietnam--a matter of great concern to Indonesia--are a
derivative of U.S. policy toward China.[18]

In general, however, the negative perceptions
voiced about America today usually lack the venom of
the late Sukarno years. Nevertheless, even Indonesian
politeness and good nature cannot obscure the misgivings about the United States that many leaders feel.

Malaysia

Almost two decades ago I subtitled a study of
Malaysian foreign policy "The Dilemmas of a Committed
Neutral,"[19] and today, although the rhetoric and the
arguments are considerably different, the dilemmas are
much the same. Malaysia still aspires to steer a
foreign-policy course equidistant from the major and
middle-range powers, but today, as in the mid-1960s,
there is a general consensus that some powers must be
kept at a greater distance than others.

An American over-the-horizon presence is probably
just as welcome in Malaysia as it is elsewhere in
ASEAN, although under Prime Minister Mahathir, Malaysia has often seemed reluctant to admit it. In an
interview with a United Press International correspon-
dent not long after assuming the office of prime
minister Mahathir responded to a question about the
role the United States should play in Southeast Asia
with an ambivalence that is not confined to Malaysia:
"We don't think having a sort of armaments race in

this region is going to help. On the other hand, the
lack of interest is also bad. It gives the feeling the
Russians can do what they like." In response to a
specific question about the future of American bases
and an American presence in the Philippines, Mahathir
was equally noncommittal when he responded that Malaysia could not say what role the United States should
play, but since the United States was already in the
Philippines, "I suppose it should stay there."[20]

Malaysian ambivalence apparently stems from its
acceptance of the benefits from "what is," at the same
time that it points with hope to the benefits accruing
from what it would like the political situation to be.
On the one hand, most Malaysian leaders agree that the
ASEAN region benefits from a slight, but not overwhelming, imbalance of power that favors the West. But
on the other hand Malaysia prides itself in being the
architect and major proponent of ZOPFAN, which, if
effected, would eliminate the present imbalance. The
present is familiar. ZOPFAN seems an ideal solution,
but it is thus far untested and unfamiliar.[21]

As far as bilateral relations with the United
States are concerned, the two countries have had their
differences but there have been no serious ruptures.
The American proclivity for disposing of rubber and
tin from its strategic reserves, sometimes when prices
are already depressed, provides a frequent irritant in
Malaysian-American relations,[22] but at the same time
the United States has replaced Britain as the major
source of training for students on government scholar-
ships.[23] To compound the ambivalence, the United
States is often subjected to verbal criticisms similar
to those levelled against the USSR and the PRC. In the
view of the Malaysian prime minister all major powers
are intent on meddling in Malaysian domestic affairs,
and the United States is no exception.[24] At the same
time, the newfound cordiality between America and the
People's Republic of China is a cause of some concern.[25]

To add to Malaysia's frequently voiced frustration, policy makers often express the view that Malaysia is too small and too insignificant to influence
American policy in any important way. Prime Minister
Mahathir lamented that although he has met "a number"
of Americans who were "very sympathetic," he could not
see that these sympathizers had had much influence in
Washington. In fact, in the prime minister's words,
"I have the feeling that there is a great deal of
ignorance about Malaysia in Washington. I think that
for some officials . . . Malaysia doesn't exist at
all."[26]

Trade statistics alone provide grounds for the
prime minister's concerns. As for many other small
nations, trade with the United States constitutes a
significant proportion of Malaysia's total foreign

trade. The United States has consistently been Malaysia's second or third largest trading partner, behind
Japan and sometimes behind Singapore, but Malaysia's
proportion of the total volume of U.S. trade is almost
insignificant.[27] Kuala Lumpur must be knowledgeable
about the United States, but Washington can afford to
be ignorant of Malaysia--and in the perceptions of
Malaysian leaders, Washington acts as if it knows it.

Thailand

The United States has gained a position of fairly
high esteem in the institutional memory of Thailand.[28]
In one of the few systematic surveys in the ASEAN
region of the images of other nations conveyed through
school textbooks and curricula Asadakorn Eksaengsri
has observed that American advisors to Thai kings (the
appointment of foreign advisors was common practice
from Rama V, 1868-1910, onward) were singled out for
especially favorable treatment[29] and that many texts
selectively reported and favorably interpreted such
historically controversial and often criticized U.S.
policies as the Monroe Doctrine and the Open Door in
China.[30] The Thai scholar concludes that in the history books read by Thai students the United States is
treated well, probably better than it deserves.[31]
In the modern era, Thai relations with the United
States, which were very close after the close of
World War II, underwent a radical change following the
collapse of Saigon and the accompanying chaos of the
final American withdrawal from Vietnam in 1975. This
was dramatic evidence to the Thais that postwar power
relationships had changed and that their policy calcu-
lations must change accordingly. Relations between
Thailand and the United States were very cold during
much of the Carter administration, but they improved
following the Vietnamese invasion of Kampuchea, the
rekindling of American interest in Asia following the
nadir of the post-Vietnam disillusionment in the
United States, and the emergence of an ASEAN-American
coalition opposing the Vietnam-USSR coalition. The
willingness of the United States to accelerate greatly
the delivery of promised armaments only hours after
the Vietnamese border crossings of June 1980, and U.S.
support for Thai villagers displaced by the Kampuchean
conflict considerably improved the climate of Thai-
U.S. relations.[32]
If current policy pronouncements are to be accepted at face value, Thailand may not again allow
itself to become as closely allied to the United
States as it was at the height of the Vietnam War. Yet
two Thai scholars have offered statistical evidence
contradicting many of these official statements. Thailand has been a recipient of advanced weapons, including Redeye and Harpoon missiles, M114 howitzers, and

the U.S. has approved the export of F16/A100 jets; the U.S. Seventh Fleet has increased its number of port calls to Thailand (fifty were reported in 1982); joint U.S.-Thai military exercises ("Cobra Gold," held annually) have increased in magnitude and complexity; U.S. bilateral aid has increased significantly each year; the United States provided 75 percent of all Thai arms during the period 1976-80; and the Chulalongkorn elite survey "found that an overwhelming majority . . . still cherish the relationship with the U.S. and *expect the latter to lend aid and comfort in all exigencies and in all manners possible.*"[33]

In the context of the unrest and uncertainty of the final months of the Marcos government numerous rumors surfaced about the possibility or probability that some American forces might be moved from the Philippines to Thailand, but denials were quickly forthcoming. The army chief of staff reportedly felt concerned about the U.S. position in the Philippines, but added that Thailand should not be considered an alternative,[34] and the deputy defense minister was quoted as saying that in view of their previous "Yankee-go-home experience" in Thailand it seemed unlikely that the United States would want to risk another attempt to base troops in Thailand.[35]

Despite considerable evidence of an increased presence in Thailand it is nevertheless improbable that America will seek to dominate the politics of the region as it did during the Vietnam War. Without this perception of commitment Thailand seems determined to leave its options as open as is possible for a front-line state that needs a superpower ally.

The Philippines

Until recent times the Philippines has been cut off from the rest of Asia--physically, culturally, and historically. For a half-century the colony fell under the wing of American foreign policy, and after independence Philippine policy tended to parallel that of its colonial mentor.

Events of February 1986 may have altered the main course of Philippine history. When People Power overthrew the entrenched regime of President Ferdinand Marcos it may have set the Philippines off in new historical directions. Perhaps it will be remembered as a major turning point in Philippine politics. Yet, for all the drama and significance of this truly remarkable event, the People Power Revolution cannot obliterate the nation's previous political history. Although this is not an appropriate place to argue the case, it is evident that there are elements of both continuity and discontinuity in the new regime. It is sufficient to point out that the Philippines today is the sum total of what it is and what it has been.

The memories of the American colonial period in the Philippines are still very much alive, though in recent years they have undergone some reinterpretations by both supporters and critics of Philippine-U.S. ties. Most of the Filipinos who were in positions to influence policy under President Marcos, and--although there is less empirical evidence available at this early date--many of those helping to shape policy around President Aquino believe that a "special relationship" derived from the almost half-century association between the two countries exists, even in the troubled times of the mid-1980s. Although optimism about the likely benefits of this often romanticized special relationship has waxed and waned, most Filipino policy makers view it as more of an asset than a liability.[36]

The impact of the special relationship varies in an almost cyclical manner. In the wake of the cordial reception given to President and Mrs. Marcos in Washington on the occasion of their state visit in 1982 (with saturation media coverage in the Philippines), fond memories of the relationship were rekindled, just in time to bring the bases negotiations to a successful conclusion for both parties during the following year. However, events from mid-1983 onward--the assassination of opposition leader Benigno Aquino in August 1983, the rapid downturn in the Philippine economy, demonstrations, American pressures for free elections, and some effort on the part of Washington to distance itself from the Marcos regime--cooled the fervor of the memory of the special relationship for some, but not for all.[37] Nevertheless, applications for visas to the United States continue unabated as Filipinos seek to visit friends and relatives in the U.S. or to emigrate if possible.[38]

The United States has always been the cornerstone of Philippine foreign policy, despite periodic chills and the expansion of Philippine diplomatic contacts following the withdrawal of the United States from Indochina in 1975.[39] The "Indochinese debacle," as it was termed in the controlled martial-law press,[40] triggered a new wave of concern about the provincialism of Philippine foreign policy, and during 1976 and 1977 the Philippines concentrated on extending its diplomatic contacts with the socialist bloc, with which it had had no previous ties. It also exchanged missions with many Third World countries.

Notwithstanding these departures, relations with the United States still dominate Philippine foreign policy, and the military bases at Subic and Clark still serve as both an irritant and a bond. They provide an issue around which the political opposition and nationalists of all political convictions can rally, and at the same time they are the cement of the Philippine-American alliance. The Marcos administration sometimes spoke glumly about possible termination of the Military Basing Agreement, and occasionally the president would hint darkly that the bases should perhaps be made available to other interested nations. Less than a year before People Power deposed Marcos, the minister for defense, later to be a key figure in the February revolution, denounced the congressional maneuverings to amend the makeup of the compensation package and suggested that the Philippines might view this as a reason for repudiating the agreement.[41] However, despite some vacillation, often to gain political bargaining power, Filipino policy makers during the Marcos era seemed to feel comfortable with the highly visible American presence represented by the bases, particularly after it was discovered that the bases were not a contentious issue in relations with the Philippines' Asian neighbors.[42]

Many well-placed Philippine officials during the Marcos years conceded that the American bases increased the likelihood of Philippine involvement in big-power disputes, that the Sino-American thaw was not in the Philippines' best interests, and that the desire of the United States to have Japan play a larger defense role in Asia posed a long-term threat to the Philippines. However, even after cataloging these problems--and perhaps criticizing American heavyhandedness in dealing with their country--the same officials usually reaffirmed the importance to the Philippines of its alliance with the United States.[43]

The present Philippine administration has transmitted mixed signals on the issue of the bases. Before the election campaign got underway Corazon Aquino seemed to be strongly opposed to the bases, but candidate Aquino took an increasingly moderate stance on the issue as the campaign proceeded. She seemed to fall in line with the position taken by her vice-presidential running mate, now also the foreign minister, that no actions would be taken until the present agreement expired in 1991, and to this Laurel added that a popular referendum should determine if Filipinos want the bases to remain on Philippine soil. After the downfall of Marcos, President Aquino in her statements made at home has been noticeably silent on the bases question, a silence that has itself attracted media attention,[44] and in her visit to the United States in September 1986 she avoided all but the most general statements. However, former Defense Minister Enrile surfaced as an apparently strong supporter of the American presence.[45]

There is more diversity of views concerning U.S.-Philippine relations within the Aquino government than was the case under Marcos, but, on balance, it seems that in both Foreign Affairs and Defense there is little desire to effect any fundamental changes in the relationship. There are of course exceptions, perhaps because differing opinions are now accepted, and there are differing suggestions about the nature and extent of the restructuring that should take place.[46] However, the fundamental perceptions of the United States held by policy makers seem not to have been been significantly affected by the change in administrations. Of course, the president has not yet asserted her authority in the foreign-policy process, and she therefore remains an unknown factor.

Singapore

Singapore-American relations did not get off to a good beginning in 1965.[47] At the time of independence Lee Kuan Yew had some doubts that the Americans belonged in Southeast Asia at all. Two years later he had come to feel that Americans by their commitment to South Vietnam were destined to be a significant force in the region, but he sometimes seemed uncertain whether history would prove the Americans to be a blessing or a curse. This early ambiguity toward Americans, in contrast to a more abstract American presence, has continued to surface at various times.

On the one hand, American forces were a welcome addition to Southeast Asia. In London in 1966 the prime minister told a capacity audience of Singapore and Malaysian students that an American presence in the area was crucial to the survival of the Singapore with which they were familiar: "If the Americans decide to pack it up because their position is untenable in South Vietnam; and if the Thais . . . decide not to resist . . . then it is very pertinent what happens to the 500 armed communists wandering around the borders of Thailand and Malaysia. And if Malaysia cannot be held, then Singapore must make adjustments accordingly."[48]

On the other hand, though an American presence was desirable in Southeast Asia in general, it was not desirable in Singapore in particular. The prime minister regarded the British, in contrast to Americans, as "part of the landscape of Southeast Asia . . . , unobtrusive . . . and effective in a quiet sort of way," and he spoke warmly of the "quiet, . . . peaceful situation at the Britannia Club." If the Americans replaced the British in Singapore he could foresee "U.S. marines involved in rows outside Raffles Hotel."[49]

Despite his concern about the probable behavior of American troops, by about this time (mid-1967) Mr. Lee seems to have concluded that the die was cast in Southeast Asia. As he told visiting American journalists in April 1967, "if you can just hold . . . and prevent the other side from winning, you would have made a valuable contribution to the long-term stabili-

ty of the region."[50] Today the prime minister may
remind a critic of the Vietnam War that the American
presence "bought time" for Singapore and her neighbors.

From Singapore's perspective if the Soviet grand
strategy for Asia and the world is to be thwarted it
is the United States that must provide the leadership.
Every non-communist state must recognize and resist
Soviet thrusts, but only the United States is large
enough and powerful enough to lead the way. However,
Singapore's leaders are not convinced that the United
States is emotionally capable of leading. In short,
America has the strength, but it may not have the
will. The United States is seen as inconsistent (the
abrupt abandonment of South Vietnam and the incremental retraction of commitments to Taiwan are often
cited as evidence), given to foreign-policy fads, and
because of domestic political and social factors un-
able to "stay the course."

Despite these serious and often voiced misgivings, Singapore has consistently remained one of America's strongest supporters among the membership of
ASEAN, and the foundations of this support are to be
found in Singapore's appraisal of its national interests. The Soviet Union constitutes a serious long-term
threat to Singapore, and the United States is the only
noncommunist state with the capability of countering
Soviet ambitions of world domination. Perhaps at times
the will of the U.S. is weak; but no other country
approaches America's predominant strength, and thus
the United States must be the leader of the free
world, even if by default. "The United States presence
is the only counterweight to a Soviet presence. If we
have no American presence . . . we have a very different world."[51] "The Soviet Union . . . take[s] advantage of any untoward development in this part of the
world. . . . A U.S. presence . . . [is] needed to
keep the balance of power."[52]

ASEAN AND THE U.S.: A RISKY BUT NECESSARY ALLIANCE

All of the ASEAN states perceive the United
States as a friendly power, probably less reliable
than desirable, but a friendly power nevertheless.
Continuity is not an American strength. The U.S. is
given to rapid policy shifts. These are sometimes
attributed to domestic political pressures, to American governmental structure and processes, to a fickle
(and to some ASEAN leaders overly indulged) American
public that has little regard and less interest in
events outside fortress America.[53] On the other hand,
the United States is a force that must be reckoned
with, and having America on one's side, on balance, is
far better than having it as an enemy.

In at least one general area of foreign policy the United States cannot please all of the ASEAN members. Some Indonesian officials, particularly Foreign Minister Mochtar Kusumaamadja, have labored diligently to bring the United States and Vietnam closer together. The foreign minister has apparently urged his SRV counterpart to take more seriously American determination to pursue a systematic accounting of forces missing in action in the war, and to U.S. officials he seems to have urged a softer line and eventual rapprochement.[54] Yet the possibility of a Vietnamese-American thaw before the SRV agrees to a total withdrawal of its troops from Kampuchea is very disturbing to Thailand and Singapore. A "premature" settlement of outstanding issues between the United States and Vietnam, in the views of Thailand and Singapore, would remove one of ASEAN's important bargaining chips for a favorable resolution to the Kampuchean problem.[55]

The United States economy also dominates the international marketplace, and prosperity in America is essential if the ASEAN states are to prosper. American protectionist policies, or even discussions of proposals for protectionist legislation, are widely reported and greeted with great apprehension in most ASEAN countries. The proposal to curb textile imports, which passed Congress but was vetoed by President Reagan, sent shock waves throughout the region. Concern stemmed not only from the actual damage that would be done to ASEAN textile exports, but also from the realization that the Jenkins Bill (introduced in the House of Representatives by Ed Jenkins, Democrat, Georgia), if successful, might be the beginning of a wave of protectionist legislation that could disrupt the international marketplace for decades.[56] Prime Minister Lee Kuan Yew of Singapore was particularly concerned about protectionist sentiments in the United States and the disruption of world trade that could result. Because of these concerns he took the opportunity of his state visit to Washington in October 1985 to speak out frequently about the benefits of free trade. Mr. Lee devoted most his speech before a joint session of Congress to an appeal for support of the principles of free trade.[57] Economic barometers in New York and political pronouncements in Washington are watched with almost equal intensity in the ASEAN states.

The United States does not constitute a perceived threat in the ASEAN region in the same sense that the USSR is seen as a threat to Singapore, or the PRC is considered to be a threat to Indonesia. Indeed, for at least several of the ASEAN members, and to some extent for all, the United States is valued as a counterweight to the more serious threats facing the region. But, as an Indonesian policy maker observed

in the opening quotation to this chapter, the United
States does pose a potential danger. Many thoughtful
Southeast Asian leaders who are on friendly terms with
Americans and sympathetic to the goals and aspirations
of the United States agree. The United States would be
a formidable enemy, but it is a risky friend.

NOTES

1. Wanandi, "Indonesia: Domestic Politics and
Foreign Policy," 20.
2. This principle was reiterated by U.S. Secretary of State George Shultz in his address at the
ASEAN postministerial consultations in Kuala Lumpur in
July 1985. "The U.S. and ASEAN," 2.
3. Pringle, *Indonesia and the Philippines*, 17-23.
Pringle adds a fourth category of interests that
chiefly involve encouraging a higher level of trust
between Japan and insular Southeast Asia.
4. Bundy, "New Tides in Southeast Asia."
5. "X" [Kennan], "The Sources of Soviet Conduct."
6. Secretary Shultz could therefore say at the
ASEAN postministerial consultations in Kuala Lumpur
that "in East Asia the most immediate threat to peace
comes from Vietnam." "The U.S. and ASEAN," 3.
7. See chapter 6 for a discussion of the Japanese
"lifeline" through the ASEAN region. Although these
sea lanes are intrinsically important to the U.S.,
their availability to Japan constitutes the more vital
American interest.
8. Information in the three preceding paragraphs
dealing with U.S. facilities in the Philippines has
been taken from Keehu, "United States Military Bases
in the Republic of the Philippines," Appendix B. The
author utilized various sources, but he was most indebted to Grinter, *The Philippine Bases*.
9. "The U.S. and ASEAN," 5.
10. Ibid., 1 and throughout.
11. This paragraph and the one that follows have
been drawn chiefly from Weinstein, *Indonesian Foreign
Policy*, 66-82.
12. Arrogance was not confined to one side. Weinstein reports that one "pro-American general" declined
to be interviewed immediately because, as he apparently explained to a colleague, "these Americans think
that if they walk in everyone must stop what he is
doing and talk to them. I want this fellow to know
that I am not one of their Vietnamese generals."
Ibid., 143.
13. These were the words used by a young but
senior member of Parliament in an interview in Jakarta
in 1983. This response is not novel. In the Weinstein
survey more than a decade earlier the United States
was found to be as guilty of instigating and continu-

ing the cold war as was the USSR. Both superpowers, in the view of Weinstein's respondents, want to dominate the world and the contest is to see who can do it. *Indonesian Foreign Policy*, 114-15.

14. Indonesian feelings were also hurt by the manner in which Washington dealt with the proposed visit to Washington of the Indonesian minister of defense.

15. Paul Wolfowitz was named ambassador to Jakarta in late 1985 and took up his post in the following March.

16. *The Star* (Penang), 25 October 1982.

17. This concern is manifest in the work of two scholars associated with the influential Centre for Strategic and International Studies in Jakarta. See Wanandi and Soesastro, "Indonesian Security and Threat Perceptions," 27-28.

18. *Indonesian Times*, 2 March 1985, 1.

19. Tilman, "Malaysian Foreign Policy."

20. The interview with Paul Wedel was reported in full in two parts on 5 and 6 July 1981 in the *The Star* (Penang). Both quotations have been taken from part one.

21. A senior military officer in Manila in June 1986 pointed out what he saw as conflicting interpretations of ZOPFAN among the ASEAN leadership. He felt that for some leaders it meant a major-power standoff in the nature of a traditional balance of power. For others it was viewed in idealistic terms as a major-power withdrawal from the affairs of the region.

22. At the Pacific Forum symposium on national perceptions of international threats, a Malaysian scholar noted that in December 1980 the GSA released 1,415 tons of tin within four days and the international price dropped 55 cents per kilo. The point was made in the context of Malaysia's need for economic stability and growth if the New Economic Policy is to achieve its social goal of bringing the communities into better balance. See Abidin, "Malaysian Security Perceptions," 4. This theme--external threats in the context of internal threats--is addressed in the final chapter of this study.

23. The number of Malaysian students taking the English examination (a mandatory requirement of foreign students applying for admission to most American universities) increased dramatically in the late 1970s and early 1980s. The 1982 figure was 60 percent above the figure for the previous year (*The Star* [Penang], 7 March 1982), and the number of students leaving for the United States was up 73 percent in the same year. Two-thirds of these students received Malaysian government support. *New Straits Times*, 28 October 1982.

24. However, if the findings of Llewellyn D. Howell are valid, most Malaysian elites do not agree with the view that the United States and the USSR are

alike. On a measure of "international political distance" Howell found that Malaysians perceive themselves to be much closer politically to the United
States than to the USSR. Howell's Malaysian respondents placed the United States, along with Australia,
Great Britain, and France, politically close to Malaysia, but the USSR was placed at the extreme end of the
scale, the greatest distance politically from Malaysia. See "The International Political Attitudes of
Malaysians," table 2.

25. At the Commonwealth Heads of Government Conference in Nassau in October 1985 Prime Minister Mahathir again warned about warming Sino-American relations. He told his fellow Prime Ministers that American weapons sold to China might someday be used
against Southeast Asia. He urged the United States to
be "very careful about supplying arms to China."
Straits Times, 22 October 1985, 36.

26. Quoted by Lazarus, "Foreign Policy Is People," 14. Except for a brief introductory chapter, the
Pathmanathan and Lazarus volume is made up chiefly of
reprinted speeches of the prime minister. The prime
minister made similar observations in his interview
with me in April 1983.

27. Economic Intelligence Unit, *Quarterly Economic Review of Malaysia and Brunei*, 22. Exports to
Singapore, Japan, and the United States in 1983 represented respectively 22.5, 19.7, and 13.2 percent of
Malaysia's total exports. Comparable percentages for
imports from Japan, the United States, and Singapore
were 25.3, 16.1, and 13.9 for the same year. According to International Monetary Fund, *Direction of Trade
Statistics*, in 1984 of Malaysia's total world trade
14.8 percent was with the United States. For the same
year Malaysia accounted for only 2.0 percent of the
total world trade of the United States.

28. In addition to the sources cited this summary
of Thai-U.S. relations has relied on some facts and
interpretations taken from Xiang, "Thailand Foreign
Policy."

29. Asadakorn Eksaengsri, *Foreign-Policy Making
in Thailand*, 32.

30. Ibid., 43-44.

31. Ibid., 73. For a critical review of the
American impact on the printed media in Thailand, see
"American influences on Books, Magazines, and Newspapers in Siam," in *Siam in Crisis*, edited by Sivarsaka,
280-331.

32. During the period 1980-85 the United States
reportedly gave Thailand $32 million in resettlement
assistance. See *FBIS: APS*, IV, 009 (14 January 1986),
J-2.

33. Suchit Bunbongkarn and Sukhumbhand Paribatra,
"Thai Politics and Foreign Policy in the 1980's," 32-
33. Emphasis in original.

34. General Chaovalit Yongchaiyut, *Bangkok Post*, 7 November 1985, 3. Hints of the reappearance of American troops on Thai soil predate the most recent Philippine crisis. In 1982 Ambassador John Gunther Dean apparently suggested the desirability of reopening one of the former U.S. air bases, but the Thai government quickly vetoed the suggestion. It was reported that the government had agreed to refueling privileges for American military aircraft, but at the same time it was pointed out that it would be inappropriate to consider stationing aircraft on Thai soil. *Straits Times*, 1 April 1982.

35. *FBIS: APS*, IV, 033 (19 February 1986), J-2. A proposal may have been made to stockpile American weapons in Thailand in a regional "munitions center." This suggestion seems to have been better received by the Thai military, but even they were reported to have said publicly that this would not lead to any basing arrangements. See *FBIS: APS*, IV, 051 (17 March 1986), J-1, 2.

36. Although not mentioned, this "special relationship" frame of mind was very evident in the well reported remarks of Foreign Minister Laurel at Bali when he made his "cobwebs of doubt" comment and when he argued that the United States was not giving the Aquino government the financial aid it had a right to expect. On several occasions President Aquino has also made comments about the lower-than-expected level of U.S. economic assistance. The influence of the special relationship on both parties was apparent during the state visit of President Aquino in 1986. During the dispute with Defense Secretary Enrile in October 1986 President Aquino's press secretary, Teodoro Benigno, commented that the president's position had been strengthened by Washington's support for her government. This assertion of the influence of the special relationship drew sharp criticism in some Manila newspapers as another example of the negative effects of the special relationship. See *New York Times*, 30 October 1986, 6.

37. During the Marcos years the Statehood USA movement argued that the crises faced by the Philippines could be resolved only by joining the American federation. The leader of the movement, a retired U.S. air force major, is often dismissed as an unrealistic romantic, which he probably is. Nevertheless, his romanticism would probably prove not to be unique if ever put to a test.

38. On 11 May 1984, for example, 1,170 Filipinos applied for nonimmigrant visas and 250, for immigrant visas. *Bulletin Today*, 14 May 1984, 6. The U.S. consulate in Manila approved 15,200 nonimmigrant visas in April 1984, up considerably from previous Aprils. The annual totals of nonimmigrant visas approved are as follows: 1981, 71,006; 1982, approximately 80,000;

1983, 76,729. When this information was published,
1984 figures were running about 30 percent ahead of
those for 1983. *Daily Express*, 19 June 1984, 19.
Figures are not yet available for the period of the
new Aquino administration, but comments made by embassy personnel, and personal observations of intense
activity at the entrance to the visa section of the
embassy compound, suggested that in June 1986 there
had been no significant decrease in applications.
Pringle, *Indonesia and the Philippines*, 56-58, points
out that by 1979 there were between five-hundred thousand and one million Filipino immigrants in the United
States, that in virtually every Philippine barrio
there are Filipinos with relatives living in the U.S.,
and that although "many Southeast Asians . . . look
toward their capital city as a locus of upward mobility . . . , [for Filipinos] Manila is often only a way
station on the road to New York or Chicago" (58).
According to comments made to me by an American official, most visa applications are not approved. To
receive a visa a Filipino, in addition to the usual
requirements of financial responsibility etc., generally must be able to convince the examiner that he has
strong and compelling reasons to return to the Philippines. Thus, Pringle's observations are even more
revealing.
    39. The process actually began in 1972 with the
decision of the Foreign Policy Council to exchange
ambassadors with Romania and Yugoslavia. *Philippines
Herald*, 17 January 1972.
    40. *Times Journal*, 14 June 1975, 5.
    41. Juan Ponce Enrile, quoted in *Straits Times*,
28 March 1985, 6.
    42. As early as 1975 the Marcos government sought
reassurances from its Asian neighbors that the bases
were internationally acceptable. See AFP release 1078,
24 November 1975, which reported President Marcos's
desire to gain Chinese approval of the basing agreement. It has been reported off the record that several
of the ASEAN states at about this time were also
advising Marcos to avoid actions that might further
reduce U.S. involvement in the region.
    43. The responses in 1983 of a senior MFA offi-
cial to my questions about the threat from the United
States are illustrative and instructive even today.
("Does the U.S. constitute a 'threat' to the Philippines?") "Yes, in terms of the bases because they are
a lightning rod that invites intervention by others.
Yes, in terms of U.S. support for an increased Japanese presence in Southeast Asia. Yes, in terms of
shortsightedness in not linking broader development
issues with the question of the bases. Yes, in the
sense that the Philippines cannot count on the U.S. in
the long-term. Yes, perhaps, if the Philippines gets
caught between the U.S. and the USSR in a limited

nuclear war." In the end, however, the same official, after considering possible policy alternatives, could suggest no drastic changes that might provide the Philippines with better security against outside threats.

44. *Malaya* (Manila), 12 June 1986, 12.

45. In a major speech before members of the diplomatic community at the Intercontinental Hotel on 30 May 1986, although committing the Philippines to self-reliance and to ZOPFAN, the former minister argued that the bases were important to maintain political equilibrium in Southeast Asia. *Manila Bulletin*, 31 May 1986, 5. In another report of the speech Enrile was quoted as saying that any other position would amount to "daydreams or wishful thinking," that "issues involving national security do not partake of ideal situations but of stark realities," and that in international politics the Philippines must align itself with nations with whom it shares "common ideals and aspirations." *Malaya* (Manila), 12 June 1986, 12. A similar balance-of-power argument was put forward by Deputy Foreign Minister Samuel Ramel when he observed that the necessity of maintaining political equilibrium in the region will mean that "the American bases at Clark and Subic will have a longer existence than what is agreed upon." *Business Day* (Manila), 12 June 1986, 7. The draft constitution produced by the Constitutional Commission in October 1986 contains the provision that the basing agreement will continue in force until its expiration in 1991. Thereafter it can be renegotiated but the new terms must be approved in a popular plebiscite.

46. A senior military officer suggested that the bases might be privatized or might be made available to other friendly powers in the region. A senior official of the Ministry of Foreign Affairs in Manila, in a remark quoted later in this study, suggested that the bases should be removed so Filipinos will have to stop blaming foreigners for all of the country's problems.

47. Here I have relied more on contemporary interviews with foreign journalists, but Lee, "Singapore and East Asia," 339, makes a similar point about the rocky beginning to Singapore-U.S. relations. He attributes this to the "extreme anti-Western and anti-American posture adopted by Singapore in the early months of its independence."

48. Lee, International Student House, 22 April 1966, 2.

49. The information in this paragraph is derived chiefly from the interview of 11 April 1967 with Simms and Kraar.

50. Discussion with a panel of foreign journalists moderated by Dennis Bloodworth of the *London Observer*, 5 July 1967.

51. Prime Minister Lee Kuan Yew in response to questions posed by foreign journalists, 9 October 1984, 33.

52. Foreign Minister Dhanabalan, responding to a question in Parliament, *Sunday Times*, 24 March 1985, 10. This is also the source of the opening quotation in this chapter. Of course, there is also an economic rationale for Singapore's desire for good relations with the United States. As Prime Minister Lee told the Commonwealth Heads of Government meeting in Melbourne, Australia, on 1 October 1981, "My choice is obvious. If I went along with the Chinese or the Soviets I would be poor. . . . Can they provide me with the exchange of goods and services, the capital, the technology? . . . We have plugged into a free-world trading system which, despite its shortcomings, provides us with an opportunity to achieve [our] potential" (10-11). The United States is the dominant force in this "free-world trading system" and thus good U.S.-Singapore relations are of paramount importance.

53. An unnamed Thai official is quoted in an AFP release as saying that "Ronald Reagan is a good man. But if public opinion changes or if the Republicans lose an election then anything can happen." *FBIS: APS*, IV, 018 (28 January 1986), J-1.

54. After completing his visit to Washington in February 1986 Foreign Minister Mochtar seemed encouraged that U.S.-SRV relations were improving. He reportedly did not rule out the possibility of eventual U.S. assistance to Vietnam. *FBIS: APS*, IV, 034 (20 February 1986), N-1.

55. An unnamed Thai official commented that Thailand was very suspicious of American attempts to resolve the MIA issue and of Hanoi's apparent receptiveness to U.S. initiatives. He reasoned that if the MIA issue were resolved and U.S.-SRV relations improved, the United States might lose its enthusiasm for resolving the larger issue of Kampuchea. See *FBIS: APS*, IV, 018 (28 January 1986), J-1, 2. Singapore ambassador to Washington, T. B. Koh, in an address before an Asia Society audience in New York on 4 December 1984, commented that "this is not the right time" for the United States "to normalize its relations with Vietnam" because "to do so would send Vietnam the wrong signal" (7).

56. When eight American congressmen visited Bangkok in August 1985, while the Jenkins Bill was being considered, they received strong representations on behalf of both Thailand and ASEAN. They were told that the ASEAN states could lose U.S.$1.2 billion in textile trade if the bill passed and that this would come at the worst possible time for ASEAN. *Straits Times*, 28 August 1985, 14. However, figures released some four months later showed that for the first time

in a decade Thailand enjoyed a trade surplus with the
United States during the first eight months of 1985.
FBIS: APS, IV, 006 (9 January 1986), J-2.

57. The full text of the prime minister's speech
was released by the Singapore embassy in typescript.
Excerpts appeared in the *New York Times* and *Washington
Post* on 10 October 1985. Both newspapers credited the
prime minister's arguments with swaying enough congressmen to make it difficult to gather the votes
needed to override the president's veto of the Jenkins
Bill. At the state dinner in his honor Lee spoke
warmly of President Reagan's "courageous stand"
against protectionism "in the face of strong popular
pressures" favoring it.

8

Tigers at the Door and Tigers in the Kitchen: External and Internal Threats in Perspective

Threats to regional security are two-pronged. . . .
The first threat is domestic subversion, which is
rooted in the process of modernization. . . .
These pains of modernization-- . . . uneven growth
between the rural and urban sectors . . . , skewed
income distribution, and the rebellion of those who
feel left out . . . --have been exploited by sub-
versive groups.

Air Chief Marshall Siddhi Savetsila
Thai Minister for Foreign Affairs
New York, 1983

A real external threat, a security threat? No I
don't think we face that kind of problem. External
forces may exploit our internal problems, but the
causes are internal and not external.

Senior member of Parliament
Jakarta, 1983

Yes, I'd like to get rid of Clark and Subic because
then we could stop blaming others for our own
problems. Our real problems are right here in the
Philippines. Foreign bases don't help us solve
those.

Senior official
Ministry of Foreign Affairs
Manila, 1986

ASEAN's leaders perceive real, menacing, and
identifiable enemies beyond their shores. Perceptions
vary greatly within ASEAN on detail, motivations, and
timing, but on the fundamental question of identity
most ASEAN perceptions of tigers agree. But these
perceptions of external threats must be put into perspective. In some cases they are but extensions of
internal threats, or they exploit and complicate
otherwise unrelated domestic issues. On the other
hand, some crucial internal threats are simply unrelated to external threats, and they will probably

remain unrelated. In the hierarchy of governmental priorities they deserve to be placed at the top, though they often are not. This concluding chapter addresses these two issues--significant similarities and differences in ASEAN perceptions of external threats and the nature of the perceived internal threats.

TIGERS AT THE DOOR AND TIGERS IN THE JUNGLE

Most ASEAN leaders think they recognize tigers when they encounter them, and there is some agreement within the membership of the association on which animals are tigers and which are not. However, there is less agreement on the proximity of particular tigers to the various front doors. Some think the tiger is at their doorstep; others think it is still in the jungle.

Some of the most important leaders in every ASEAN state harbor long-range fears of a powerful China. But Thailand, at one end of the spectrum, is willing to accept China as an ally so long as present conditions demand it; Indonesia, at the other extreme, views the PRC as a short-range as well as a long-range threat to the security of the region. For Thailand the PRC is a tiger in the jungle; for Indonesia the PRC tiger is lurking menacingly at the doorstep. Between these two extremes lie the remaining three ASEAN partners. Malaysia is closest to Indonesia; Singapore, to Thailand; and the Philippines, at the middle of the spectrum.

Every ASEAN state is concerned about the long-term intentions of the USSR. All are convinced that the Soviet Union is intent on increasing its presence in Southeast Asia. There are different explanations for the origins of these concerns, and there are different ways of expressing them throughout ASEAN. Some important leaders in the military in Indonesia and Thailand view the Russian naval buildup as a security threat. The Philippine military--in addition to being ideologically anticommunist--has a vested interest in confirming this Russian threat, and under General Ver's leadership the Soviet threat was often trumpeted at opportune times. The New Armed Forces of the Philippines (New AFP) under General Fidel Ramos have publicly expressed greater concerns about internal problems, but some officers are troubled by the potential for external support for the New People's Army, to which the potential donors are considered to be the USSR or China.

The Marcos Ministry of Foreign Affairs contained some strongly committed anticommunist officials, but these individuals are no longer in policy-making positions. Perhaps ministry perceptions of the USSR changed little in the transition from Marcos to Aquino, but it is difficult to be certain. In any case, the level of concern in the Foreign Ministry in Jakarta seems much lower than that in Manila. The USSR is one of the world's great powers, and the great powers can be expected to demand a presence in the region. Malaysia is likely to cite the threat of a Russian buildup in the ASEAN region as evidence that every major power seeks to dominate Southeast Asia, thus emphasizing the need for ZOPFAN and strengthening the argument for its acceptance. The Singapore position on the USSR has been frequently and consistently voiced by the PAP leadership for some two decades: the Soviet Union is a predator, and if not stopped from carrying out its grand designs it will eventually dominate Southeast Asia. There is nothing wrong with supporting ZOPFAN, but in the end, force and not doctrine will block the ambitions of the Soviet Union.

So far as the Vietnam-USSR partnership is concerned, the Indonesians, and with less conviction the Malaysians, view the entente as out of character for independent-minded Vietnam and therefore of a temporary nature. Other ASEAN members tend to view it as a long-term association, though not permanent. Long-term or short-term, the alliance presents a serious and immediate threat to the Thai perceptions of the country's physical well-being. Indonesia, far removed from the conflict and with much more confidence in Vietnam, enjoys the luxury--in the Thai view--of casting Vietnam as the long-term buffer against a hostile China. Singapore leaders think that the present generation of Vietnamese leaders have designs on Indochina, and that the USSR is helping them to attain their goals, just as Vietnam is helping the USSR achieve its larger objective, becoming the dominant power of the world. However, in the Singapore view, the Vietnam-USSR entente is unlikely to become a permanent arrangement because, as one senior official put it, "the next generation of Vietnamese will grow weary of seeing all the country's resources dissipated for a political cause while they fall behind the rest of the region in material benefits."

As it was succinctly put by an Indonesian author whose views are not unique to Indonesia, the Soviet threat is more amenable to precise calculation than the Chinese threat. The threat from the USSR is primarily military "and thus concretely visualized." By contrast, the Chinese threat "is more or less a mystery" because it involves "a set of beliefs about intentions." It is not concrete, "but it is felt to be there," and because of this lack of definition "the Chinese threat is seen to be greater, more urgent, and more immediate."[1]

Every ASEAN state has some concern about Japanese rearmament. The concern is greatest in the Philip-

pines, but it is not totally absent in any ASEAN
country. The Indonesian military is concerned about
the type of weapons being considered; others are concerned that with added responsibilities may come significant changes in Japanese behavior. Some Singaporeans are concerned not with rearmament for protec-
tion of the sea lanes, but with what this may portend
for the future. In several ASEAN states the danger of
Japan becoming an exporter of weapons has been brought
up, and fears have been expressed in both economic and
political terms. Economically, there is concern that
Japan will again demonstrate its superiority in applied technology and in aggressive competitiveness in
international marketing. Politically, there is concern
about another arms merchant on the scene. In Malaysia,
despite Prime Minister Nakasone's reassurances, Mahathir has continued to stress that Japanese defense
commitments must not include the Straits of Malacca.
And General Prem in Thailand has expressed reservations about the presence of Japanese warships in Thai
waters. The Japanese tiger now seems tame, even house-
broken, and it is tempting to accept it as a member of
the family. Occasionally, however, something happens
to remind the ASEAN leadership of its past behavior,
and it is then that the ferocity of the Japanese tiger
is remembered.

Every ASEAN state also expresses concerns about
the United States as a threat in one way or another.
America is urging Japan to rearm without considering
the latent security threat that Japan may pose to the
ASEAN region. It is the United States that "irratio-
nally"--so the critics charge--has allied itself with
China because the PRC is anti-USSR, because Americans
are hopelessly sentimental in their dealings with
China, and because Southeast Asia is viewed by
Washington policy makers as a region of low priority
and as an appendage of East Asia.

Most ASEAN members feel that the United States
does not adequately understand, or even try to understand, their unique situations. For them Americans
fail to understand Southeast Asian misgivings about
China, the emotional appeal of nationalism, or the
desire on the part of people for change. It may be
attributed to a communications gap between the bottom
and the top of the governmental machinery, American
sentimentality, American inexperience as a world
power, or typical superpower arrogance.

Many ASEAN policy makers also regard as a threat
the unpredictability and discontinuities of American
foreign policy produced by the four-year election
cycles and the almost-continuous campaigning that
accompanies them. For these policy makers America
behaves like a loose cannon on a rolling deck. It is
powerful but not predictable, and in this sense it is
a "danger" even if it is not a "threat."

The Philippines must be treated as a separate case because U.S.-Philippine relations tend to be more of an internal than an external issue. However, even some of America's most steadfast and articulate Filipino supporters concede stoically and almost fatalistically that with Soviet missiles aimed at Subic Bay Naval Base and Clark Air Force Base the United States constitutes a threat to the security of the Philippines. Occasionally policy makers have somewhat bitterly complained that America was prepared to fight a limited nuclear war, which they felt means a war in which the principals survive and the proxies die. In this sense the United States poses an external threat to the Philippines, an indirect threat, but a threat nonetheless.

Two related questions cannot be answered with quantitative specificity in this study: to what extent, in what proportions, and in what manner do the various "dimensions" put forward initially actually influence leaders' perceptions of the powers beyond their shores; and, second, to what extent and in what manner do elite perceptions drive the engine of policy? Circumstantial evidence abounds, and on the bases of such evidence this study has attempted to speculate on possible answers to both complex questions. As the reader was warned early, if the conclusions are less than fully satisfying it is because the evidence is elusive and the processes are complex.

To put our study of threat perceptions in perspective, one last subject must be considered. ASEAN's external enemies are important, but their significance is eclipsed for most leaders by other more pressing threats.

TIGERS IN THE KITCHEN: THE ENEMIES WITHIN

No ASEAN country expects to be invaded, and no country anticipates the arrival of an enemy fleet in its territorial waters. The greatest threats to national security are threats that begin as external, but work their destruction from within. ASEAN leaders are concerned about foreign economic penetration, the unplanned importation of alien cultural values and practices that destroy indigenous value systems, and the political and economic implications of technology transfer. All of these constitute threats of greater destructive potential than external military threats.

When asked which was more threatening to their countries in the coming decade, the world beyond or the world within, almost all ASEAN leaders responded without hesitation that their most serious challenges were internal, not external. It was put succinctly in one capital--"Our biggest problems are internal to us and must be solved internally by us"--a view that was repeated in different words with different emphases in every ASEAN capital. When quizzed about the nature of these internal threats the specifics varied, but there was still striking agreement in general terms. Most concerns involved uncertainties arising during a period of rapid technological, economic, and social change within the setting of a volatile, troubled, and unpredictable world. Most felt that external forces could make their internal challenges more difficult, and all felt that one or more of the major powers would exploit their internal problems to further the major power's larger international objectives. In the end, however, the most serious threats perceived by the leadership of the ASEAN states are domestic and not foreign,[2] and the problems that these threats create must be resolved internally.

Many of the internal threats facing the ASEAN states, and indeed the most significant of the domestic threats, stem more from their fortes than from their foibles. Without excluding the country currently most troubled by its foibles, the Philippines, ASEAN is made up of states that have enjoyed more successes than failures. ASEAN members have a legitimate claim to Third World status--that is, each ASEAN member can break into the First World in one or several generations if present trends continue. When examining ASEAN there is no cause for the hopelessness and despair that plagues observers of countries such as Somalia and Ethiopia. ASEAN members are high achievers.

But success produces its own problems, and my conversations over the past five years confirm that many of the area's leaders and thinkers understand this very well.[3] These new problems, however, cannot be considered in a vacuum. Perhaps the analogy is too facile, but each member of ASEAN can be likened to the hero of a Shakespearean tragedy, whose "fatal flaw" set him apart from others in the play. Perhaps the fatal flaw makes the hero more interesting, or more amusing, but ultimately it also makes him more tragic because the hero contains within himself the seed of his own destruction. Throughout Southeast Asia each country seems to have its own fatal flaw, which, if allowed to develop to its logical conclusion without intervention, might ultimately bring about its destruction. Fortunately, here the analogy ends. Unlike Shakespeare's tragic heroes, for whom the end is inevitable from the beginning, nations can, and do, change their historical courses. ASEAN's modern problems, the problems associated with success, are compounded by their fatal flaws, their primordial givens,[4] but unlike characters in a play their self-destruction is not foreordained.

TIGERS IN THE KITCHEN: THE PRIMORDIAL GIVENS

Geography, history, language, and culture have all conspired against the countries of ASEAN to make their tasks of nation building and economic development more difficult. Of the five countries considered here only Thailand has any reasonable claim to nationhood, described in its ideal form by Rupert Emerson as "a single people, traditionally fixed on a well-defined territory, speaking the same language and preferably a language all its own, possessing a distinctive culture, and shaped to a common mold by many generations of shared historical experience."[5] Within the ASEAN states, the search for nationhood has been, and continues to be, a major concern of every regime.

Malaysia

Malaysia's social heterogeneity is apparent and well documented in virtually every scholarly and popular treatment. Welding a nation from diverse and potentially antagonistic communities of Malay Muslims, Hindu Indians, and eclectic but predominantly Buddhist Chinese would be difficult enough. However, when other social cleavages tend to reenforce communal compartmentalization rather than crisscross the clearly demarcated communal boundaries, the challenge is even greater. In the case of Malaysia, the two major communities, Chinese and Malay, have more than the critical mass needed for each community to perpetuate its own traditions.

Interethnic tensions constitute Malaysia's most pressing internal threat. Communalism has been the mother's milk of Malaysian politics since the first municipal elections were held in 1952. No noncommunal party has enjoyed more than very modest success at the polls; no noncommunal party has achieved more than temporary and passing success; and noncommunal parties that have succeeded in perpetuating themselves have ceased to be noncommunal except for the labels and trappings.[6]

Today Malaysia's major internal challenges—occasional outbursts of militant Islam, the continuing pressure to push politics out of mid-stream and toward a more traditional Islamic republic, major disparities in the distribution of wealth, and different perceptions of long-range goals—are all directly or indirectly related to its social heterogeneity. Together all of these threats (or "challenges," as Malaysian leaders are more likely to call them) dwarf the external threats perceived to be facing the country. Perhaps, as some fear, foreign powers may someday try to take advantage of these problems, just as a more revolutionary China exploited the predominantly Chinese Communist Party of Malaya and its associated "liberation army." However, such a threat is far more domestic than international. In fact, in the minds of many Malaysian leaders, both Malay and Chinese, were it not for the fertile and inviting internal situation no foreign power could pose a serious external threat.

Singapore

When Singapore was in the process of achieving independence it was often commented that Malaysia needed a port and Singapore needed a hinterland. And to many it seemed apparent that Singapore needed Malaysia more than Malaysia needed Singapore. Logic suggested that a hinterland could develop its own ports, but a port could not create a hinterland. This, however, is precisely what Singapore had to do, and did, after it separated from Malaysia in 1965.

By its trade policies and its development programs the world became Singapore's hinterland. Yet some harsh primordial realities remained. The Republic of Singapore is literally a 227 square-mile island, but it is also, figuratively, an island of ethnic Chinese in a sea of Malays. The leadership of the newly independent republic had to create conditions to encourage the development of a Singapore national identity among an immigrant Chinese population, and they had to convince their Malay neighbors that this process was producing results. The task was formidable.

The leadership faced a large proportion of the Chinese population who were very reluctant to part with their Chinese identity, and they faced an opposition leadership eager to exploit the alienation of the Chinese to achieve their own political ends. Sometimes opposition leaders and followers went to considerable lengths, including shedding blood, to protect and defend a real or imagined Chinese heritage.

Insofar as Singaporeans succeeded in defending their Chinese heritage, they provided further proof to their Malay neighbors that they were transplanted Chinese and not fellow Southeast Asians. Singapore leaders faced a delicate task. They had to push their constituents to shed their Chinese identity and acquire a Singaporean identity fast enough to convince their neighbors that Singapore was not a threat, but the process had to be slow enough to avoid a possible backlash that might wipe out their gains.

At the international level the current state of relations with neighboring Malaysia and Indonesia, and at the national level governmental programs encouraging Singaporeans to rediscover their Confucian roots, suggest that the leadership is confident of its success in overcoming its major primordial obstacle to nation building. Yet, the process is never complete, and retrogression is always a possibility. Moreover,

Singapore, despite its success in forging a nation from immigrants, remains a minuscule state, and no government policy can alter significantly this primordial fact.[7]

Philippines

Political problems stemming from primordial givens are legion in the Philippines. A country of seven thousand islands speaking a dozen major languages and dialects faces a monumental task of political integration, and the catalogue of forces tearing at the fabric of Philippine society does not end with territory and language. The Muslims of the south have never considered themselves a part of the various Manila-centric regimes, and in turn most regimes--Spanish, American, and Filipino--have treated the Muslim minority as outsiders and second-class citizens of the Philippine nation.

The dichotomy of wealth and poverty is common throughout the world, but in the Philippines the extremes tend to be separated by a void rather than joined by a middle class. The current patterns of wealth and poverty have roots deep in the Spanish colonial regime. Despite some notable exceptions--families who have made it from the bottom to the top in several generations--today's wealth is in the hands of a wealthy class of landowners who emerged under the Spanish and have survived every successive change of regimes for the past several centuries. The distribution of wealth has undergone some changes in the past decade, but the general pattern is so old as to be considered a primordial given, at least for the present generation of political leaders.

Until recently there was little evidence that the average Filipino felt much responsibility for other faceless Filipinos who were not members of his own family, extended family, or dialect group. Only rarely did Filipinos demonstrate a sense of overarching civic responsibility, a responsibility for fellow countrymen with whom they were not linked by some real or constructed bond of kinship or language. Without this unifying force national political integration was difficult if not impossible. Perhaps, however, the People Power Revolution of February 1986 revealed a newly found sense of national responsibility that will transcend the dyadic structure of politics that prevailed for almost a half-century in the Philippines.[8] It is too soon to judge whether the recent revolution was a national phenomenon, or was confined largely to traditionally oppositionist Manila. Time will also tell whether the revolution reflects a deep change in a Filipino psyche that placed the family at the top of the hierarchy of values or a shallow victory for the

opposition brought on by peculiar and unique circumstances not likely to be repeated again.

Thailand

Of all the ASEAN countries Thailand alone escaped
a colonial history, and, perhaps not coincidentally,
today Thailand faces fewer internal political threats
stemming from primordial givens. The monarchy provides
an overarching unity that sets Thais apart from those
outside their borders. The language of Bangkok is not
spoken universally throughout the kingdom, but there
is less variation than is to be found in other ASEAN
states. With a few significant exceptions, Thais are
followers of Theravada Buddhism, and the institution
of the monkhood, through which all young Thai males
must pass, is a powerful homogenizing force in the
country.

The most serious primordial obstacle to nation-
building in Thailand is the presence of an unassimi-
lated Malay community on the Thai-Malaysian border.
Historically the south was ignored until recent
times, and the results of this neglect are apparent
without reference to economic data. Malays on the
Thai side of the border resent the relative prosperity
of the Bangkok Thais and look with envy at their
Malaysian cousins to the south. Malays in Malaysia are
better off economically, and they are members of a
vast political majority and not a minuscule minority.
In the early years of television it was difficult if
not impossible for the south to receive Thai programs
from Bangkok, but Malay-language programs from government relay stations in northern Malaysia were readily
available. For years the situation had been similar in
radio broadcasting.

It is not surprising that southern Thailand developed an aloofness from Bangkok. In this environment
a Malay separatist movement with deep roots in history
prospered for a time, and the presence of other elements not in sympathy with the Bangkok government were
ignored or tolerated by the Malay population.[9] The
Bangkok government in recent years has devoted considerable attention to the economic problems of the
the south, and new development in the southern towns
has dramatically altered their appearance. Nevertheless the legacy of years of neglect has not been
overcome. Regionalism, though not as pronounced, in
the east and the north as well as in the south, remains a serious primordial problem for Thailand.

Indonesia

Regionalism is similarly a problem for Indonesia,
and there is no equivalent of a traditional force like

the Thai monarchy to forge unity among the disparate regions. When President Sukarno proudly proclaimed that even a child could look at a map and see the natural unity of Indonesia, he was giving expression to his own vision of the republic and not reflecting the geographic realities of the region.[10] This is commonly recognized by Indonesian leaders. In Jakarta in 1983 one senior official answered my question about Indonesia's major achievements since the revolution with the candid comment: "We have survived as a single nation against great odds. That has been a major accomplishment."

The national language, Bahasa Indonesia, and Islam provide two of the few unifying traditions counteracting the divisive forces of Indonesian regionalism. The language, a hybrid Malay used originally by traders in their travels through the islands, is a powerful unifying force. Although local dialects differ, Bahasa Indonesia can be understood and freely used throughout the republic by both Indonesians and Chinese. Islam is also universal, but it can be as much a force of disunity as unity.

Many respected Indonesian leaders genuinely fear the destructive potential of renascent Islam, and this often puts them at odds with their more traditional constituents. Although rarely a matter of public record, in private (and occasionally in public) many Indonesians have watched developments in neighboring Malaysia with considerable concern. Many of the more senior military officers remember with pain their experiences fighting the radical Islamic revolts in the Outer Islands, and they do not want to repeat the experience. For most political leaders politics must be insulated from renascent Islam for the good of Indonesia. It is difficult to escape the conclusion that *Panca Sila*, as is often alleged by its critics, has been supported officially largely to create and maintain a wall of separation between religion and politics, at least so far as this is possible.

TIGERS IN THE KITCHEN: THE PRICE OF SUCCESS

The member states of ASEAN have amassed impressive records of economic development. The worldwide economic recession of the eighties has slowed this development, and it is probable that the halcyon days of the 1960s and early to mid-1970s are not likely to be repeated. Nevertheless compared with the progress of economic development elsewhere in the Third World, or indeed on any standard of comparison, ASEAN economic performances throughout their years of independence have been strong. Table 8.1 indicates these strengths.

Table 8.1

ASEAN Economic Performances:
Average Annual Growth of GDP at Constant Prices,
1970-75, 1975-80, 1980-83, 1984

	1970-75	1975-80	1980-83	1984
Thailand	7.11	8.79	5.69	5.9
Malaysia	12.80	10.21	6.62	6.9
Singapore	11.51	10.41	8.73	8.2
Indonesia	9.45	9.27	5.00	4.5
Philippines	6.97	7.04	2.70	-5.5

Source: Figures for 1970-83 were tabulated
from data contained in United Nations, Statistical
Office, *Monthly Bulletin of Statistics*, special
table 1, p. xcviii. Figures for 1984 from Alburo,
"The Region in in 1984," figure 1, p. 23.

Thailand

Economic performances have been strong, but development alone does not assure domestic tranquillity.
Indeed, economic development can itself contribute to
internal unrest. When Thai Foreign Minister Siddhi
commented in his Asia Society address, quoted at the
beginning of this chapter, that Thailand's domestic
unrest was rooted in "uneven growth . . . , skewed
income distribution, and the rebellion of those who
feel . . . left out,"[11] he was citing problems associated with economic success, not failure. Between
1960 and 1983 the Thai gross domestic product (GDP)
generated by the agricultural sector almost tripled,
but its performance lagged considerably behind the
other sectors. The tertiary sector recorded an almost
six-fold increase and the industrial, an almost eight-
fold increase.[12] In 1984 two Thai scholars, noting the
political implications of available economic data,
reported that in 1976 the average annual income of
workers in agriculture was one-fifth of those in the
service sector, one-seventh of those in industry, and
one-tenth of those in commerce.[13] The Thai case is not
unique.

Malaysia

Of all the ASEAN countries Malaysia has most
actively sought to redistribute wealth through its New

Economic Policy (NEP). A major goal has been to steer
Malays into the modern sector of the economy, and to
this end the NEP has encouraged Malays to buy and hold
share capital in the corporate sector. Despite their
aggressive efforts, in 1983 Malays held only 18.7
percent of all shares, and of these most were held by
government-run "trust agencies," rather than by individuals.[14] In 1970, 67.6 percent of those Malaysians
in agriculture, forestry, hunting, and fishing were
Malays; in 1980 the figure had risen to 68.2 percent.[15]

The New Economic Policy has not been a great
success in statistical terms, but it is apparent to
any seasoned observer that Malaysian attempts to
create a Malay entrepreneurial class have borne fruit.
The old style "Ali-Baba" relationship (a Chinese firm
with a Malay front) is now more the exception than the
rule. Today Ali is more likely either to own the firm
or, at least, to have a strong voice in its management.

Success, however, has produced a new set of political problems for incumbent governments. Much of the
current political unrest--political factionalism
within the Malay community and the rejection of the
Chinese leadership by many Malaysian-Chinese voters--
can be directly attributed to the government's success
in changing the traditional lifestyles and roles of
many Malays.

Philippines

Historically the Philippines has faced problems
stemming from the unequal distribution of the nation's
wealth. Several presidents made halfhearted attempts
at land reform, and President Marcos repeatedly cham-
pioned his New Society Movement as a vehicle for
economic and social reforms. However, the evidence
that was available even before the People Power Revolution seemed to suggest other results.

Comparable statistics are not available for the
entire Philippines, but in Metro Manila after 1978 the
rich got richer and everyone else got poorer. The
lowest 20 percent of the income-producing population
received 5.3 percent of all income earned in 1978 and
only 3.4 percent in 1984. At the other extreme the top
20 percent of income earners took home 53.7 percent of
the income generated in 1978 and 59.6 percent in
1984.[16] President Marcos's New Society Movement might
have created new wealth for some, but it did nothing
about the problem of its skewed distribution.

The most serious internal threat now facing the
Philippines has both primoridal and modern roots. The
New People's Army (NPA) feeds on the economic and
social inequities of Philippine society, and at the
same time it is the direct descendent of the communist

insurgency that plagued the Philippines immediately after World War II. President Aquino has pledged herself to seek peaceful solutions to an insurgency that has spread throughout the country, but her efforts have been only modestly successful. The soft-line approach has become a major issue in the internal politics of her administration and provided the ammunition for her major rival, former minister Enrile, whose power base probably remains in the army. Although Chief of Staff General Fidel Ramos has consistently pledged support for the President, his statements and actions on the eve of President Aquino's departure for Japan in November suggest that Ramos is concerned about the loyalty of some commanders.[17] The murder in November 1986 of a leader of the left-wing opposition, followed by the apparent retaliation of the left with the assassination of a close associate of Minister Enrile on 18 November add a somber new dimension to the internal dissention in Manila.[18]

Singapore

The major economic success story in ASEAN has been Singapore, whose statistics on almost every measure outstrip those of its neighbors. Today Singapore has a standard of living second only to Japan in Asia, and the island republic has become a much publicized model in environmental management, public housing, transport, and communications--in fact in almost everything related to modern urban living. Yet, success has produced its own problems.

To achieve its remarkable success Singaporeans have had to accept a degree of discipline that many in the West would find intolerable. Singaporean parents well remembered the difficult days of the fifties and early sixties, and most gladly exchanged the prospect of more personal freedom for concrete manifestations of material advancement. Perhaps it was the Chinese way; perhaps it was a rational choice. Whatever the reasons the vast majority of an older generation of Singaporeans enthusiastically followed orders given by their paternalistic government, and together they and the PAP created an economic and social miracle in a minuscule state with few resources other than its location and the wits of its people.

Today a generation of young Singaporeans have known nothing but affluence, and for them affluence seems to be the natural and expected condition in Singapore. Now that physical well-being is not an issue, many have turned their attentions elsewhere. Some, but as yet not many, are questioning the right of the PAP overwhelmingly to dominate Singapore government and politics, and some--more perhaps, but still not many--are insisting that the government should consult its constituents before instituting

policies that will significantly change their lives.
In short, in its own way a younger generation of
Singaporeans is beginning to rebel. The manifestations
of this rebellion are so innocuous at present that
most Western visitors would probably miss them completely, but for an older generation of Singaporeans--
and for the leadership of the PAP--they are painfully
apparent. Many Singaporeans wonder if this is only
the beginning, and where it might lead. Success has
its rewards, and these are very apparent in Singapore.
It also has a price, and the exact costs are not yet
evident.[19] This is the tiger in Singapore's kitchen.

Indonesia

Indonesia's economic successes, after the almost ruinous period of rule by Sukarno, have largely
been connected with the discovery and extraction of
its petroleum resources. Its failures have stemmed
largely from the same source. Internal mismanagement
of the government agency overseeing the petroleum
industry and the rapid deterioration of international
oil prices have combined to deal a severe setback to
Indonesian development plans. Yet, despite the gloomy
economic forecasts often put forward today, three
facts stand out: first, the resource base exists for
long-term development; second, by international comparisons the Indonesian record is good; and, finally,
for the next decade Indonesia's problems are likely to
be more political than economic.
The transition from Sukarno to Suharto was difficult, violent, and totally outside any constitutional
framework. The Suharto era is coming to a close, and
there is much speculation that the next transition may
also be difficult. No obvious successor is in sight,
and President Suharto has made no apparent attempt to
identify and promote the next generation of Indonesian
leadership. The movement supporting the president,
Golkar, is held together chiefly by President Suharto;
without him its long-term viability seems question-
able. Moreover, the next political transition will
probably take place in the context of economic difficulties occasioned by the failure of development plans
based on the expectation of large oil revenues, a
government that is still viewed as Java-centered and
Javanese dominated, and Islamic movements that may
increasingly demand and receive political attention in
Jakarta. There are many tigers in the Indonesian
kitchen.

TIGERS AND POLITICS

For every ASEAN member there are tigers at the
door, tigers in the jungles, and tigers in the kit-

chen. The future is fraught with risks for every
state in the region. The association is a fragile
organization, and every state belonging to it is also
fragile. Outside forces over which each has no control
could loose centrifugal forces tugging at ASEAN unity.
Outside forces might also set off internal chain reactions that could topple any of the current regimes and
wipe out the gains of the last several decades. On the
other hand, a Shakespearean fatal flaw might play
itself out to its logical conclusion, and any ASEAN
state could collapse without outside help. There are
many defensible reasons for pessimism about the future
of ASEAN and the membership of the association, but
there is also no reason to eschew an optimistic conclusion.

Two decades ago no one who predicted the current
situation in the ASEAN region would have been believed. The chaos of the mid-1960s was foreboding.
The world was polarized by the American involvement in
Vietnam and no solution was in sight. The new Federation of Malaysia had already lost one of its most
important members and some thought others might de-
fect. Newly independent Singapore faced a host of
skeptics inside and outside who doubted that it could
survive as an independent ministate. Indonesia had
just undergone a bloody internal pogrom and was in the
painful process of changing governments. Midway in
1966 "confrontation" with Malaysia came to a formal
close, but Indonesia was still distrusted by many
leaders, and within the country the disastrous effects
of Sukarno's economic policies were apparent as infla-
tion soared so high that the numbers became meaning-
less. Many Thais were speculating that in allying
themselves with the American efforts in Vietnam Thailand had lost its historic flexibility, and an author
wrapping up events of 1966 asked in the title of his
essay if Thailand was to be "another Vietnam."[20] In
the Philippines an immensely popular Ferdinand Marcos
and his beautiful first lady were viewed as a hopeful
sign that at last Malacanang Palace was occupied by a
Philippine president who cared about the worsening
plight of the Filipino people.[21]

ASEAN, and most of the association's members--
Thailand, Malaysia, Singapore, Indonesia, the Philippines, and, for historical accuracy, Brunei--have come
a long way in the last two decades. Of course, on most
measures newly autonomous Brunei and the troubled
Philippines still have a long way to go. Brunei will
probably discover, as other successful Third World
states have learned, that change cannot be confined to
those sectors not considered threatening to the government. In the Philippines there is more cause for
optimism than before the overthrow of Marcos, but
latent revolutionary forces could still be triggered
by as yet unidentified catalytic agents. Not only in

the Philippines, but elsewhere in ASEAN, prophets of doom can cite considerable evidence to support pessimistic predictions. But there is an optimistic side.

Few, if any, ASEAN leaders sense impending doom emanating from outside their borders, and probably only the most committed foreign ideologues would disagree. Then too, most of ASEAN's leaders have candidly appraised the nature and extent of their threats from within, and many have taken steps to resolve some of the most pressing of these issues lest they unleash destructive forces that cannot be controlled.

There has also emerged an embryonic sense of ASEAN regionalism. Perhaps the embryo will die; perhaps it will live and thrive. That it exists at all is itself revolutionary. The historical impact of ASEAN will thus be significant, even if the organization were to die. This study has found both agreement and disagreement on the nature of external threats facing the ASEAN members. Given the diversity of the region, disagreement is to be expected; agreement is not. In fact, in regard to the most crucial issues involving the major powers and the region, there lies a remarkable degree of agreement on the presence or absence of threats. This congruence of views probably owes much to ASEAN. Leaders are at last interacting with one another through the vehicle of ASEAN, and, at least on some issues, they are beginning to view the world about them in similar ways. This alone is reason for optimism.

NOTES

1. Soesastro, "The U.S. and the USSR in the Second 'Cold War,'" 52-58, esp. 57-58. This is a brief but very perceptive essay. The emphases reflect an Indonesian perspective, but the general themes are applicable throughout ASEAN.

2. A Japanese scholar has made a similar observation about the greater significance of domestic threats. He comments that threats emanate "from the internal foibles of each nation, such as the weak legitimacy of the government and extensive reliance on high-handed rule, rather than a menace from the outside, such as the Soviet Union, China and Vietnam." Kamiya, "The World and Asia," 7. His observations about the relative importance of internal and external threats are valid, but his explanation of the origins of domestic threats is superficial and incomplete, as is discussed below. Federspiel, "A Comparison of Security Concerns," 1967 45-62 also found that with only two exceptions concerns about internal threats exceeded concerns about those from outside their borders. The two exceptions were Singapore and Thailand

in 1983. Federspiel used events data drawn from several common sources and set up a ten-point scale that ran from least (1) to most (10). On his measure the two exceptional cases fell only slightly on the side of greater concern for external threats. It should also be noted that in this study "external" included possible threats from neighbors as well from the major powers. Federspiel's general findings tend to confirm my own observations based on interviews, but his quantified tabular conclusions are not as convincing as his textual observations.

3. See, for example, the comments of Jusuf Wanandi, director of the Centre for Strategic and International Studies, in "Current Political Situation in the ASEAN Countries," 3-8. Wanandi gets to the heart of a major genre of internal problems facing most of the ASEAN states--coping with success. These views are shared by many of the political leaders of ASEAN.

4. The term and the concept are borrowed from Geertz, "Primordial Sentiments and Civil Politics in the New States."

5. Emerson, *From Empire to Nations*, 103.

6. The United Malays National Organization (UMNO) and the Malayan Chinese Association (MCA) joined in a temporary preelection alliance to fight the Kuala Lumpur municipal elections in 1952. By the time of the first general elections in 1955 this agreement had been formalized into the Alliance and had incorporated the Malayan Indian Congress (MIC), which represented the remaining identifiable Malayan community. Three facts are significant: the Alliance was created because of a fear of the popular appeal of the noncommunal Independence for Malaya Party (IMP), the noncommunal IMP was overwhelmingly defeated, and the Alliance was precisely what it name indicated--a coalition of three communally based parties that retained their individual identities and characteristics. Every alliance since that time, including the current *Barisan Nasional* (National Front) has retained this organizational format.

7. "Alter significantly" is used advisedly. Singapore has grown from a 225-square-mile colony to a 227-square-mile republic. There are few opportunities remaining for additional land reclamation projects, but a roughly 1 percent territorial growth without acquiring a neighbor's land is certainly unusual, if not unique.

8. On the dyadic structure of Philippine politics see Lande, *Leaders, Factions, and Parties*.

9. In the course of a visit to Yala and Betong in 1967 I was able to observe firsthand some manifestations of this aloofness. In patent contradiction of Thai law and Ministry of Education guidelines, Chinese-language education using banned curricula and textbooks was readily available, and the largest Chi-

nese school in Thailand was operating openly in Betong. Similarly, Pondok (Islamic religious) schools
were flourishing and in many cases providing the only
education the children were receiving. Officers of the
Malaysian-Chinese Communist guerrilla forces based
across the border moved about freely on the streets of
Betong, and many apparently kept their families in
Betong.

10. This remark, without direct quotation, is
attributed to Sukarno in Emerson, *From Empire to Nations*, 125.

11. Siddhi, Address before the Asia Society, 13,
14. This also the source of the opening quotation of
this chapter.

12. Narongchai Akrasanee, Sukhumbhand Paribatra,
and Chalermpoj Iamkamala, "Economic Change and National Security in Thailand," table 1, 18.

13. Ibid., table 14, 63.

14. Ahmad and Osman-Rani, "Economic Change and
National Security: The Malaysian Case," table 6, 34.
Malaysian citizens hold 66.4 percent of the share
capital; foreign nationals, 33.6 percent.

15. Ibid., table 3, 31. Some success was recorded, however, in moving Malays into the secondary
and tertiary sectors.

16. These figures and others on income distribution in Metro Manila were provided from unclassified
sources by the U.S. Embassy, Manila, in 1985.

17. General Ramos placed the military on "red
alert" and warned commanders about the risks of dis-
loyalty.

18. David Puzon, a former member of the National
Assembly and a supporter of Enrile, was slain in his
car in the outskirts of Manila, apparently in retaliation for the murder of Rolando Olalia, a labor union
leader, six days earlier.

19. In a sometimes culture bound but otherwise
perceptive essay T. D. Allman, a roving journalist
with a keen eye for major issues, assessed the costs
and benefits of Singapore economic success and concluded with a series of unanswered questions that
seemed generally optimistic in nature. "The Failure
of Singapore's Success."

20. Nuechterlein, "Thailand: Another Vietnam?,"
126-30. In fairness to the author, he concludes that
contrary to the prevailing view, Thailand was not
likely to become "another Vietnam."

21. Wurfel, "The Philippines: Intensified Dialogue."

Acronyms and Abbreviations

AFP	Armed Forces of the Philippines
ASA	Association of Southeast Asia
ASEAN	Association of Southeast Asian Nations
COMECON	Council for Mutual Economic Aid
CPM	Communist Party of Malaya
CPP	Communist Party of the Philippines
CPT	Communist Party of Thailand
CSIS	Center for Strategic and International Studies (Jakarta)
DPR	*Dewan Perwakilan Rakyat.* Parliament (Indonesia)
EEC	European Economic Community
GESTAPU	*Gerakan Tiga Puluh September.* September 30 Affair (Indonesia)
GESTOK	*Gerakan Satu Oktober.* October 1 Affair (Indonesia)
Golkar	*Golangan Karya* ("Functional Groups"-- political party, Indonesia)
ISEAS	Institute of Southeast Asian Studies (Singapore)
ISIS	Institute of Security and International Studies (Bangkok)
JEI	Japan Economic Association

MAPHILINDO	Political association of *Malaysia*, *Philippines*, and *Indonesia*
MBA	Military Basing Agreement (Philippines-U.S.)
MCA	Malayan Chinese Association
MIC	Malayan Indian Congress
MPR	*Majelis Permusyawaratan Rakyat*. People's Consulatative Congress (Indonesia)
NEP	New Economic Policy (Malaysia)
NPA	New People's Army (Philippines)
ODA	Official Development Act (Japan)
PAP	People's Action Party (Singapore)
PKI	*Partai Komunis Indonesia*. Communist Party of Indonesia
PRC	People's Republic of China
SEATO	Southeast Asia Treaty Organization
TCIA	Thai Central Intelligence Agency
UMNO	United Malays National Organization
VOMR	Voice of the Malayan Revolution
ZOPFAN	Zone of Peace, Freedom and Neutrality (ASEAN)

Bibliography

BOOKS AND MONOGRAPHS

Asadakorn Eksaengsri. *Foreign Policy in Thailand: ASEAN Policy, 1967-72.* Ann Arbor: University Microfilms, 1980.

Axelrod, Robert, ed. *Structure of Decision.* Princeton: Princeton University Press, 1976.

Boulding, Kenneth E. *The Image.* Ann Arbor: University of Michigan Press, 1956.

Buchanan, William, and Headly Cantril. *How Nations See Each Other.* Urbana: University of Illinois Press, 1953.

Chen, Peter S. J., ed. *Singapore: Development Policies and Trends.* Singapore: Oxford University Press, 1983.

Chia Lin Sien and Colin MacAndrews, eds. *Southeast Asian Seas: Frontiers for Development.* Singapore: McGraw Hill, 1981.

Cohen, Raymond. *Threat Perceptions in International Crises.* Madison: University of Wisconsin Press, 1979.

Coughlin, Richard. *Double Identity: The Chinese in Modern Thailand.* Hongkong: Oxford University Press, 1960.

Doy Laurel in Profile: A Philippine Political Odyssey. Manila: LAHI, Inc., 1985.

Economic Intelligence Unit. *Quarterly Economic Review of Malaysia and Brunei, Annual Supplement, 1984.* London: *The Economist*, 1985.

Emerson, Rupert. *From Empire to Nations.* Cambridge: Harvard University Press, 1960.

Fairbank, John King, ed. *The Chinese World Order: Traditional China's Foreign Relations.* Cambridge: Harvard University Press, 1968.

Falkowski, Lawrence S., ed. *Psychological Models in International Politics.* Boulder: Westview Press, 1979.

Far Eastern Economic Review. *Asia 1977 Yearbook.* Hongkong: Far Eastern Economic Review, 1977.

Fifield, Russell J. *National and Regional Interests in ASEAN: Competition and Cooperation in International Politics.* Singapore: Institute of Southeast Asian Studies, 1979.

Fitzgerald, Stephan. *China and the Overseas Chinese.* Cambridge: Cambridge University Press, 1972.

Geertz, Clifford, ed. *Old Societies and New States.* New York: Free Press, 1962.

Girling, J. L. S. *The Bureaucratic Polity in Modernizing Societies.* Singapore: Institute of Southeast Asian Studies, 1981.

Grinter, Lawrence E. *The Philippine Bases: Continuing Utility in a Changing Strategic Context.* National Security Affairs Monograph Series 80-2. Washington, D.C.: National Defense University, 1980.

Howell, Llewellyn D. *The International Political Attitudes of Malaysians, 1971-1981.* In American University Papers in Asian Studies. Washington, D.C.: American University Center for Asian Studies, 1982.

Institute of Southeast Asian Studies, *Southeast Asian Affairs 1982.* Singapore: Heinemann Asia for Institute of Southeast Asian Studies, 1982.

_____. *Southeast Asian Affairs 1985.* Singapore: Institute of Southeast Asian Studies, 1985.

International Monetary Fund. *Direction of Trade Statistics Yearbook, 1984.* Washington, D.C.: IMF, 1984.

Japan Economic Institute. *Report 27A.* Washington, D.C.: Japan Economic Institute, July 1985.

Japan External Trade Organization. *A Survey of Japanese Firms Operating in ASEAN Countries.* Tokyo: Foreign Press Center, Japan, 1982.

Jervis, Robert. *Perceptions and Misperceptions in International Politics.* Princeton: Princeton University Press, 1976.

Jha, Ganganath. *Foreign Policy of Thailand.* New Delhi: Radiant Publishers, 1979.

Katano, Hikoji. *Japanese Enterprise in ASEAN Countries.* Kobe: Research Institute for Economics and Business Administration, 1981.

Kelman, Herbert C. *International Behavior.* New York: Holt, Rinehart and Winston, 1965.

Knorr, Klaus, ed. *Historical Dimensions of National Security Problems.* Lawrence: University of Kansas Press, 1976.

Lande, Carl. *Leaders, Factions, and Parties.* New Haven: Yale University Southeast Asia Studies Monograph Series, 1965.

Laurel, Salvador. *Laurel Report: Mission to China.* N.p., [ca. 1972].

Lee Ngok and Leung Chi-keung, eds. *China: Development and Challenge.* Hongkong: University of Hong Kong, Center of Asian Studies, 1979.

Leifer, Michael. *Indonesia's Foreign Policy*. London: Allen and Unwin, 1983.

Loh Kok Wah, et al. *The Chinese Community and Malaysia-China Ties: Elite Perspectives*. Tokyo: Institute of Developing Economies, 1981.

Matsumoto, Shigekazu. *Southeast Asia in a Changing World*. Tokyo: Institute of Developing Economies, 1980.

Milne, R. S. *Government and Politics in Malaysia*. Boston: Houghton Mifflin, 1967.

_____, and Diane K. Mauzy. *Politics and Government in Malaysia*. Vancouver: University of British Columbia Press, 1978.

Montgomery, John D., and Albert O. Hirschman, eds. *Public Policy, XVI*. Cambridge: Harvard University Press, 1967.

Morrison, Charles E., ed. *Threats to Security in Asia-Pacific*. Lexington: D. C. Heath, 1983.

Mountbatten, Vice Admiral. *Report to the Combined Chiefs of Staff by the Supreme Allied Commander, South-East Asia, 1943-1945*. London: His Majesty's Stationery Office, 1951.

Ozaki, Robert S., and Walter Arnold. *Japan's Foreign Relations: A Global Search for Economic Security*. Boulder: Westview Press, 1985.

Pathmanathan, Murugesu, and David Lazarus, eds. *Winds of Change: The Mahathir Impact on Malaysia's Foreign Policy*. Kuala Lumpur: Eastview Publications Sdn. Bhd., 1984.

Phuangkasem, Corrine. *Thailand's Foreign Relations, 1964-80*. Singapore: Institute of Southeast Asian Studies, 1984.

Pringle, Robert. *Indonesia and the Philippines: American Interests in Island Southeast Asia*. New York: Columbia University Press, 1980.

Riggs, Fred W. *Thailand: The Modernization of a Bureaucratic Polity*. Honolulu: East-West Center Press, 1966.

Roeder, O. G. *The Smiling General: President Soeharto of Indonesia*. Jakarta: Gunung Agung Ltd., 1980.

Rothstein, Robert L. *Planning, Prediction, and Policymaking in Foreign Affairs: Theory and Practice*. Boston: Little, Brown and Co., 1972.

Sarasin Viraphol. *Tribute and Profit: Sino-Siamese Trade, 1652-1853*. Cambridge: Harvard University Press, 1977.

Scalapino Robert A., and Jusuf Wanandi, eds. *Economic, Political, and Security Issues in Southeast Asia in the 1980s*. Berkeley: University of California, Institute of East Asian Studies, 1982.

Sivaraksa, S. *Siam in Crisis*. Bangkok: Komol Keemthong Foundation, 1980.

Skinner, G. William. *Chinese Society in Thailand: An Analytical History*. Ithaca: Cornell University Press, 1957.

Steinbruner, John D. *The Cybernetic Theory of Decision*. Princeton: Princeton University Press, 1974.

Suryadinata, Leo. *Pribumi Indonesians, the Chinese Minority, and China*. Kuala Lumpur: Heinemann Asia, 1978.

Tilman, Robert O. *In Quest of Unity: The Centralization Theme in Malaysian Federal-State Relations*. Singapore: Institute of Southeast Asian Studies, 1976.

_____. *Malaysian Foreign Policy*. McLean, Va.: Research Analysis Corporation, 1969.

_____, ed. *Man, State, and Society in Contemporary Southeast Asia*. New York: Frederick A. Praeger, 1969.

United Nations Statistical Office. *Monthly Bulletin of Statistics*. New York: United Nations, 1985.

Weinstein, Franklin B. *Indonesian Foreign Policy and the Dilemma of Dependence: From Sukarno to Soeharto*. Ithaca: Cornell University Press, 1976.

Wertheim, W. F. *East-West Parallels*. The Hague: van Hoeve, 1964.

Wu Yuan-li. *The Strategic Land Ridge*. Stanford: Hoover Institution, 1975.

Xiang Chai Shad. *Thailand Foreign Policy: An Analysis of Its Evolution since World War II*. Nanyang University, Institute of Humanities and Social Sciences, Occasional Papers Series, no. 73. July 1977.

NEWSPAPERS AND NEWS MAGAZINES

Agence France Presse
    Release 1078, 24 November 1975
Asiaweek (Hongkong)
    23 July 1982
    5 November 1982
    10 December 1982
    11 February 1983
Bangkok Post (Bangkok)
    27 February 1983
    7 November 1985
Bulletin Today (Manila)
    2 May 1984
    14 May 1984
    10 June 1984
Business Day (Manila)
    12 June 1986
Business Times (Manila)
    23 March 1985
Daily Express (Manila)
    19 June 1984
Far Eastern Economic Review (Hongkong)
    3 September 1982

Far Eastern Economic Review (Hongkong)
    20 January 1983
    7 March 1984
    23 May 1985
    5 December 1985
    10 July 1986
Foreign Broadcast Information Service: Asia/Pacific Series
    28 May 1985 (IV, 102)
    29 November 1985 (IV, 230)
    9 January 1986 (IV, 006)
    14 January 1986 (IV, 009)
    28 January 1986 (IV, 018)
    19 February 1986 (IV, 033)
    20 February 1986 (IV, 034)
    24 February 1986 (IV, 023)
    17 March 1986 (IV, 051)
Free Philippines (Manila)
    22 February 1945
Indonesian Times (Jakarta)
    2 March 1985
Japan Times (Tokyo)
    Special supplement, "ASEAN at the Crossroads," 31 October 1985
Malaya (Manila)
    12 June 1986
Manila Bulletin (Manila)
    27 May 1986
    31 May 1986
The Nation Review (Bangkok)
    16 February 1983
    17 February 1983
New Nation (Manila)
    29 November 1979
New Straits Times (Kuala Lumpur)
    12 January 1981
    28 March 1981
    14 July 1981
    10 August 1981
    16 September 1981
    7 January 1982
    6 February 1982
    15 February 1982
    10 June 1982
    7 July 1982
    22 July 1982
    11 September 1982
    28 October 1982
    30 November 1982
    8 December 1982
New York Times
    10 October 1985
    30 October 1986
Philippines Herald (Manila)
    17 January 1972

The Star (Penang)
    5 July 1981
    6 July 1981
    7 March 1982
    25 October 1982
Straits Times (Singapore)
    13 March 1980
    25 April 1980
    16 March 1981
    23 March 1981
    25 September 1981
    16 January 1982
    11 February 1982
    1 April 1982
    20 September 1982
    15 May 1984
    28 March 1985
    25 April 1985
    1 June 1985
    25 July 1985
    2 September 1985
    2 October 1985
    22 October 1985
Sunday Mail (Kuala Lumpur--Malaysian edition)
    2 April 1972
    9 April 1972
Sunday Star (Penang)
    16 August 1981
Sunday Times (Singapore)
    24 March 1985
Times Journal (Manila)
    14 June 1975
Washington Post (Washington, D.C.)
    10 October 1985

ARTICLES, PAPERS, ESSAYS, INTERVIEWS, AND ADDRESSES

Abidin, Zainal. "Malaysian Security Perceptions."
    Paper presented at the Pacific Forum Symposium,
    "National   Threat   Perceptions   in East Asia/
    Pacific," Waikola, Hawaii, 6-8 February 1982.
Ahmad, Zakaria Haji and H. Osman-Rani. "Economic
    Change and National Security: The Malaysian
    Case."   Paper presented at a workshop on "Eco-
    nomic Change and National Security in ASEAN Coun-
    tries," Bangkok, 23-25 August 1984.
Allman, T. D. "The Failure of Singapore's Success."
    Asia (May/June 1983): 20-27, 48.
Axelrod, Robert. "The Analysis of Cognitive Maps." In
    Structure of Decision, edited by Axelrod, 55-73.
    Princeton: Princeton University Press, 1976.
Benda, Harry J. "The Structure of Southeast Asian

History: Some Preliminary Observations." *Journal of Southeast Asian History* 3 (March 1962): 103-38.

Bird, Kai. "Inside the Manila Embassy." *Foreign Service Journal* 61, 8 (September 1984): 24-27.

Boulding, Kenneth E. "The Learning and Reality-Testing Process in the International System." *Journal of International Affairs* 21, 1 (1967): 1-15.

Bundy, William P. "New Tides in Southeast Asia." *Foreign Affairs* 49, 2 (January 1971): 187-200.

Chan Heng Chee. "The PAP in the Nineties: The Politics of Anticipation." Paper presented at the Third U.S.-ASEAN Conference, "ASEAN in the Regional and International Context," Chiangmai, Thailand, 7-11 January 1985.

Chin Kin Wah. "A New Assertiveness in Malaysian Foreign Policy." In *Southeast Asian Affairs 1982*, 273-82. Singapore: Heinemann Asia for Institute of Southeast Asian Studies, 1982.

Cristobal, Adrian E. "U.S. As a Threat." Address to the Second Joint Seminar on Philippine-U.S. Relations, Manila, 6-7 December 1983. In *Bulletin Today* (Manila), 14 December 1983.

Dhanabalan. "Why Singapore Needs an Active Foreign Policy." In Government of Singapore, Ministry of Culture, *Speeches*, 5, 6 (December 1981): 30-39.

_____. "Opening Statement." 18th ASEAN Ministerial Meeting, Kuala Lumpur, 8 July 1985. Singapore Government Press Release, 09-1/85/07/08, 8 July 1985.

Djiwandono, J. Soedjati. "An Analysis of the Use and Role of a Third Party in the Settlement of International Disputes with Special Reference to Indonesian-Soviet Relations." D.Phil. thesis, University of London, London School of Economics, 1982.

_____. "The Soviet Presence in the Asia-Pacific Region: An Indonesian Perspective." *Indonesian Quarterly* 12, 4 (October 1984): 52-58.

Elsbree, Willard H., and Khong Kim Hoong. "Japan and ASEAN." In *Japan's Foreign Relations: A Global Search for Economic Security*, edited by Robert S. Ozaki and Walter Arnold, 119-32. Boulder: Westview Press, 1985.

Eto, Shinkichi. "Japanese Perceptions of National Threats." Paper presented at the Pacific Forum Symposium, "National Threat Perceptions in East Asia/Pacific," Waikola, Hawaii, 6-8 February 1982.

Federspeil, Howard M. "A Comparison of Security Concerns of Noncommunist Southeast Asian Nations in 1967 and 1983." *Asian Affairs* 10, 4 (Winter 1984): 45-62.

Feurwerker, Albert. "Chinese History and the Foreign

176

Relations of Contemporary China." *Annals of the American Academy of Political and Social Science* 402 (July 1972): 1-14.

Geertz, Clifford. "Primordial Sentiments and Civil Politics in the New States." In *Old Societies and New States*, edited by Geertz, 105-57. New York: Free Press, 1962.

George, Alexander L. "The Causal Nexus between Cognitive Beliefs and Decision-Making Behavior: The 'Operational Code' Belief System." In *Psychological Models in International Politics*, edited by Lawrence S. Falkowski, 95-124. Boulder: Westview Press, 1979.

Goh Chok Tong. Opening address before the Singapore Institute of International Affairs/National University of Singapore, "Conference on the Security of the Sea Lanes in the Asia-Pacific Region," Singapore, 2 May 1985. Singapore Government Press Release, 05-1/85/05/02, 2 May 1985.

_____. "Singapore and the Region." Address before the Harvard Club of Malaysia, Kuala Lumpur, 21 August 1985. Singapore Government Press Release, 05-1/85/08/21, 21 August 1985.

Hashim, Shafruddin. "Malaysian Domestic Politics and Foreign Policy: The Impact of Ethnicity." Paper presented at the Third U.S.-ASEAN Conference, "ASEAN in the Regional and International Context," Chiangmai, Thailand, 7-11 January 1985.

Herman, Margaret G. "Explaining Foreign Policy Behavior Using The Personal Characteristics of Political Leaders." *International Studies Quarterly* 24, 1 (March 1980): 7-46.

Hernandez, Carolina G. "Domestic Politics and Foreign Policy." Paper presented at the Third U.S.--ASEAN Conference, "ASEAN in the Regional and International Context," Chiangmai, Thailand, 7-11 January 1985.

Holsti, Ole. "Foreign Policy Formulation Viewed Cognitively." In *Structure of Decision*, edited by Robert Axelrod, 18-54. Princeton: Princeton University Press, 1976.

Howell, Llewellyn D. "Looking East, Looking West: The International Political Attitudes of Malaysia's Successor Generation, 1971-1981." *Journal of Southeast Asian Studies*, in press.

Joewono, Lt. Gen. Soetopo. "Mutual ASEAN-Japanese Interests in the Field of Regional Security." Position paper prepared for delivery at the "4th Japan-ASEAN Symposium," Jakarta, 3-5 September 1981.

Kamiya, Fuji. "The World and Asia: A Japanese View on 1984." Paper presented an the 11th Japanese-Indonesian Conference, Bali, 23-25 January 1984.

Keehu, Ioane. "United States Military Bases in the Republic of the Philippines: Their Role in the

Regional Balance of Power." Master's thesis, North Carolina State University, 1985.

Knorr, Klaus. "Threat Perception." In *Historical Dimensions of National Security Problems*, edited by Knorr, 78-119. Lawrence: University of Kansas Press, 1976.

Koh, T. B. Address before the Asia Society, New York, 4 December 1984, typescript.

Kuntjoro-Jaki, Dorojatun, and Juwono Sudarsono. "Economic Change and National Security: The Indonesian Search for a Concept." Paper presented at a workshop on "Economic Change and National Security in ASEAN Countries," Bangkok, 23-25 August 1984.

Lang, David Chiang-Kau. "Japan's ASEAN Gaiko: A Reassessment." *Asian Profile* 22 (April 1983): 153-65.

Lao Tek Soon. "National Threat Perceptions: A Singapore Perspective." Paper presented at the Pacific Forum Symposium, "National Threat Perceptions in East Asia/Pacific," Waikola, Hawaii, 6-8 February 1982.

Laurel, Salvador H. Address at a reception for foreign diplomats, Manila, 20 March 1986. In *MFA Newsletter*, 4, 2 (March 1986): 1-2.

_____. "New Directions in Philippine Foreign Policy." Address before the Philippine Council for Foreign Relations, Manila, 10 April 1986. In Philippines, Ministry of Foreign Affairs, *Information Bulletin*, n.d.

Lee Kuan Yew. Address at International Student House, London, 22 April 1966, typescript.

_____. Television interview with foreign journalists, Singapore, 8 November 1966, typescript.

_____. Discussion with a panel of foreign journalists moderated by Dennis Bloodworth of the *London Observer*, Television Singapura studios, Singapore, 5 July 1967, typescript.

_____. Address to the American Association of Singapore, Singapore, 10 November 1967, typescript.

_____. Interview with Singapore journalists, Xiamen, China, 23 November 1980. In Government of Singapore, Ministry of Culture, *Speeches* 4, 6 (December 1980): 11-17.

_____. Interview with *Asahi Shimbun* (Tokyo), Singapore, 5 January 1981. Singapore Government Press Release, 02-1/81/01/07, 7 January 1981.

_____. Opening address before the Commonwealth Heads of Government meeting, Melbourne, 1 October 1981. Singapore Government Press Release, 02-1/81/10/01, 1 October 1981.

_____. Interview with Lester Tanzer of *US News and World Report*, Singapore, 7 December 1981. Singapore Government Press Release, 02-1/82/02/01, 2 January 1982.

_____. Interview with *Asahi Shimbun* (Tokyo), Singapore, 30 October 1982. In Government of Singapore, Ministry of Culture, *Speeches* 6, 7 (January 1983): 1-5.

_____. Response to questions posed by foreign journalists, Singapore, 9 October 1984. In Government of Singapore, Ministry of Culture, *Speeches* 8, 5 (September/October 1984): 25-34.

_____. Address to a Joint Session of Congress, Washington, D.C., 9 October 1985, typescript.

Lee Lai To. "Singapore and East Asia." In *Singapore: Development Policies and Trends*, edited by Peter S. J. Chen, 335-59. Singapore: Oxford University Press, 1983.

Lee Poh Ping. "ASEAN: The Answer to Japan's Search for a Role in Southeast Asia in the 1980's?" Working paper prepared for delivery at a seminar on "The Politics of Southeast Asia in the 80s," Universiti Kebangsaan (Malaysia), 23-24 February 1983.

Leifer, Michael. "The Security of the Sea Lanes in Southeast Asia." *Survival* 25, 1 (January/February 1983): 16-23.

Liddle, R. William. "Soeharto's Indonesia: Personal Rule and Political Institutions." *Pacific Affairs* 58, 1 (Spring 1985): 68-90.

Lie Tek-tjeng. "China's Policy toward Southeast Asia: A View from Jakarta." Paper presented at the German-Indonesian Conference, Samur, Bali, 5-7 July 1982.

_____. "Indonesia in China's Foreign Policy 1949-1977." In *China: Development and Challenge*, edited by Lee Ngok and Leung Chi-keung, 331-40. Hongkong: University of Hong Kong, Center of Asian Studies, 1979.

_____. "Indonesia and the World Powers, an Indonesian Perspective." In *Southeast Asia in a Changing World*, edited by Shigekazu Matsumoto, 36-46. Tokyo: Institute of Developing Economies, 1980.

_____. "Indonesian-PRC Relations: A View from Jakarta." *ASEAN Forecast* (Singapore). Special Supplement, July 1983: 89-92.

_____. "Security Problems in Southeast Asia and the Role of the Great Powers, Especially the PRC." Paper presented at the Ninth Japan-Indonesia Colloquim, Surabaya, 20-22 August 1981.

_____. "The Sinic East Asian Image in Southeast Asia as Seen from Jakarta." Paper presented at the Korean Institute of International Studies, 13th International Conference, Seoul, 4-9 July 1983.

_____. "Vietnamese Nationalism: An Indonesian Perspective." Paper presented at the Frederich Ebert Stiftung Round Table Conference, "Crisis Region Indochina--Causes and Effects," Jakarta, 4-6 March 1981.

Lim Hua Sing. "Japan in ASEAN: Potential Trade Frictions." *ASEAN Economic Bulletin* 1, 2 (November 1984): 115-35.

Lim, Joo Jock. "The South China Sea: Changing Strategic Perspectives." In *Southeast Asian Seas: Frontiers for Development*, edited by Chia Lin Sien and Colin MacAndrews, 225-38. Singapore: McGraw Hill, 1981.

Mahathir bin Mohamed. Address to the 7th Conference of the Heads of States and Heads of Governments of the Non-Aligned Countries, New Delhi, 1 March 1983. In *Winds of Change: The Mahathir Impact on Malaysia's Foreign Policy*, edited by Murugesu Pathmanathan and David Lazarus, 198-210. Kuala Lumpur: Eastview Publications Sdn. Bhd., 1984.

_____. Interview with Robert O. Tilman, Kuala Lumpur, 3 April 1983.

_____. Opening remarks at a conference of the Malaysian-Japanese Economic Association, Kuala Lumpur, 8 February 1982. In *Winds of Change: The Mahathir Impact on Malaysia's Foreign Policy*, edited by Murugesu Pathmanathan and David Lazarus, 109-16. Kuala Lumpur: Eastview Publications Sdn. Bhd., 1984.

_____. Transcript of an interview on the eve of the Prime Minister's first visit to Singapore. In *Straits Times* (Singapore), 7 December 1981.

_____. Transcript of an interview with Malaysian journalists discussing the Prime Minister's first year in office. In *New Straits Times* (Kuala Lumpur), 16 and 17 July 1982 (two parts).

_____. Transcript of an interview with Malaysian journalists. In *New Straits Times* (Kuala Lumpur), 27 October 1981.

Mangahas, Mahar, and Felipe B. Miranda. "Economics and Security in the Philippines." Paper presented at a workshop on "Economic Change and National Security in ASEAN Countries," Bangkok, 23-25 August 1984.

Morrison, Charles E. "Southeast Asia in a Changing International Environment: A Comparative Foreign Policy Analysis of Four ASEAN Member Countries." Ph.D. dissertation, The Johns Hopkins University, 1976.

Narongchai Akrasanee, Sukhumbhand Paribatra, and Chalermpoj Iamkamala. "Economic Change and National Security in Thailand." Paper presented at a workshop on "Economic Change and National Security in ASEAN Countries," Bangkok, 23-25 August 1984.

Neuchterlein, Donald E. "Thailand: Another Vietnam?" *Asian Survey* 7, 2 (February 1967): 126-30.

Niksch, Larry K. "Philippine Domestic Politics and Foreign Policy." Paper presented at the Third U.S.-ASEAN Conference, "ASEAN in the Regional and International Context," Chiangmai, Thailand, 7-11 January 1985.

Nivera, Carlos F. "Threats to National Security: The Philippine Perspective." Paper presented at the Pacific Forum Symposium, "National Threat Perceptions in East Asia/Pacific," Waikola, Hawaii, 6-8 February 1982.

Pathmanathan, Murugesu. "Readings in Malaysian Foreign Policy." Typescript, n.d.

Philippines, President's Center for Special Studies. "Global and Regional Issues." Briefing paper for the president, n.d. [1982?].

_____. "The Strategic Position of the Philippines." Briefing paper for the president, n.d. [1982?].

Pike, Douglas. "Vietnam and Its Neighbors: Internal Influences on External Relations." Paper presented at the Third U.S.-ASEAN Conference, "ASEAN in the Regional and International Context," Chiangmai, Thailand, 7-11 January 1985.

Prasong Soonsiri. Interview with journalist Tony Davis on Thai external threats. In *Business in Thailand* (Bangkok), June 1981.

Rajaratnam, S. Speech before the 17th Annual Chief Executive Officers' Roundtable, Puerto Vallarta, Mexico, 9 January 1981. In Government of Singapore, Ministry of Culture, *Speeches* 4, 8 (February 1981): 30-37.

_____. Address to the NUS Democratic Socialist Club, Singapore, 21 December 1981. In Government of Singapore, Ministry of Culture, *Speeches* 5, 7 (January 1982): 22-30.

Ramsay, Ansil. "Thai Domestic Politics and Foreign Policy." Paper presented at the Third U.S.-ASEAN Conference, "ASEAN in the Regional and International Context." Chiangmai, Thailand, 7-11 January 1985.

Rithauddeen, Ahmad. "Meeting the Challenge of Change." Keynote address, colloquium on "Regional Trends and the Role of Diplomacy in Southeast Asia in the 80s," Frayser's Hill (Malaysia), 2 November 1979. Malaysian Ministry of Foreign Affairs, pamphlet, 1979.

Rose, Leo E. "The Soviet Union and Southeast Asia." Paper presented at the Third U.S.-ASEAN Conference, "ASEAN in the Regional and International Context," Chiangmai, Thailand, 7-11 January 1985.

Sarasin Viraphol. "Domestic Considerations of Thailand's Policies toward the Indochina States." Paper prepared for the "SOAS/FCO Seminar on ASEAN and Indochina," London, 15-17 July 1982.

_____. "The People's Republic of China and Southeast Asia: A Security Consideration for the the 1980s." In *Economic, Political, and Security Issues in Southeast Asia in the 1980s,* edited by Robert A. Scalapino and Jusuf Wanandi, 147-55. Berkeley: University of California, Institute of East Asian Studies, 1982.

_____. "Thailand's Perspectives on Its Rivalry with Vietnam." Paper prepared for a workshop, "The Future of ASEAN-Vietnam Relations," Institute of Strategic and International Studies, Chulalongkorn University (Bangkok), 7-9 February 1983.

Saravanamuttu, J. "Malaysia-China Ties, Pre- and Post-1974: An Overview." In *The Chinese Community and Malaysia-China Ties: Elite Perspectives*, edited by Loh Kok Wah, 39-45. Tokyo: Institute of Developing Economies, 1981.

Seah Chee-Meow. "Soviet Interest in Southeast Asia: Issues in the Eighties." In *Economic, Political, and Security Issues in Southeast Asia in the 1980s*, edited by Robert A. Scalapino and Jusuf Wanandi, 197-205. Berkeley: University of California, Institute of East Asian Studies, 1982.

Shafie, M. Ghazali. "Indochina Crisis: The Threat to ASEAN and the Implications of the Crisis." Working paper prepared for delivery at a seminar on "The Politics of Southeast Asia in the 80s," Universiti Kebangsaan (Malaysia), 23-24 February 1983.

_____. "ASEAN: Contributor to Stability and Development." Keynote address at the Fletcher School of Law and Diplomacy conference on "ASEAN--Today and Tomorrow." Boston, 11 November 1981. Malaysian Ministry of Foreign Affairs, typescript.

Shultz, George. "The US and ASEAN: Partners for Peace and Development." Address at the post-ministerial ASEAN consultations, Kuala Lumpur, 12 July 1985. In U.S., Department of State, *Current Policy Series* 722 (July 1985): 1-5.

Siddhi Savetsila. Address before the Asia Society, New York, 6 October 1983. In Thailand, Ministry of Foreign Affairs, *Foreign Affairs Newsletter* 1619/83 (September/October 1983): 13-14.

_____. Address at the Cosmos Club, Washington, D.C., 7 October 1983. In Thailand, Ministry of Foreign Affairs, *Foreign Affairs Newsletter* 16-19/83 (September/October 1983): 15-16.

Simon, Sheldon. "China and Southeast Asia: Protector or Predator." Paper presented at the Third U.S.-ASEAN Conference, "ASEAN in the Regional and International Context," Chiangmai, Thailand, 7-11 January 1985.

Singh, L. P. "Thai Foreign Policy: The Current Phase." *Asian Survey* 3 (November 1963): 535-43.

Soesastro, Hadi. "The U.S. and the USSR in the Second 'Cold War' and Its Implications for Southeast Asia." *Indonesian Quarterly* 10/1 (January 1982): 52-58.

Sprout, Harold, and Margaret Sprout. "Environmental Factors in the Study of International Politics." *Conflict Resolution* 1, 4 (December 1957): 305-28.

Suchit Bunbongkarn, and Sukhumbhand Paribatra. "Thai

Politics and Foreign Policy in the 1980s: *Plus ca change, plus cest la meme chose?*" Paper presented at the Third U.S.-ASEAN Conference, "ASEAN in the Regional and International Context," Chiangmai, Thailand, 7-11 January 1985.

Sudarsono, Juwono. "Security in Southeast Asia: The Circle of Conflict." In *Economic, Political, and Security Issues in Southeast Asia in the 1980s*, edited by Robert A. Scalapino and Jusuf Wanandi, 63-68. Berkeley: University of California, Institute of East Asian Studies, 1982.

Sukhumbhand Paribatra. "Irreversible History? ASEAN, Vietnam, and Polarisation of Southeast Asia." Paper presented at the Third U.S.-ASEAN Conference, "ASEAN in the Regional and International Context," Chiangmai, Thailand, 7-11 January 1985.

Tan Teng Lang. "Economic Change and National Security in Singapore." Paper presented at a workshop on "Economic Change and National Security in ASEAN Countries," Bangkok, 23-25 August 1984.

Thailand, Ministry of Foreign Affairs. *Foreign Affairs Newsletter*, 16-19/83 (September/October 1983).

Thanat Khoman. "National Threat Perceptions in East Asia--Pacific." Opening address before the Pacific Forum Symposium, "National Threat Perceptions in East Asia/Pacific," Waikola, Hawaii, 6-8 February 1982.

Tilman, Robert O. "Malaysian Foreign Policy: The Dilemmas of a Committed Neutral." In *Public Policy, XVI*, edited by John D. Montgomery and Albert O. Hirschman, 115-59. Cambridge: Harvard University Press, 1967.

_____. "The Enemy Beyond: Threat Perceptions in the ASEAN Region." Singapore: Institute of Southeast Asian Studies Working Paper, 1984.

_____. "Philippine-Chinese Youth: Who Are They?" *Solidarity* 7, 10 (October 1972): 25-33.

_____. "Philippine-Chinese Youth: The Perpetuation of the Chinese Subculture." *Solidarity* 8, 11 (November 1982): 42-54.

_____. "Philippine-Chinese Youth: Political Orientations." *Solidarity* 10, 12 (December 1975): 65-73.

Wanandi, Jusuf. "Current Political Situation in the ASEAN Countries." Paper presented at the 11th Japanese-Indonesian Conference, Bali, 23-25 January 1984.

_____. "Indonesia: Domestic Politics and Foreign Policy." Paper presented at the Third U.S.-ASEAN Conference, "ASEAN in the Regional and International Context," Chiangmai, Thailand, 7-11 January 1985.

_____. "The United States and Southeast Asia in the 1980s." In *Economic, Political, and Security Issues in Southeast Asia in the 1980s*, edited by Robert A. Scalapino and Jusuf Wanandi, 111-23.

Berkeley: University of California, Institute of East Asian Studies, 1982.

_____, and Hadi Soesastro. "Indonesian Security and Threat Perceptions." Paper presented at the Pacific Forum Symposium, "National Threat Perceptions in East Asia/Pacific," Waikola, Hawaii, 6-8 February 1982.

Wang Gungwu. "Early Ming Relations with Southeast Asia: A Background Essay." In *The Chinese World Order: Traditional China's Foreign Relations*, edited by John King Fairbank, 34-62. Cambridge: Harvard University Press, 1968.

Weinstein, Franklin B. "Japan and Southeast Asia." In *Economic, Political, and Security Issues in Southeast Asia in the 1980s*, edited by Robert A. Scalapino and Jusuf Wanandi, 184-94. Berkeley: University of California, Institute of East Asian Studies, 1982.

Wolfowitz, Paul D. "Developments in the Philippines." Statement before the Senate Foreign Relations Committee, Washington, D.C., 30 October 1985. In U.S., Department of State, *Current Policy Series* 760 (November 1985): 1-4.

Wurfel, David. "The Philippines: Intensified Dialogue." *Asian Survey* 7, 2 (February 1967): 46-52.

"X" [George Kennan]. "The Sources of Soviet Conduct." *Foreign Affairs* 25 (July 1947): 566-82.

Index